FRESH START!

■ Surviving Money Troubles ■
■ Rebuilding Your Credit ■
■ Recovering Before or After Bankruptcy ■

John Ventura

Dearborn
Financial Publishing, Inc.

While a great deal of care has been taken to provide accurate and current information, the ideas, suggestions, general principles and conclusions presented in this text are subject to local, state and federal laws and regulations, court cases and any revisions of same. The reader is thus urged to consult legal counsel regarding any points of law—this publication should not be used as a substitute for competent legal advice.

Publisher: Kathleen A. Welton
Acquisitions Editor: Patrick J. Hogan
Associate Editor: Karen A. Christensen
Cover Design: Salvatore Concialdi

Published by Dearborn Financial Publishing, Inc.

Printed in the United States of America

92 93 94 10 9 8 7 6 5 4 3 2 1

Library of Congress Cataloging-in-Publication Data

Ventura, John.
Fresh Start! / John Ventura.
p. cm.
Includes index.
ISBN 0-79310-394-0
1. Finance, Personal–United States. 2. Consumer credit–United States. 3. Bankruptcy–United States. I. Title
HG179.V46 1992 92-81432
332.7'5—dc20 CIP

dedication

To my mother, Lucille Ventura, who provided the prayers; Mary Ellen Ventura, who provided the love and understanding; and Mary Reed, who gave more to this project than can ever be repaid.

acknowledgments

Special thanks to the following people for helping to make Fresh Start! *a reality:*

Susan Stotesbery—BANK ONE, TEXAS

Bob Arrington—CSC Credit Services in San Antonio, Texas

Harvey Corn—CPA, Austin, Texas

Patrick Hogan—Editor, Dearborn Financial Publishing, Inc.

contents

preface

"You may have a fresh start any moment you choose, for this thing that we call 'failure' is not the falling down, but the staying down."

Mary Pickford

Millions of Americans currently are facing the hardest financial times in recent memory. Approximately 40 million Americans have credit problems or no credit at all. According to *The Wall Street Journal*, 70 percent of all Americans live from paycheck to paycheck, risking disaster if their incomes are suddenly reduced or stopped.

According to the American Bankruptcy Institute, 944,000 American individuals and businesses filed bankruptcy in 1991—the highest number in the history of the United States. Ninety-two percent of these bankruptcies were individuals. This is the seventh time since 1978 when the new bankruptcy code went into effect that annual numbers increased dramatically. And the Administrative Office of the United States Courts predicts that bankruptcies are expected to increase in the coming years.

Evidence of continuing hard times means that there will be millions of Americans struggling to rebuild their lives after financial difficulty. As they do so, they will discover what so many consumers have already learned—that successful recovery from financial hard times is complicated by three factors.

First, financial troubles usually affect not only a person's sense of economic well-being but also his or her personal relationships, self-image and emotional health.

Second, American society routinely turns its back on those people who go through financial hard times. No one focuses on this growing segment of our population. This cannot continue to happen. An overwhelming number of people are in serious economic trouble and their ranks will grow in the next few years.

Third, there are few resources available to assist consumers who are struggling to rebuild their fiscal and emotional lives after serious financial trouble. Although attitudes are slowly beginning to change, most businesses will not work with the recovering or bankrupt consumer. While there are nonprofit organizations and government agencies available to offer advice and assistance, their numbers are still few. Furthermore, the impact is hindered because people do not know these organizations exist, much less how they can be of help.

Americans are facing the greatest challenge of the decade—learning the skills necessary to rebuild their lives and live sanely in these precarious financial times. If you are on the financial edge, this book will give you the information you need to avoid falling over. If you have already fallen, due to loss of credit or even bankruptcy, you deserve a second chance.

This book gives you that chance—it provides practical, up-to-date information and advice about how to deal with the issues you face every day, including:

- How to live successfully without credit
- How to manage money, rebuild credit and use it wisely
- How to clean up credit records and deal with credit bureaus
- How to deal with the emotional and psychological upset caused by the stress of severe financial difficulty
- How to protect against creditor harassment and credit bureau foul-ups and
- How to increase income or change careers

This book also provides you with information about the organizations, companies and individuals that can help you make a fresh start.

I know how important these issues are because the people I consult with on a daily basis tell me. I have been a practicing consumer bankruptcy attorney since 1978 and during that time have worked with an average of 60 financially troubled clients a month. Throughout my professional career I have watched more than 10,000 people struggle to put their lives back together after financial crisis. What I have learned is that there is a real need for good, helpful information in one source.

That is what motivated me to start my newsletter, *Fresh Start!*, and write this book. I have learned that no one is immune to financial difficulty. Once you experience it, however, you find yourself an outcast in this society with little guidance to help you reinstate yourself in the community. The *Fresh Start!* newsletter and this book are intended to do just that.

A major goal of this book is to create an awareness of the resources available to you to restore you and your family to financial health. I have included hundreds of names of books, periodicals, organizations, companies and consumer groups that can assist in your recovery.

Starting over isn't easy, but you *can* do it if you have the skills, information and persistence. Good luck with your Fresh Start!

John Ventura, May 1992

"You didn't think when you got up this morning that this would be the day when your life would change, did you? But it's going to happen because the only thing that stands between you and grand success in living are these two things: Getting started and never quitting! You can solve your biggest problem by getting started, right here and now."

Robert H. Schuller

one

Picking Up the Pieces

"The witch doctor succeeds for the same reason all the rest of us succeed. Each patient carries his own doctor inside himself. They come to us not knowing that truth. We are best when we give the doctor who resides within each patient a chance to go to work."

Albert Schweitzer

I hardly recognized Sid and Marla M. when they came to see me. A year before, I had met with them when they were going through an especially difficult bankruptcy. The couple I remembered could hardly stand to be in the same room together during those uneasy times.

Now here they were, making jokes about the past and obviously enjoying each other's company. I saw something in their relationship that I had not seen a year ago—respect for one another. They had stopped by to get some advice about rebuilding their credit, but I was so amazed and curious about the change in their relationship that I had to ask them what had happened to make such a big difference.

"You're right," Sid said, "when our financial world was collapsing, we couldn't stand to be around each other and almost got a divorce. I was

angry with Marla for not being supportive enough and blaming everyone and everything for my misfortunes. Fortunately when things were the bleakest, we went to see our parish priest.

"He helped us out in a very practical way. It had less to do with religious beliefs and more to do with common sense—something I was short of at the time. First he helped me get through the emotional upset of finding myself in a situation that I didn't think I had control over. Then, he helped Marla and me figure out the cause of our problems.

"For us it was a lack of knowledge about how we used money combined with unrealistic goals and expectations about the role money should play in our lives. The priest helped us clarify our values and identify the things that are most important to us. In our case, a happy family life turned out to be our number one priority. So now if there are things in our lives that do not contribute to our happiness in a very fundamental way, we do what we can to change or get rid of them."

This chapter is about the importance of understanding the role that attitudes about money can play in creating financial difficulties as well as the importance of dealing positively with the emotional repercussions of financial trouble.

Getting a fresh start in life often requires an adjustment in one's attitude toward money. Sid and Marla found help by going to their priest. Others may want to turn to a group like Debtor's Anonymous, or seek psychological counseling. The bottom line, however, is that a fresh start always begins inside of you.

Someone once said that "it's not the events of life that determine its quality; it's how you respond to those events." I have found that to be very true. This chapter is designed to help you look beyond your financial troubles, develop a healthier relationship with money and create a happier, more balanced life.

Understanding the Cause of Your Financial Difficulty

There are many reasons why people get into financial trouble, including:

- events beyond their control—serious illness or job loss;
- poor decision making;
- irresponsible use of credit;
- compulsive spending behaviors.

It is important to spend time analyzing why you got into trouble with money and then do whatever is necessary to address the root causes of your financial problems. You need to honestly assess your lifestyle, your money management skills and the role money plays in your life. If you don't, you risk either failing at financial rebuilding or experiencing a recurrence of your financial problems at some point in the future.

Events or Circumstances beyond Your Control

Your financial misfortune may be due to things beyond your control: you got laid off or your employer shut down, and there are no jobs in your area paying an equivalent salary. Or your spouse or child became seriously ill, and you were saddled with expensive medical bills that used up all of your assets. If unforeseen events triggered your financial difficulties, make sure that other factors—overspending or poor money management skills—did not contribute to your troubles. It's up to you to take charge as you begin the rebuilding process.

Poor Decision Making

Most consumers are relatively uninformed about issues relating to credit, money management and investments. As a result, many people find themselves pushed into financial crisis because they lack the skills and knowledge necessary to make informed financial decisions.

If this applies to you, it is important that you learn more about personal finance. By reading this book you have already started your education. However, you need to do more. Read other books and magazines. (The Resources section at the end of this book provides suggestions for additional readings.) Take a money management class at your local community college. Attend low-cost/no-cost seminars on the basics of money management. Ask your banker about such seminars or call the Consumer Credit Counseling office closest to you; find out if they will be sponsoring a money management seminar or know of anyone who will.

Irresponsible Use of Credit and Compulsive Spending

Many financial problems are rooted in the irresponsible use of credit and compulsive spending. Often, people who get into trouble because they misuse credit are unaware that they are not managing their money responsibly. For years they paid their bills and were late only occasionally; they saved little if anything, figuring that there would be time for that later. Since bankcard companies kept sending them cards, they believed that they must be in control of their finances. Once they experienced a drop in their income or a loss of income entirely, their financial world fell apart since they had too much debt and little if anything to fall back on.

Irresponsible spending was a significant problem during the 1980s when the ethos was to spend, spend, spend and live for the present. Few Americans saved to pay for big-ticket items in anticipation of the unexpected. If we wanted something, we bought it, all too often on credit. Making money and spending it blinded us to the fact that our economic house of cards might one day come tumbling down, and we would be without a financial safety net. Not only did this approach to money get a lot of people in serious trouble, it also skewed their perspectives about money and the role that it should play in their lives.

Compulsive spenders have psychological problems with money. While irresponsible spenders may not experience stress or problems as a result of their spending patterns until their income begins to decline, compulsive spenders frequently continue to spend even though they are aware that their financial and personal lives are deteriorating due to overspending. Although they may resolve to change their ways, compulsive spenders usually return to their old habits unless they get counseling or psychological help.

Money often plays an inordinately important and inappropriate role in the lives of both irresponsible and compulsive spenders. Typical roles may include:

Mood Enhancer Money may be used to overcome boredom, loneliness or to help irresponsible or compulsive spenders forget their problems and worries.

Reward Money is used by some people to provide a *pat on the back.* If they've had a hard day, they may spend money to reward themselves for getting through it. If they finish an important project, they may decide that they deserve to spend some money on themselves. They worked so hard—they definitely earned the right to spend!

Entertainment Rather than exercising, enjoying friends, pursuing a hobby or reading a book, recreation for some people involves spending money.

Ego Booster Many people use money to help themselves overcome feelings of inferiority or low self-esteem. Surrounding themselves with material possessions, going out to expensive restaurants and taking costly vacations, make them feel better about themselves. Spending can also be a way to *buy* the admiration or approval of one's peers.

A Way To Get Love People who feel unlovable may spend money on others in order to buy approval and love.

Getting Help

A number of resources exist for consumers who think that they have emotional problems with money and are seeking help. Resources include professional counselors such as psychologists and psychiatrists, publicly and privately funded mental health centers and Debtors Anonymous (DA).

DA is a nonprofit organization that uses the proven techniques and principles of Alcoholics Anonymous to help people overcome their spending problems. Through group and individual counseling, consumers are helped to understand the reasons for their problems and are encouraged to systematically gain control of their finances by creating and living with a spending plan. Some consumers find DA's discipline, support and sharing of experiences and insights sufficient for them to change their relationship with money. Others combine DA with emotional counseling.

Attendance at DA meetings is free. Look in your telephone directory for the Debtors Anonymous chapter in your area. If you cannot find one, write Debtors Anonymous at: General Service Board, P.O. Box 20322, New York, NY 10025-9992.

The Stages of Grief

"The longer we dwell on our misfortunes, the greater their power to harm us."

Voltaire

As you confront the seriousness of your financial difficulties and begin to rebuild your life, you, like many others in your situation, are likely to experience a variety of emotions. Knowing what to expect and how best to deal with each emotion can help you cope day-to-day and speed your financial recovery.

When experiencing a major loss—of a job, a loved one or financial security—people go through several different stages of grief. Generally, complete emotional recovery will not take place unless you are able to work though each stage of grief—shock, anger, depression and resolution.

Shock

Most people experience an initial sense of shock or disbelief when confronted with the loss of their financial security. The loss is so overwhelming that it can shake your very core.

Shock may cause you to question the fundamental *truths* and values upon which you've based your life. These might include: "If you work hard, pay your bills and stay out of trouble, life will be good," or "Bad things only happen to bad people." Suddenly the American dream that having more is always better is shaken. Confronted with events that contradict one's long-held beliefs and assumptions, it is not uncommon to begin wondering whom and what to trust, what to believe in, etc.

Although such doubt is often unpleasant, it is not necessarily bad. Fundamental upheaval can and should be treated as a chance to reexamine your lifestyle and your values, test old assumptions and figure out what is really important to you. It is also an opportunity to make some positive changes in your life. Through soul-searching you may discover that your old beliefs and the ways that you have been living your life have not helped you and have in fact contributed to your current troubles.

Anger

Feelings of anger commonly follow shock. At this point, you may begin looking for scapegoats for your troubles: the real estate industry, the politicians, your boss, your spouse, bad luck. This is the stage in which people are most likely to get stuck when recovering from a major loss.

When your situation begins to get to you, allow yourself to express your anger, being sure to direct your annoyance toward the situation rather than toward scapegoats. Focusing on scapegoats is ultimately a nonproductive use of your energy and emotional resources; it implies that you have no control over your life and that what you can do won't make a difference. Looking for scapegoats can cause you to lose confidence at the very time you need it most.

Get angry. Acknowledge that something terrible has happened and mourn what you have lost. Through anger you lay the groundwork for emotional healing and lasting financial recovery.

Hot Tip

Research shows that painful events ultimately cause most people to discover more meaning in their lives. As Henry Ford once said, "Life is a series of experiences each of which makes us bigger even though sometimes it is hard to realize this."

Depression

Depression is another stage in the grieving process, often appearing when you give in to feelings of guilt, anger and anxiety. Soon you are feeling hopeless, helpless and desperate, as though your life is falling apart.

Depression saps you of your energy and initiative—the very things you need to get your life back together. Giving in to it only makes you more depressed. Therefore, when you begin to feel depressed, remind yourself that you are not helpless and that you can improve your life. Take stock of all the good things in your life and draw positive energy from them, rather than dwelling on the bad. Here are some other things you can do to avoid self-pity and drive depression away:

- Acknowledge that you have responsibility for your own life and begin making things happen for yourself.
- Understand that the quality of your life is most important, not the things that money can buy. Think about the things in your life that give it quality—a loving spouse, happy children, good health, your surroundings, etc.
- Experience each day fully. Don't dwell on the past or yearn for the future.
- Surround yourself with the people you care about. As often as possible, put yourself in enjoyable situations that are free of stress.
- Do something active. Get some physical exercise, work in the yard or tackle a project in your house that you've been meaning to do for a long time.
- Get involved in a worthy cause. Taking part in a good cause or helping people less fortunate than yourself can help put your situation in perspective and take your mind off your own troubles.
- Pamper yourself. Take a long, hot bubble bath, eat a favorite meal, listen to some good music.

If despite all your efforts, you are unable to shake your depression, you may need to seek professional help.

Resolution

This is the stage when healing can begin. Once you've experienced shock, anger and depression, and have begun to confront the reality of what has happened, you are ready to begin putting your life back together. You have accepted your situation and are ready to focus on the future rather than on the past. You are ready to begin creating a new and better life for yourself.

Even when you reach the stage of resolution, you will likely experience emotional ups and downs as you rebuild financially. Periodic feelings of anxiety, frustration, fear and anger are only normal. Therefore, when you hit low points, don't get discouraged. Instead, remember the advice and information in this chapter, talk with friends and family members about what you are feeling and keep moving forward.

Friends and Family

When caught up in a crisis and under pressure, it is easy to direct anger and frustration at other people—often your family and friends—the very people you need most during difficult times. As a result, you may cause people to pull away from you, creating even more stress in your life. To prevent alienating or angering your friends and family, be open and honest with them. Tell them what you are feeling and what you are worried about. You may also want to write about your emotions or even talk about them on tape. Professional counseling can be helpful at this stage of the grief process.

Consider calling regular family meetings to talk about the situation. Discuss what you are doing to resolve your household's financial problems, ask everyone for their patience and support and ask them if they have questions about what is going on. Don't forget that your children are probably experiencing some anxiety too, and it can help them if they are encouraged to talk about their feelings. When appropriate, use these meetings to apologize for any rude or difficult behavior on your part, and assure family members of your love for them and their importance to you.

Have similar conversations with your close friends. Maintaining an open and honest dialogue with both family and friends can make you feel better about any unpleasant behavior you may demonstrate. It can reassure everyone that you are the same person as the one they loved and cared for before the financial crisis. Being open with your feelings also helps you to hold on to the comfort and support of your family and friends throughout your financial rebuilding.

Some of your friends and extended family may also be experiencing financial troubles but have been reluctant to talk about them. By being frank about your own troubles, you may encourage them to open up.

Talking with each other, sharing experiences, concerns and ideas for recovery including job leads, and sources of good quality, well-priced food and clothing, can be therapeutic and healing. Through such sharing can come the realization that you are not alone in your troubles; you will begin to feel less isolated and alienated. This sharing of experience can help foster a new sense of community, a feeling that "we're all in this together."

Figure 1.1 Common Negative Reactions of Children to Financial Trouble

Some children may demonstrate no particular or obvious reaction to a family's financial crisis, while others, depending on their ages, may respond in one or more of the following ways:

Younger Children

- Bad dreams
- A return to more infantile behaviors
- Excessive crying or clinging

Older Children

- Anger
- Discipline problems in school or at home
- Use of drugs or alcohol

Children and Financial Crisis

A major problem for many parents in financial crisis is how best to deal with their children. Should they pretend that nothing has changed? Should they be honest—and if so—how honest should they be? Most experts agree that if you are in serious financial difficulty it is always best to talk about it with your children. It is much better for children to have a clear understanding of what is going on than for them to sense that there is something wrong and worry about exactly what the problem is and how it may affect them.

The best way to explain financial trouble to your children is to tell them that things have changed, and describe why and how they have changed. Explain that the situation is temporary and that it is one that you can deal with as a family. Children usually understand and are anxious to help in whatever way they can.

Make your children part of the solution. For example, ask your older children for their ideas about how household expenses could be reduced and specifically about where they might cut back—perhaps they might get along on a smaller allowance. An older high school student might be asked to help out by getting a temporary, part-time job after school or on weekends as long as it won't interfere with studies. Also, if both parents are working in order to bring in more money, ask your children to help with household chores like cooking and cleaning.

When discussing your household's financial situation, be as honest as you think is best for your child, remembering that every child is different. Like adults, each child has a different capacity for dealing with change and stressful situations. See Figure 1.1 for possible reactions to financial trouble.

One way to alleviate your children's fear and stress is to show them articles about other families who are having financial difficulty. Knowing that their family is not alone can reassure them and may encourage them to talk openly with their friends about what is happening to them.

A particularly difficult problem for parents of children old enough to be subject to peer pressure is how to help those children cope with the fact that they may not be able to do all of the things that their friends are doing, or wear the latest styles. There are no easy solutions to this problem. Let your children know that you realize it may be difficult for them right now. Remind them that everyone is making sacrifices and that each of you must do what you can to put the family's money troubles behind you. You may want to suggest ways for your children to earn extra money around the house or places where they can get part-time jobs so that they can buy some of the things their peers are enjoying. Use the situation as an opportunity to teach older children how to get the most for their money and how to shop sales. Take the children to retail outlets and resale shops; teach them how to read the classifieds.

Hot Tip

Your family's financial difficulties offer you an opportunity to help your children develop a healthy perspective about money and material possessions. If they can begin to understand that people should be valued and judged for who they are and the good things they accomplish in life, rather than for what they wear, drive or buy, they will be less subject to peer pressure and will have learned a very valuable lesson.

Try to spend some special time every week alone with each of your children; also try to do something as a family. Use your time together to have fun and show affection, rather than only discussing finances. This is especially important if your financial situation has forced you to cut back on special lessons or activities that your children once enjoyed. Spending time together can help reassure your children that there are things in their lives that have not changed—your love and family togetherness.

The Importance of Perspective

> *"I've never been poor, only broke. Being poor is a frame of mind. Being broke is only a temporary situation."*
>
> ***Mike Todd***

As I indicated in the introduction to this chapter, perspective is critical to one's ability to cope successfully with a difficult situation. Different people perceive the same problem in entirely different ways. One person's perspective toward the problem can help him or her work through the trouble and lead to a successful resolution. Another person can take a totally different perspective and never resolve the same problem.

People typically react to events with one of two basic perspectives. Some people respond with "why did this happen to me?" They tend to see things outside themselves as contributing to their problems and in turn, view themselves as victims. Because as victims they feel relatively powerless to help themselves, they often limit their access to the information and the assistance that could help them deal with their problems. This approach to life tends to trigger feelings of self-pity, frustration and depression and rarely encourages productive problem-solving.

Others recognize that life is a series of ups and downs. They believe that if things were good once they can be good again, and they tend to have confidence in themselves and their ability to deal with difficult challenges. They believe that *they* can make things better. People with this perspective are more apt to seek out sources of help and advice and are open to testing new strategies and approaches to their lives.

In this rapidly changing, unpredictable world, no one can afford to view life from the first perspective. Those who can *roll with the punches,* and learn from their mistakes and misfortunes, rather than getting bogged down in them are most apt to succeed. Such individuals view the cycles of change not as threats, but as opportunities for personal growth. Change also offers persons in financial crises an opportunity to begin anew.

Maintaining a Positive Attitude

Maintaining a positive attitude in the face of adversity may not always be easy, but it is absolutely essential. The way you think about what has happened to you affects your ability to deal successfully with your circumstances and problems. Your attitude can transform a difficult situation into a destructive one. Here are some typical self-destructive attitudes:

- "I can't stand to be out of control of my life."
- "The present is awful, and I don't even want to think about the future."
- "I can't stand having other people know about my financial situation."
- "I must have done something terrible to be in this situation."

To maintain a positive attitude about your financial problems and your ability to rebuild, keep your situation in perspective. Recognize that as difficult as your life may be right now, there are other people who have it worse.

Realize that although it may not happen quickly and without some sacrifices, you *can* change your life. Focus on the good things in your life; don't dwell on the negatives. For example:

- "I am in control of my life. I can make things happen. I am still me—no creditor, bankruptcy court or debt collector can take away my self, my pride, my identity."
- "The present is difficult but the future can be better, and I can make it better."
- "I made some mistakes, but I can learn from those mistakes and create a happier life for myself and my family."

See Figure 1.2 for more ways to maintain a positive attitude.

Figure 1.2 Things You Can Do To Maintain a Positive Attitude

- Find reasons to laugh and smile.
- Each day, visualize a happy experience from your past and relive the good feelings you had at that time.
- Make a list of all the people who have befriended you or helped you over the years. Each day call or write one of them. Thank them for their kindness and offer to help them.
- Take the time to reestablish old friendships you may have neglected.
- Get involved in volunteer work. Helping others can help you keep your situation in perspective and make you feel good about yourself.
- Make a list of all the positive things in your life right now.
- Every time something good happens to you, write it down in a diary or a notebook. Don't limit *something good* to things related to money. A beautiful sunset, a good conversation, an enjoyable book are all *good things.* Doing this not only broadens your capacity for happiness and pleasure, it also helps you recognize that happiness is not necessarily something you buy.
- Find one thing that you keep telling yourself you can't do because of money, and find a way to do it anyway. For example, if you have stopped entertaining at home because you can no longer afford to, invite your friends over for a potluck meal.
- Envision yourself a year from now, happier, free of guilt and other negative emotions, and closer to financial recovery.

Don't Give in to Guilt or Shame

"How can they say my life isn't a success? Have I not for more than 60 years got enough to eat and escaped being eaten?"
Logan Pearsall Smith

Feelings of guilt and shame can be especially hard to deal with for people in serious financial difficulty. Such feelings can be so overwhelming they can affect one's ability to move forward and rebuild. To deal with these feelings, consider the following:

- What kind of people get into serious financial trouble? All kinds do—the rich and poor, the famous and not-so-famous, the financially responsible and the financially irresponsible. Countless individuals and companies are contributing to our economy today after having recovered from financial difficulty.
- What will my family and friends think? The way you deal with your financial troubles to a great extent affects the way your friends and family think about you and your problems. It may not be necessary for anyone to know about your troubles. If they need to know, be up front about your problems, and talk in terms of the opportunities that your troubles present you—opportunities to reexamine your values and priorities, create a more stable financial life, and learn more about money management. When you act as though what has happened to you is shameful and bad, that is how your friends and family are apt to perceive your situation. However, if you acknowledge that you are in trouble, talk about the lessons you have learned and affirm your determination to rebuild and create an even better life for yourself, your friends and family are more likely to view you with respect and concern.

If some of your friends ostracize you after they learn about your troubles, they were never really very good friends and losing them is not a great loss. True friends will stick by you.

Hot Tip

If you have friends or acquaintances who are also in financial trouble, consider starting a support group. Schedule regular meetings to offer one another advice about how to live frugally, how to deal with any problems your financial troubles may create for your children, how to cope with stress, rebuild credit, etc. Out of this sharing can come new and stronger friendships as well as a deepening sense of community.

- There are many definitions of success. A happy family life and a life full of friends are two important types of success that money can't buy! Remember, there are many people who have had great monetary success but who have never experienced much personal happiness. Instead of getting hung up on money as the arbiter of success, examine your life, focus on the things you have done well and your achievements—in your personal relationships, in sports, in the way you have raised your children, in your volunteer work, in sticking to your convictions and values—in order to figure out how you can enjoy even greater success.
- You are only a failure if you allow yourself to think like one. You, like millions of other people who have ended up in financial trouble due to money problems, made some mistakes and now you are paying the price. That's all! Also, stop and think of all the people you hear about and read about who are in bankruptcy or struggling financially. Surely they are not all failures! Rather than dwelling on the mistakes you may have made, think about what you've learned from those mistakes. Then, act on that new knowledge. Remember, positive change and a brighter future can come out of hard times. Figure 1.3 highlights success stories from this author's legal practice.

Set Goals and Work toward Them

It is not enough to believe in something; you have to have the stamina to meet obstacles, to overcome them, to struggle."

Golda Meir

Figure 1.3 People Who Have Overcome Financial Adversity

In my job I often have the pleasure of watching people recover from financial difficulty and use those hard times to create new and happier lives for themselves. Here are a few success stories:

- A client of mine had a regular job and was running a business on the side. He hoped that someday his business would become his sole source of support, however, he had difficulty juggling both. Ultimately he lost his business and ended up in personal bankruptcy. His financial troubles caused him to assess the toll that his business had taken on his and his family's life, and he decided to redouble his efforts at work rather than trying to pursue another business. Through hard work and initiative, he revived his career and has received two promotions and significant salary increases. He now uses the time he used to spend working on his business doing things with his children and his wife and pursuing woodworking as a hobby—something he hasn't had time for since he was a young man.
- Another client had once had a very large and successful clothing business. Due to a sluggish economy and too much debt, she had to file for both personal and business bankruptcy. Undeterred, she took her knowledge of the clothing industry, her understanding of the mistakes she had made in her own business and what she would have done differently and began consulting to small and mid-size retailers to help them avoid what had happened to her. She now works out of a small office in her home, is more relaxed, and, after scaling back her spending, has a very comfortable lifestyle.

Figure 1.3 People Who Have Overcome Financial Adversity (Continued)

- One client was a struggling writer who for years had worked on a part-time basis because she wanted to concentrate on her writing and because her husband made a good income. However, a divorce and her husband's subsequent bankruptcy pushed her into bankruptcy as well. Undiscouraged, she drastically scaled back her life, found a job that afforded her a basic living and continued to pursue her writing in the early morning hours. Today she is a successful novelist with four published books who is able to support herself doing what she likes best.
- A successful commercial architect saw the collapse of his business when the economy in his city deteriorated. He and his wife had to file bankruptcy since his wife did not make enough to support their family, they had little in savings and he was unable to find a job in his profession. After reading several career planning books, he thought back to a part-time teaching job he had when he was in graduate school, remembering how much he enjoyed working with the students. He decided to pursue a teaching career and today teaches drafting to high schoolers. He has never felt so fulfilled.

When rebuilding, it is important to establish goals for yourself and to work toward them. Moving toward your goals reinforces the fact that you do have control of your life and that you can do things to improve it. Your progress also helps drive depression out of your life.

At first what you are able to accomplish may seem very small and insignificant in view of the seriousness of your situation.

However, the important thing is to do what you can. Little by little, step by step, you will make progress. Each series of little steps adds up to big steps.

As you analyze what needs to be done to achieve your goals, don't allow yourself to become overwhelmed. Break each problem or challenge into small, doable tasks and accomplish one at a time.

Hot Tip

Use physical conditioning and a sport like biking or race walking to overcome feelings of low self-esteem. Intense absorption in a physical activity that requires a focus on the here-and-now can help you detach your feelings of self-worth from your monetary problems and encourage you to feel good about yourself by creating a more fit and physically stronger you.

Stress

Expect to experience a considerable amount of stress as you begin to rebuild your life. Feeling *stressed out* is only normal given the sorts of things you may be dealing with: how to pay your bills, how to find a new job, the toll your family's financial troubles are taking on your children and on your relationship with your spouse, not to mention all the emotions you are probably feeling. Sometimes the stress may become almost suffocating, causing you to lose valuable sleep, making it difficult to think clearly and making you worry constantly.

There is a lot of tension in your life, and few people can go through what you are without experiencing some level of stress. However, too much stress can be debilitating, draining you of the physical and mental strength you need to get through difficult times. If you find that stress is interfering with your ability to cope, consider some of the following stress beaters:

- Exercise regularly.
- Read a good book.
- Take up yoga.
- Learn to meditate.
- Spend time with friends.

- Listen to relaxing music.
- Rediscover nature. (Take walks in the woods, listen to the sounds of nature, smell the out-of-doors, stop and admire the sunset or the sunrise.)
- Take up an inexpensive hobby.
- Get involved in a worthy cause.

Not only can these stress beaters help you relax, they can contribute to a healthier, spiritually richer, happier life.

Dealing with the Holiday Season

Perhaps the most emotionally difficult time of year for families in serious financial trouble, particularly those with children is December. Whether you celebrate Christmas or Hanukkah, the pressure to give presents and to spend money on special food and entertaining is intense at this time of year, making most parents feel guilty when they can't afford to buy their children toys and other gifts.

There are, however, other ways to create a happy, joyful holiday season. Families can rediscover the true spirit and forgotten pleasures of a simpler, old-fashioned era. The holidays can once again become a time for homemade gifts and *gifts from the heart,* for relaxing with family and friends, for carolling and doing something special for those less fortunate.

The key to creating a *new-fashioned* holiday season is to shift your family's focus away from what can be bought and how costly the presents toward what is given and the sentiment and thought behind those gifts. *New-fashioned* holidays need not mean an end to store-bought gifts and toys. They do place a greater emphasis on *gifts from the heart*: gifts that are homemade, gifts of one's time, thoughtful gestures or favors. This approach to the holidays not only helps create a more relaxed, less expensive holiday season, it also teaches your children invaluable lessons about the true spirit and pleasure of giving. This approach works just as well for birthdays. Specific ideas for *new-fashioned* holiday and gift giving basics are discussed in detail in Chapter 6, "Smart Spending."

Conclusion

Financial disaster is nearly always difficult. Not only must you cope with the practical realities like how to deal with your debt, where the money will come from to pay for your family's basic needs and how you can rebuild your credit, you must also deal with the emotional repercussions of financial failure. You must come to terms with how and why you got into trouble and work through a range of emotions coupled with feelings of self-doubt, shame and confusion. As you do, never stop believing in yourself and your ability to triumph over adversity. You, like others, *can* do it, with hard work and determination, and by using the information and ideas in this book.

As you rebuild, never lose sight of the following:

- You are a worthwhile person who may have made some mistakes with your money.
- Money problems have nothing to do with your integrity as a human being.
- You are not alone in your troubles.

Remember the advice of the great psychologist Albert Ellis: "Be kind to yourself and do not harm others." These few simple words represent a sane approach not only to recovering from financial difficulty and getting a fresh start but also to living in general, before and after financial trouble.

two

Surviving Collection and the IRS

"I know God will not give me anything I can't handle. I just wish that he didn't trust me so much."

Mother Teresa

Kathy and Bill B. looked worried as they told me what had brought them to my office. Bill worked in the assembly department of an electronics firm, and Kathy was a secretary in a downtown insurance company. They were upset. They told me that they had struggled for over a year to solve their financial problems with no luck. Even though their combined salaries provided good income, they had barely enough money to cover their expenses and were beginning to get cash advances from their credit cards to pay other ongoing debts. They were not getting ahead, and any unexpected expense could be a disaster. They had no savings and were living from paycheck to paycheck. Their credit was still good, but it would not last long at this rate.

"We were doing fine a year ago," Bill said. "We had a nice house; we each drove a fairly new car, and we had all the major credit cards. Then my company cut out overtime, and things started to get tight. I never

thought there would be a time when we couldn't earn enough money to buy whatever we wanted."

Kathy said, "When I heard that there was a chance I was going to lose my job or at least have my hours cut back, I knew we had to do something. I can't take living like this. If my son gets sick, I worry that we won't have the money to take him to the doctor, and Bill has been holding off going to the dentist because we don't have the money."

I asked Kathy and Bill questions about their income, their debts and the status of those debts. Although they were barely making it, they were not candidates for bankruptcy. They just needed some advice and help in avoiding bankruptcy and getting ahead. They also needed to know how to deal with creditors and debt collectors, and where to go for help.

Today, there are many people living on the edge of financial disaster just like Kathy and Bill. We Americans have believed for a long time that plenty of jobs would always be available, and enough money to buy what we wanted. Now we are finding that we cannot count on those old expectations. We have to back away from the edge and live saner, less credit-dependent lives. But how do we do that? First, take the advice of Jerrold Mundis in his book *How To Get out of Debt, Stay out of Debt and Live Prosperously*, (Bantam Books, 1988): "For today, just today, do not go into another penny of debt. You have to stop increasing your debt if you are ever going to get ahead."

We all must learn to become less dependent on credit and, until we are certain that we have permanently backed away from the edge and are stabilized, we must avoid the use of credit entirely except in the case of an emergency. If Kathy and Bill's situation sounds similar to yours, it's time for some aggressive action. The issues you now face and how best to deal with them are addressed in this chapter.

How To Recognize Financial Trouble

> *"There comes a time in the affairs of men when you must take the bull by the tail and face the situation."*
>
> ***W.C. Fields***

How best to deal with your financial situation depends upon the seriousness of your particular problems and the condition of your credit record. The more money you owe, the more serious your situation and the more badly damaged your credit record, the fewer the options available to you. The sooner and more decisively you address your financial troubles, the better.

Signs of Moderately Serious Financial Trouble Include:

- You are regularly late on many of your payments and are incurring a lot of late penalties.
- Your outstanding credit card balances are increasing.
- You are using cash advances to pay consumer debt or for day-to-day living expenses.
- You are paying only the minimum due on your credit cards.
- You are close to or over your credit limit on at least some of your accounts.
- You are behind at least a month on some of your accounts.
- You are using savings or borrowing from friends or relatives to make ends meet.

Signs of Serious Financial Trouble Include:

- You are so far behind on most of your payments that you don't see how you can get caught up.
- You are having trouble paying even the minimum on your accounts.
- You are over your credit limit on most of your accounts.
- You are paying numerous late charges each month.
- You are getting phone calls and letters from creditors and debt collectors asking you to pay up.
- You are always worried about money, and money troubles are straining your marriage or other key relationships.

Responding to Moderate Trouble

If your financial situation is moderately serious, you need to take immediate steps to avoid further damage to your credit record. Stop using all of your credit cards, and live on a cash only basis until your situation has stabilized. Once you stop charging, it may be possible to get your finances under control by simply cutting back on your day-to-day spending for a while and using the money you save to catch up on your bills. As you catch up, be sure to make all payments on time since continued late payments will further damage your credit record. You or your spouse may also want to take an extra job for a while, or look into working additional hours at your current jobs. Be sure that you contact the credit managers for the accounts that you are behind on, and let them know what you are doing to get caught up.

It is generally not advisable to borrow money from friends or relatives to get yourself out of debt. They usually cannot afford to give you money so asking for it may create an uncomfortable situation; if they do lend you money, it may cause them hardship. If you do borrow money from a friend or a relative, make sure the loan is secured by collateral, and the lien is properly perfected. Your family member or friend will then have a better position with creditors if you later file for bankruptcy.

If you have several delinquent accounts with one creditor—a bank for example—explore the possibility of refinancing those debts, collapsing them into a single loan. Your goal in doing so would be to lower the amount of money you are paying to that creditor each month by extending the length of time you have to repay what you owe. This can be a particularly attractive option if you are able to refinance your debts at a lower rate of interest than the interest rates on your current debts with that creditor. However, if a higher rate of interest is applied to the refinanced debt, refinancing may not be advisable.

It is usually unwise to trade one kind of debt for another in order to deal with financial troubles. However, a debt consolidation loan, or a home equity loan, may be a reasonable option for those of you who still have relatively good credit, whose household incomes are stable and who have firmly resolved that once you have paid off your debt with the loan proceeds, you will not let your finances get out of control again. If you lost your job but now have a new one at a good salary, or if your financial troubles were caused by an unexpected medical crisis that is now over, a debt consolidation or home equity loan may be a viable possibility.

Hot Tip

Beware of advance-fee loan brokers. They will charge you a substantial up-front *application* fee in exchange for promising to help you find a loan. They will then pocket the fee without ever finding you a loan.

Debt Consolidation Loans

A debt consolidation loan allows you to borrow money to get rid of your miscellaneous debt, leaving you with a single large loan to pay off. These loans are typically unsecured, usually made for a maximum of three years. In order for it to be a good deal, the monthly payment on a debt consolidation loan should be smaller than the total payments on the individual debts you are going to pay off. Also, the interest rate on a debt consolidation loan should be lower than the rates on individual debts.

A debt consolidation loan has several advantages besides helping you get out of debt. By paying off a single large debt rather than several smaller ones, you are less apt to damage your credit record with numerous missed or late payments. You no longer pay late fees, and your creditors stop calling you.

If you want to apply for a debt consolidation loan, your best bet is to contact a bank, savings and loan or credit union. As a general rule, steer clear of finance companies or other businesses that advertise debt consolidation loans. They often charge high rates of interest or require you to pledge your home as collateral. Sometimes they misrepresent the terms of your loan, and as a result, you may find yourself in danger of losing your home.

Another good reason to avoid finance companies and other firms that offer debt consolidation loans is that working with such companies can actually hurt your credit record. Many businesses are reluctant to extend credit to consumers who have had loans with such companies since they are known for having such lenient credit standards.

Home Equity Loans

In 1986 when changes in the federal tax laws began phasing out interest deductions on most consumer loans, other than property loans, the popularity of home equity loans grew rapidly. Not legal in all states, a home equity loan allows you to borrow money on the equity in your home. Equity is the difference between your home's current market value and the amount you owe on your home. For example, if you owe $50,000 on your home and its current market value is $85,000, your equity is $35,000. Most equity loans are made for up to 80 percent of a home's equity value with your home used as collateral.

Home equity loans come with either a fixed or a variable interest rate. With a variable rate, the interest rate changes as the economy changes. When the prime rate goes down, your rate goes down, and when the prime rate goes up, your rate goes up, as does the monthly amount you pay on the loan. Since interest rates can fluctuate sharply and unpredictably, you may find that the variable rate home equity loan you initially felt was the answer to your problems suddenly becomes another debt you have trouble paying off.

Some home equity loans are structured to allow for an initial series of relatively small monthly loan payments, or even interest-only payments, followed by one or more balloon payments at the end of the loan period. Credit terms like this can sound extremely attractive to anyone anxious to get out of debt. It is your home that is being used as collateral, so you need to be absolutely certain that your financial situation will be so improved by the time the balloon payments become due that you will have no trouble making them. Otherwise, you risk defaulting on the loan and possibly losing your home.

Keep in mind that getting a home equity loan is not going to be cheap. You usually have to incur a number of up-front costs including an appraisal and application fees.

Home Equity Fraud

As the popularity of home equity loans has increased, so too has the incidence of home equity fraud. Victims—in many cases women—are often homeowners in serious financial trouble who have little access to conventional credit.

Generally the companies perpetrating this fraud are finance companies, not legitimate financial institutions. The company salesperson typically approaches a homeowner about the benefits of a home equity loan but fails to make clear that the person's home is to be used as collateral. Often unsuspecting homeowners do not fully understand the terms of the loan and obligate themselves to monthly payments and terms they cannot meet. Ultimately, they lose their homes.

When considering any type of loan, *do not* sign anything you do not read first and thoroughly understand; *never* sign a blank form. Treat with great skepticism anyone who comes to your home, calls on the phone or contacts you by letter about a home equity loan. Without taking these precautions, you open yourself up to the possibility of victimization.

Pawnshop Loans

Don't overlook a pawnshop loan as a quick source of money for an unexpected expense or to tide you over until the next paycheck. Pawnshops specialize in quick, small, short-term loans and don't require a credit check before working with you. Also, pawnshop loans are not reported to credit bureaus so they have no effect on your credit record.

Pawnshops give you cash for a wide variety of merchandise. Items most frequently pawned are tools, electronic equipment, color TVs, musical instruments (especially guitars), cameras and jewelry. Most pawnshops hold your item for 90 days. If you don't reclaim it during that period of time, the shop sells it.

Although pawnshop loans are a convenient source of cash, they are also expensive in part because when you pawn an item, you generally get only about one-fourth of its new product value. This percentage is influenced somewhat by the condition of the items you pawn. Figure 2.1 gives tips for getting the best deal at pawnshops.

Pawnshops charge very high rates of interest—varying from state to state to as much as 60 percent per annum. Assume that you live in a state where pawnshops may charge 20 percent per year on the money they loan. If you borrow $25, and need to redeem that loan in a month, you must pay $30 to get your pawned merchandise back. If you wait 90 days, or the maximum amount of time, to get your item back, you pay $40—three months worth of interest plus the cash value of the loan.

Responding to Serious Financial Trouble

> *"Annual income twenty pounds, annual expenditure nineteen nineteen six, result happiness. Annual income twenty pounds, annual expenditure twenty pounds ought and six, result misery."*
>
> ***Charles Dickens***

Serious financial trouble demands immediate action. First, if you still have any credit cards, stop using them. Keep one in case of an emergency and either cut up the rest or put them in an inaccessible place—in a safe deposit box perhaps.

Hot Tip

If you cut up your credit cards, write each of the credit card companies to tell them that you want your account closed. Request that they inform the credit bureaus they work with that you have closed your account. If you do not do this, those accounts will continue to appear on your credit record as active accounts and can harm your record by making it appear that you have more credit available than you really do.

Second, contact your creditors to see if you can negotiate new debt payment plans with them in order to reduce your total monthly payments to a level you can more comfortably manage. You can either do the negotiating yourself or secure the assistance of the Consumer Credit Counseling (CCC) office located nearest you.

It is important that you take the initiative in dealing with your debts. If you don't, your creditors' debt collection techniques will escalate, further damaging your credit record and disrupting your life. If you do nothing to resolve your financial troubles, your creditors will turn your accounts over to debt collectors who will increase the pressure on you. If that maneuver doesn't work, your wages may be garnished, your property repossessed, liens may be placed against your real or personal property, and your creditors may take you to court in order to get judgments against you. Bankruptcy may become your only option.

Initiating Debt Payment Negotiations

Write each of your creditors, directing your letters to the credit manager. Acknowledge that you are having difficulty paying your bills, succinctly explain why you are having trouble and state what you are doing to get your financial situation under control. Indicate your interest in negotiating a revised debt payment plan that would reduce the amount you have to pay each month by extending the period of time you have to pay off your debt. Refer to Figure 2.2 for an example of the type of letter to send to your creditors.

Figure 2.1 How To Get a Good Deal from a Pawnshop

- Take your pawnable items to several pawnshops to get the best price.
- Visit pawnshops in your area to see which ones have a lot of the same type of merchandise you want to pawn. Those that do probably will not be anxious to take your items. Also, ask the pawnshops you visit what types of items they need and are able to sell fast.
- Work with a pawnshop that belongs to a state or national pawnbrokers association.
- Know how much your merchandise is worth and how large a loan you need before visiting any pawnshops.
- Negotiate. Don't assume that a pawnshop's first offer is its best offer.

Most creditors would prefer to have you repay your debt in full, albeit slowly, than to have you walk the debt entirely or force them to incur the expense of collection or legal action on an account that is already a problem. Most creditors are amenable to revised debt payment plans, assuming the plans are fair. You are not likely, however, to have much success with those creditors who have already turned your account over to a debt collector or with whom you have a serious history of late payments.

Hot Tip

When you start the negotiation process, contact your secured or collateralized creditors first. These are the creditors to whom you have pledged personal property. Car, boat and computer loans are common types of secured loans, as are mortgages. In addition, you may have pledged collateral in order to get a home improvement or vacation loan.

Figure 2.2 Letter to Credit Manager Regarding a New Debt Payment Schedule

Date
Address of Credit Manager

Dear Sir or Madam:

At the present time, I am having difficulty staying current with my accounts. This is due to (explain reason/s for your financial problems.)

However, I am taking steps to get my financial situation under control. These steps include: (list what you are doing, i.e., second job, cheaper apartment, spouse now working, etc.).

As part of my effort to stabilize my financial situation, I am contacting all of my creditors to explore the possibility of negotiating reduced monthly payment plans for each of my accounts. I would like to do the same with you.

Presently, I pay you $____ per month and my account balance is $_______. I would like to propose that I begin paying you $______ per month at the same rate of interest as I'm currently paying. I realize this will mean that it will take me longer to pay off my debt to you and that I will be paying more in finance charges; however, if my payment is lowered as I am requesting, I will be able to stay current on all of my bills and will be able to pay my debt to you in full.

I believe that this proposal is fair and reasonable given my current net monthly household income of $____________ (your household income after taxes and all deductions) and my total monthly payments, $____________ .

I look forward to discussing this request with you.

Sincerely,

Signature

Before contacting your creditors, spend some time thinking about what you can realistically afford to pay out each month given your monthly net income and monthly expenses like rent, mortgage, utilities, food, day care and insurance. Budget money for unexpected expenses as well. You must be able to pay the new amounts you negotiate since your creditors are unlikely to give you a second chance if you can't pay the reduced amounts on time each month. If you need help budgeting or want to figure out where you might cut back, turn to Chapter 6.

Special Concerns Regarding Your Automobile

It is important to know that, if an owner of a car is late making payments or has stopped making them altogether, most car financing agreements allow the creditor to repossess that car without giving the owner prior notice. Also, depending upon the terms of the financing agreement, the consumer may be obligated to pay the loan in full, plus towing and storage costs before getting the car back! Therefore, when you are contacting your creditors, move the company that holds the note on your car to the top of your list.

The minute that you realize that you are going to have trouble making your car payments, contact your creditor. Explain your situation and what you are doing about it. During your conversation, explore the possibility of renegotiating your contract with the creditor to lower your monthly payments. You may also want to see if there is a way that you can catch up with the payments you missed by spreading them out over a several-month period.

If you need help doing the negotiating, ask a friend or relative to help. If you are successful at renegotiating a new agreement, be sure you get it in writing, and keep a copy in your files.

Your creditor may refuse to negotiate with you and demand that you return your car. If you agree to a *voluntary repossession,* you reduce the expenses that your creditor incurs in taking the car back—expenses that you are legally responsible for. You may still be liable for paying any deficiency (the difference between what you owe on the car and the car's selling price), and the repossession can still show up on your credit record.

Vehicle Repossession

In most cases, the contract you signed and the laws of your state give your creditor the right to seize your car as soon as you *default* on your loan. Exactly how your creditor defines *default* will be spelled out in your contract.

Most state laws allow repossession to occur at any time of day or night, without prior notice. Also, the creditor may come to your property to effect the repossession. However, the creditor may not commit a *breach of peace* by using physical force or the threat of violence to take back your car. Some states also define a *breach of peace* as taking a vehicle despite the protests of its owner or removing it from the owner's closed garage. To determine what constitutes a breach of peace in your state, call your state attorney general's office or office of consumer affairs.

Getting Your Car Back

Once your car has been repossessed, your creditor may either keep the car as compensation for your unpaid debt or resell it. You must be informed about what is happening to your car. If the creditor says that he or she is going to keep the car, you can demand that it be sold. This is a good idea if your car is worth more than what you owe on it since it can help reduce or eliminate your liability for any deficiency.

The sale of your car must be conducted in a *commercially reasonable manner,* which means that it must be made according to standard industry practices or in a manner that is considered reasonable for a given market. It does *not* mean that your creditor must get the highest possible price for the car or even a good price. If the creditor decides to sell your car at a public auction, you must be notified so that you or a friend or relative acting on your behalf can bid on it.

If your car is not sold in a commercially reasonable manner—below fair market value, for example—you may be able to use that failure as the basis for a claim against the creditor. In addition, you may be able to use it as a defense against a deficiency judgment. In this situation, get legal advice.

Whether your car is sold privately or at a public auction, you have the right to buy it back by paying the full amount you owe on it plus all expenses associated with its repossession. Some states also have laws that permit consumers to reinstate their auto loans. In other words, a consumer is permitted to reclaim his or her car by paying the total amount of arrears on the loan as well as the creditor's repossession expenses.

Your creditor is not allowed to sell or keep any personal property that may be in your car at the time of repossession. Should your creditor not be able to account for any of your property, get legal advice about your right to compensation.

Hot Tip

Any improvements that you make to a car, such as a new stereo system or a CD player, are considered a part of the car, not your personal property.

The Deficiency

The difference between what you owe on a car and what your creditor gets for selling it is called the *deficiency*. Most states allow a creditor to sue a consumer to collect the loan balance. This is called a *deficiency judgment*. To collect, however, the proper procedures for repossession and sale must have been followed.

If your creditor sues you for a deficiency judgment, a court hearing will be scheduled. If this happens, it is wise to check with an attorney to find out if you have any legal grounds for contesting the judgment, i.e., the creditor breached the peace or failed to resell your vehicle in a commercially responsible manner.

Figuring Out How Much You Can Afford To Pay Each Creditor

As you think about how much you can afford to give each creditor, bear in mind that *all* your creditors should get something each month and that no single creditor should receive a disproportionately large monthly sum. The amount each receives should be determined relative to the amounts you owe your other creditors. In other words, the more you owe one creditor (compared to what you owe other creditors), the larger that creditor's monthly payment.

The worksheet in Figure 2.3 can help you systematically determine the new minimum monthly payments you can afford. Copy the headings from the worksheet onto a piece of paper and you're ready to go. Fill in the appropriate information in columns 1, 2 and 4. Next add up the numbers in the Total Amount Owed column, and write in your Grand Total. This figure represents the total amount of money you owe your creditors.

Calculate the percentage of the Grand Total that each of the amounts listed in the Total Amount Owed column represents. To perform this simple calculation, divide each of the dollar amounts in your Total Amount Owed column by the Grand Total. The number you get will be expressed as a decimal. Convert the decimal to a percentage by moving the decimal point two places to the right. For example, looking at the sample worksheet, Company A is owed $5,000 by J. Q. Consumer. This represents .50 or 50 percent of J.Q. Consumer's Grand Total Debt.

Now, turn your attention to the Current Minimum Monthly Payments column. Add up the numbers to calculate the amount of money you are paying each month in minimum monthly payments. Look back over your records to determine, on average, how many dollars short of this figure you are each month. Next, considering your current net household income and your average monthly shortfall, figure out the total amount of money you can realistically pay out each month to get out of debt. As you'll note on the sample worksheet, J.Q. Consumer's Current Minimum Monthly Payments total is $500. Let's assume that J.Q. Consumer has decided that a more realistic total is $200. To determine how much of this $200 each creditor should get, J.Q. simply multiplies the applicable percentages on the worksheet by $200. Under the revised debt payment plan, Company A will now receive a minimum monthly payment of $100 (50 percent of $200), while Company C will get at least $46 every month (23 percent of $200).

Negotiation Tactics and Strategies

"If at first you don't succeed, find out if the loser gets anything."

Bill Lyons

When you write to your creditors to suggest reduced minimum monthly payments, let them know that you are treating all

Figure 2.3 Worksheet for J.Q.Consumer

Name of Creditor	*Total Amount Owed*	*% of Total Debt*	*Current Minimum Monthly Payments*	*Proposed New Minimum Monthly Payments*
Company A	$ 5,000	50%	$275	$100
Company B	500	5	20	20
Company C	2,300	23	95	46
Company D	1,200	12	60	24
Company E	1,000	10	50	25
Total	*$10,000*		*$500*	*$200*

of your creditors equally and fairly. Emphasize that no one creditor is receiving preferential treatment and explain how you determined the new monthly minimums you are proposing.

Some of your creditors may be more difficult to work with than others. If a particular creditor seems reluctant to work with you or wants a larger minimum monthly payment than you can afford, do not become confrontational or defensive. Instead, restate your current financial situation and reiterate your sincere interest in paying off your account. Politely but firmly remind the creditor that the best way for you to do this is through reduced monthly minimums.

One strategy to consider when first contacting your creditors is to offer them each a minimum monthly figure that is slightly less than the amount you believe you can really afford. This approach gives you some bargaining room and should result in revised payment amounts that you can handle. For example, if J.Q. Consumer has targeted a new monthly minimum of $275 for Company A, initially it may be wise to propose an amount that is perhaps 10 percent to 15 percent less than $275 and then *compromise* at $275. This approach can help create a win-win situation and leave everyone happy.

Once you have negotiated new payment plans with your creditors, ask each of them to change the information in your account record to reflect the modifications that have resulted from the negotiations. These modifications will include: a new minimum monthly payment amount; an increase in the total number of payments you'll be making (to compensate for the reduced amount of each individual monthly payment); and a past due balance of zero since the revised plan should *wipe your slate clean* and you'll therefore be starting anew.

It is essential that these changes be reflected in your account record since this information is sent to credit reporting agencies. To make certain that the changes are made, review your monthly statements once the new payment plans are in effect. If the changes have not been made, recontact the appropriate creditor and again request that the modifications be made.

Consumer Credit Counseling

"Good counselors lack no clients."

William Shakespeare

Consumer Credit Counseling (CCC) is a nonprofit organization established approximately 20 years ago by the National Foundation for Consumer Credit to educate, counsel and promote the wise use of credit. CCC offers free or low-cost financial education and guidance to consumers. Its services include assistance to people with minor budgeting problems and those who need debt management plans. CCC has over 580 offices across the country. If you don't see a listing in the phone book for a CCC office near you, call 800-388-2227.

When a CCC counselor helps you negotiate new debt payment plans, he or she contacts your creditors for you. Creditors know and respect the services of CCC so they are likely to be receptive to working with you if you are a CCC client.

Hot Tip

Some creditors may be more willing to extend future credit if you have completed CCC's debt management program. They take your involvement in the program as an indication that you are serious about getting your finances under control and about paying off your debt.

After revised payment plans have been negotiated, you begin making your payments directly to CCC who in turn pays your creditors. In other words, your CCC counselor acts as the liaison between you and your creditors, and creditors no longer contact you directly. It usually takes two to three years to complete the debt repayment plans CCC negotiates for you. You are expected to avoid incurring any new debt during this time.

If there is no CCC office close to you, contact nearby colleges, universities, military bases, credit unions or churches to find out if any no-cost / low-cost debt counseling services are offered. You might also call your bank for suggestions about such assistance.

For-Profit Debt Counselors

Whenever possible, negotiate with your creditors yourself or use the services of CCC or another nonprofit organization in your area. If none of these is a realistic option, you may have to work with a for-profit debt counselor. Unfortunately, many of these counselors make extravagant, unrealistic promises about what they can do and charge exorbitant fees for their services. Some may also offer to consolidate your debt or arrange for such a loan—typically at a very high rate of interest.

If you are considering a for-profit debt counselor, thoroughly investigate before you sign any paper work or pay any money. Ask for literature about available services and detailed cost information, as well as the names and phone numbers of several clients willing to talk to you about the value of the services.

Study all of the counselor's materials. Ask questions about anything you don't understand. Confirm all costs, making absolutely certain that all charges are clearly spelled out in the printed materials you review. If the debt counselor has no service and cost information for you to take home, if your questions are not answered to your satisfaction or if the counselor acts evasive, *do not* sign anything and *do not* hand over any money!

If, however, the counselor does provide the information you request, if you conclude that those services could benefit you and if they are affordably priced, contact your local Better Business Bureau and your state attorney general's or consumer affairs office. Find out if they have a record of any complaints against the counselor. If not, the counselor may be able to help you get your finances under control.

Debt Collectors

If a creditor turns your account over to a debt collector or a collection agency, you usually receive a letter from the collector requesting payment of the debt and telling you what to do if you do not believe you owe it or if you dispute the amount. When the debt collector's initial contact is by telephone, the Federal Fair Debt Collection Practices Act (FDCPA) requires that the call be followed within five days by a written notice stating how much you owe and to whom you owe it. The notice must also advise you of your rights under the FDCPA.

After a debt collector has contacted you, get in touch with the creditor immediately to see if he or she would be amenable to negotiating a revised debt repayment plan. At this stage in the collections process, however, creditors are seldom receptive to such a proposal since they often feel that you should have proposed such an option earlier. Some debt collectors require contractual agreements with creditors that prohibit them from contacting you directly.

You have 30 days after a debt collector gets in touch to respond in writing if you do not believe you owe the money or if you disagree with the amount you are said to owe. In your letter, state that you refuse to pay the amount due, provide any proof you may have that supports your side—cancelled checks, correspondence, receipts, etc.—and demand that all collection activities cease immediately. Be sure to indicate in your letter that you are aware of your rights under the FDCPA and that you intend to use them if necessary. Include your name, address and all relevant account information, make a copy of the letter for yourself and send the original to the debt collector via certified mail.

Upon receipt of your letter, the debt collector may not communicate with you again except to tell you that there is to be no further contact or to let you know what the next step will be if further action is planned. However, if the collector sends you proof of your debt, collection proceedings resume.

Should collection proceedings move forward, deal with the debt collector calmly, rationally and politely, realizing that emotional intimidation may be part of the collector's strategy to get you to pay up.

Explain your situation, indicate your interest in paying off the debt and explore the possibility of working out a payment plan.

Staying cool may not be easy since a debt collector's actions can sometimes be upsetting and stressful. In one instance a consumer was contacted by the same collector 20 times in one day at work! In another, a collector had other collectors in his office chant in unison, "pay your debt, pay your debt" each time the debtor answered his phone call! Figure 2.4 summarizes a few strategies for dealing with debt collectors.

Keep impeccable records of all written and verbal communications with a collector. Include the date and time of each phone conversation, the name of the collector who calls, a short summary of each conversation and a copy of all your correspondence. If you need to complain about a debt collector's tactics or end up in court such record keeping could prove invaluable.

The Fair Debt Collection Practices Act

The Fair Debt Collection Practices Act (FDCPA) governs how debt collectors and collection agencies may communicate with consumers and provides legal recourse for those consumers who feel their rights have been violated under the Act. Debt collectors, as defined by the FDCPA, are individuals who regularly collect debts owed by others as well as attorneys who handle debt collection matters as a part of their practice. If an attorney only occasionally gets involved in such matters, the FDCPA does not apply. In addition, the FDCPA does not apply to the actions of a company's in-house collections department. Personal, family and household debt, including charge accounts, auto loans and medically related expenses, are all covered by the FDCPA. Figure 2.5 summarizes the protection offered by the FDCPA.

According to the law, debt collectors may contact consumers in person, by phone, by telegram or mail. However, if they contact you by mail, they may not use a post card that mentions your debt nor may they use a see-through envelope. They are also barred from using mailing envelopes that have a return address or symbol that would indicate that the sender is a debt collector.

According to the FDCPA, debt collectors must contact consumers between 8 A.M. and 9 P.M. unless a consumer indicates that other hours of the day are better. Additionally, debt collectors

Figure 2.4 Practical Tips for Dealing with Debt Collectors

- Buy an answering machine and use it to screen your calls. This approach allows you to gain some day-to-day control over your situation.
- Record any especially abusive messages from a debt collector and use them to take action.
- Do not accept collect calls from debt collectors and do not return their long distance calls unless they leave a toll-free number.
- Never give a debt collector your phone number at work. The credit agreement you signed did not obligate you to be bothered at work or to have your boss contacted.
- In a straightforward manner, tell the debt collector what your situation is. Do not argue, bargain or engage in a discussion.
- Do not refuse to pay a debt that you know you owe. Indicate your desire and willingness to clear up the debt even if you can't pay anything at the time of the call. Say something like, "I would really like to be able to send you the $500 I owe, but I am simply not able to do so at this time."
- If you have already explained that you can't pay your debt right away, do not talk with the collector again if he or she continues to use the phone to harrass you.
- Keep a written record of all phone conversations you have with a debt collector, including the date and time of the call, the name of the collector, the subject of the call and a brief summary of what was discussed.

may not contact consumers at work if the collector is aware that the consumer's employer does not want employees interrupted during working hours.

Unless you hire an attorney to deal with a debt collector, the collector may contact people to learn where you live or work, but not for any other reason. In general, when such contacts are made, the debt collector may not indicate that you owe money.

How To Protect Your Rights

If you feel that a debt collector has violated the provisions of the FDCPA, get in touch with the collector's manager and try to resolve things yourself. If you can't, contact the creditor who hired the debt collector and get in touch with your state attorney general's office or office of consumer affairs. Many states have their own debt collection laws that may provide a remedy for your problem. You may also want to file a complaint with the Federal Trade Commission (FTC). Although this agency cannot take action on behalf of an individual, it can file a class action suit against a debt collector if a pattern of abuse can be established.

If you decide to take legal action against a debt collector, you have one year from the date you believe the violation occurred to file suit in state or federal court. You may sue for damages, court costs and attorney's fees.

Hot Tip

To file a complaint about a debt collector with the Federal Trade Commission (FTC), write the Commission's headquarter's at 6th and Pennsylvania Avenue, N.W., Washington, DC 20580, (202) 326-2222. (See Figure 3.11 in Chapter 3.) Or, you may contact the appropriate FTC regional office. The addresses and telephone numbers of FTC's regional offices may be found in the Resources section at the end of this book.

Finding Legal Assistance

If you require legal assistance but cannot afford to hire an attorney, check your local phone directory for a Legal Aid office in your area. There are 325 Legal Aid offices across the country, funded in part by the federal government's Legal Services

Figure 2.5 Important FDCPA Guidelines

The FDCPA prohibits a variety of practices and actions, including:

- Use or threat of violence or harm to a person, property or reputation
- Repeated phone calls to debtor
- Threats of arrest or imprisonment (There is no such thing as debtors prison.)
- Falsely implying that the collector is a government representative or attorney
- Misrepresenting the amount of money owed by the consumer
- Depositing or threatening to deposit a post-dated check before the date on the check
- Making the debtor accept collect calls or pay for telegrams

Corporation. If you cannot find a listing for Legal Aid in your area, write or call the Legal Services Corporation at 400 Virginia Avenue, S.W., Washington, DC 20024-2751, (202) 863-4089.

These offices offer legal assistance in areas such as credit, landlord-tenant relationships, family problems, welfare, utilities and unemployment. Each Legal Aid office establishes its own priorities regarding the specific types of cases that it focuses on.

The services of Legal Aid are free to those who qualify on the basis of income; each office establishes its own specific eligibility criteria. Legal Aid services are not available to anyone whose household income is greater than 125 percent of the federal poverty guidelines.

If you do not qualify for assistance from Legal Aid or if there is no Legal Aid office in your area, check with the Lawyer Referral Service of your city, county or state bar association for a referral to other sources of affordable legal assistance. Also, if there is a law school in your area, it may run a low-cost/no-cost legal clinic.

The Threat of Legal Action

"Next week there can't be a crisis. My schedule is already full."

Henry Kissinger

You need legal advice if you are unable to negotiate a revised debt payment plan or if you continue to dispute the validity or amount of a debt, and legal action is threatened. Unless a lawsuit has actually been filed against you, your goal in getting this advice should be to assess the seriousness of your situation in order to determine an appropriate response. If you have little or no money to spare, get in touch with one of the no-cost/low-cost sources of legal assistance previously mentioned in this chapter.

Otherwise, get the names of several general practitioners (specialists are more expensive, and you probably don't need one at this point). Call these attorneys to find out if any of them offer an initial free consultation—it's possible that you can get all the information and advice you need during this first meeting. If not, find out if any of the lawyers would schedule an initial one-hour consultation with you and how much that meeting would cost. Attorneys' rates vary depending upon their reputation, practice and the region of the country they are in. One hour of legal advice generally ranges from $40 to $125. Figure 2.6 summarizes tips for selecting a lawyer.

Prior to your first meeting, gather any background information you have about your problem as well as relevant correspondence, receipts, account statements, etc. In order to accomplish the maximum in the allotted hour, put together a list of all the questions you would like answered. When formulating your questions, keep in mind that the point of your meeting is to understand the seriousness of your situation, how strong a legal position you have, what your options are, how the attorney would handle the problem, and what you might be able to do without the lawyer's help to resolve your situation. You especially need to know:

- Does my problem merit the expense of an attorney?
- If the creditor or collector got a judgment against me, what would my liability be? What can they do to me?
- Am I judgment-proof?

After talking with the lawyer and getting as much information and advice as possible, you may decide that you can handle the situation yourself. Or, if your potential liability is significant, it may be obvious that you need professional help. If you decide to work with an attorney, be very clear about how fees are structured and ask about getting the work done for a set price. Also, if you have the time, see if you can defray your costs by doing some of the legal research or running around yourself.

If a lawsuit has already been filed or the possibility is very real, get legal assistance immediately. You should do everything possible to prevent having a lawsuit filed against you. Once a lawsuit is filed and a judgment rendered against you, the rights of the collector or creditor increase significantly, and they have the right to get a lien against your property. In addition, a judgment will further damage your credit record.

Your Taxes and the IRS

If you are in financial trouble, you may be unable to pay all or part of your income taxes by April 15, the filing deadline. If you find yourself in this situation, file your tax return by the deadline anyway. In addition, you will need to get in touch with the IRS immediately in order to avoid a serious escalation of the IRS's considerable collection powers.

Income tax extensions are extensions to file, not to pay, your taxes. If you file an extension, the IRS still expects you to send with it a check or money order for what you expect to owe in taxes. If you don't send payment, Failure To File penalties will be assessed immediately in addition to interest and other future penalties. These initial penalties are the stiffest and are calculated monthly at the rate of 5 percent of your unpaid tax balance with a cap of 25 percent. Interest and additional penalties continue to accrue until you have paid your taxes in full. The interest is compounded daily. Interest and penalties add significantly to your tax debt, so it is best to pay the IRS as quickly as possible.

A Partial Tax Payment

If you can make only a partial payment of taxes, complete and mail your tax return by April 15, and include with it a check or money order for as much as you can pay. Enclose with your

Figure 2.6 Criteria for Selecting an Attorney

- Can I afford the attorney's rates?
- Does the attorney explain my options and potential liability in terms I can understand?
- Does the attorney seem knowledgeable about the issues I'm facing?
- Do I feel that the attorney is sincerely interested in solving my problem... or just interested in the fee?

return a letter that briefly explains your current financial situation, indicates that what you are sending is all that you can presently afford and promises that you will send money each month until your taxes are paid in full. You may also call the IRS at (800) 829-1040 to convey this information. Be sure to keep a copy of your letter for your files.

If your back taxes are paid in full within a year, the IRS will take no further action, and you should receive no further communication from the agency. If at some point during that year, however, your financial situation changes and you will have to miss a payment, or you need to arrange for lower monthly payments, call (800) 829-1040 at once, and ask to speak with a Problem Resolution Officer. As a further precaution, file a Form 911, *Application for Taxpayer Assistance To Relieve Hardship.* You may file this form by telephone (800) 829-3676, in person or by mail. If you don't advise the IRS of the change in your situation, the agency views your missed or reduced payments as a violation of your agreement and begins collection proceedings.

If it will take you up to 36 months to pay your back taxes, the IRS will automatically file a lien against one or more of your assets to ensure that it will get its money if you default. This lien becomes a part of your credit record and even after you get the lien released by paying off your taxes, a record of the lien remains in your file for up to seven years, damaging your credit.

Help in Developing a Payment Plan

If you want to pay your back taxes through an installment plan but are unsure what to suggest, file your tax return by the

April 15 deadline and call (800) 829-1040. You will be asked to provide information regarding your income and expenses so that a realistic payment plan can be established. The monthly amount you pay is not driven by what you owe the IRS but rather by your current financial situation. Do not agree to bigger payments than you can realistically make. Failure to live up to your installment agreement results in an escalation of the IRS's collection proceedings, and you could experience loss of property, garnishment of wages or other unpleasant consequences. Figure 2.7 summarizes your responsibilities under an installment agreement.

The IRS personnel you talk with about an installment plan are generally very helpful—unlike the stereotypical ogre you may conjure up when you think of this agency. When dealing with IRS employees, remember that they are people just like you (possibly experiencing their own financial difficulties!) who are simply doing their jobs. Be businesslike, cooperative and polite when working with them; it is likely they will do the same.

If the IRS decides that without suffering a hardship you can pay more taxes than you feel you can pay, or recommends that you sell some property to raise the money you owe, and you refuse, it notifies you that it is about to initiate collection proceedings. If this happens, file Form 911 and get legal advice immediately. You may need to declare bankruptcy to protect your assets from the IRS.

Failure To Contact the IRS about Unpaid Taxes

If you fail to contact the IRS about unpaid taxes after you file your return, you will begin to receive a series of notices in the mail. These notices are sent over a six-month period and their tone and the actions the IRS threatens get progressively more serious. As soon as you receive a notice from the IRS, get in touch with the agency. If the IRS determines the money to be collectible, arrangements are made for payment, possibly under an installment plan. The longer you wait, the less bargaining power you have and the less amenable the IRS will be to work the problem out with you.

The first notice you receive will be a demand for your unpaid taxes. Ten days later, if you do not respond, you will receive a notice that a lien may be filed against your property. If you still don't respond, you will receive three more notices over a period

Figure 2.7 Installment Agreements

All IRS installment agreements remain in effect ONLY if the following extremely important conditions are met:

- You pay each installment on time.
- You pay all future tax liabilities on time.
- You provide the IRS with correct and complete financial information upon request.
- The IRS judges that collection of the taxes you owe is not at risk.

If any one of these conditions is not met, the IRS will notify you by mail that you are in violation of your agreement and that it will take enforcement action unless your taxes are paid in full.

of several months. After about six months, you will receive by certified mail, IRS's final notice, an intent to levy. If you do not respond within 30 days, the IRS will begin enforcement action to collect its taxes.

If you receive notification that the IRS intends to levy on your property, you are in serious trouble. Take two steps *immediately*! First, file Form 911 with your IRS District Problems Resolution Office or Service Center to temporarily stop the seizure process and give you time to get some legal advice. You may file this form over the phone, in person or by mail.

Second, call the number on the notice or the IRS Problem Resolution Office for your district. If you can't find this number in your local phone book, call the IRS taxpayer assistance number for your area, or 800-829-1040.

Levy is another term for the seizure of personal property, i.e., your home, your bank account, etc., to secure payment for taxes owed. The IRS may actually come to your home to remove property. However, unless you are presented with a court order allowing access to your home, do not allow the IRS agent inside.

If you are concerned the IRS will try to seize the funds in your bank account, here are a couple of tips for protecting those funds:

- When the IRS asks you information about your bank, do not lie. However, as soon as you can, take all of your money out of your current bank, put it in another bank and begin banking there. That way the IRS will not be able to seize your bank account.
- To pay the IRS, open an account at a bank at which you have no other accounts. That way, if the IRS ends up levying your account, the money it takes will have been intended for it anyway. Do not put any money other than funds earmarked for the IRS into this account.

If You Can't Pay the IRS Anything

Again, complete and mail your federal tax return by April 15, and call 800-829-1040 to explain your situation to the IRS. The individual you speak with will ask you to complete a financial statement to determine whether or not you can pay anything and ascertain whether you have any assets that you might sell or it might take. If the IRS determines that your account is uncollectible, collection proceedings will be suspended until your finances improve. Your situation will be reviewed in six months, and if there is no change, the IRS will continue to take no action. Each year until your back taxes plus all interest and penalties are paid, you will receive a notice from the IRS reminding you of your outstanding debt. The IRS has up to ten years to collect what you owe them.

During this time you *will* be expected to file annual tax returns. However, once a return indicates that your financial situation has improved, the IRS will contact you to negotiate an installment agreement for payment of your tax liability.

Hot Tip

Put your social security number on any check or money order you send to the IRS. Do the same if you send the IRS a letter. After your check has cleared and is returned to you with your other cancelled checks, write on it the tax period and the kind of taxes you were paying.

If you receive a bill for tax penalties and you do not understand them, contact the IRS for an explanation. The telephone number and address of the office to contact will be at the bottom of the bill. If you do owe the penalties, but you have a good explanation or *reasonable cause* for why you violated IRS rules, contact this office about the procedure for getting the penalties waived. For example, a serious illness might be considered a *reasonable cause.*

The IRS and Payroll Taxes

If you are a business owner and have fallen behind on your payroll taxes, the process for getting caught up is similar to the process for personal tax liabilities. However, if the IRS determines that your company has a pattern of nonpayment, it eventually shuts your business down, viewing your problem not as a collections matter but as one of abuse. If the IRS threatens to take this action and you are unable to prove that you can pay your back taxes, bankruptcy is probably your best course of action.

When Bankruptcy Is Necessary

> *"When written in Chinese, the word crisis is composed of two characters. One represents danger, and the other represents opportunity."*
>
> *John F. Kennedy*

Bankruptcy should *always* be considered the remedy of last resort. However, there are situations when filing for bankruptcy is your best option. If you are about to lose your home or your car, if the IRS or another creditor is ready to levy against your bank account, seize property or garnish wages, bankruptcy is a wise course of action.

Bankruptcy is a legal process that either legally eliminates your debt or allows all or part of that debt to be repaid over a period of time, usually at a lower interest rate. Bankruptcy offers protection from the IRS for up to five years, giving you time to pay that agency what it is owed. Although bankruptcy offers consumers the benefit of a fresh start, consumers who file may legally be refused credit for up to ten years and may also lose assets.

Types of Bankruptcy

There are four types of bankruptcy available to consumers.

Chapter 7 Straight Liquidation. Most debt is wiped out, but the debtor loses nonexempt property. Each state has laws that protect certain types of property from creditors. That property is termed *exempt.* A consumer bankruptcy attorney can tell you about the exemptions in your particular state. It is important to know about your state's exemptions because they help you protect your assets from creditors. The more you are able to protect, the less you lose in a bankruptcy.

Chapter 13 Adjustment of Debt. Chapter 13 allows a person or a small business to reorganize debts by lowering monthly payments and protects the debtor from creditors while the debt is being paid off. Disposition of a debt is outlined in a reorganization plan developed by the debtor's attorney and based on information provided by the debtor. The plan must be approved by the court. A person who files a Chapter 13 bankruptcy remains in bankruptcy until all debt is disposed of as indicated in the plan. Payments on this debt are made to creditors through the courts for up to five years. Chapter 13 is becoming the most popular type of individual bankruptcy.

Chapter 11 This is another type of reorganization bankruptcy and applies most frequently to very large corporations and businesses. Although individuals can file for Chapter 11 bankruptcy, they rarely do.

Chapter 12 The Family Farmer Reorganization bankruptcy is fairly new and works much the same as Chapter 13. It was created to help farmers keep their farms.

Hot Tip

Once you have filed a Chapter 13 bankruptcy you have five years to pay the IRS what you owe, but you must continue to file annual tax returns during this period. Interest and penalties do not accrue on your unpaid taxes if the IRS did not take a lien against your property prior to the time you filed for a Chapter 13.

Finding a Bankruptcy Attorney

Bankruptcy is a serious and often emotional step. It is therefore important that you find a skilled attorney with whom you feel comfortable, whom you feel will be sensitive to your concerns and whom you feel will work hard to represent you. You also want to find an attorney whose fees are reasonable. Finding such a person can be difficult; here are some tips:

- Look in the Yellow Pages of your local phone book to see if there are attorneys in your area board-certified as bankruptcy specialists. These attorneys should be your first choice.
- Contact lawyers who advertise. They sometimes offer more reasonably priced services than do other attorneys. If you find a board-certified attorney who advertises, you may have a winning combination!
- Contact an attorney whom either you or a friend knows and ask for a referral to a bankruptcy attorney.
- Call the bankruptcy court in your area and obtain the names and telephone numbers of the local bankruptcy trustees. Since trustees work in the bankruptcy system every day, they know which attorneys do the best work.
- Contact your state or local bar association. Most of them have a lawyer referral service.
- Make appointments to see several attorneys in order to judge which ones best understand your problems and can express clear solutions. Comparison shop for price, too.

Hot Tip

For more information on personal bankruptcy, read my first book, *The Bankruptcy Kit: Understanding the Bankruptcy Process, Knowing Your Options, Making a Fresh Start*, (Chicago: Dearborn Financial Publishing, Inc., 1991). This book thoroughly explains the various types of bankruptcies and describes exactly what to expect, depending upon the type of bankruptcy you file. It also explains how to find an attorney and what to expect of your attorney.

Making Ends Meet in Tight Times

"Can anybody remember when the times were not hard and money scarce?"

Ralph Waldo Emerson

Sometimes when money is tight, there is no alternative but to apply for government assistance. While the thought of such help may be repugnant or demoralizing, government assistance can help *make ends meet* until your financial situation improves. Remember, your tax dollars are helping to fund these government programs. Descriptions of some of the broader-based federal assistance programs follow.

Unemployment Insurance is a federal/state-sponsored program administered by the individual states. It makes cash payments to workers who lose their jobs. Typically, payments are available for a 26-week period, although some states offer extended benefits—up to 39 additional weeks in some cases. Each state sets its own benefit amounts and eligibility requirements.

To apply for benefits, contact the office that administers your state's unemployment insurance program. It is listed in the phone book under Unemployment Insurance, Unemployment Compensation, Employment Security or Employment Service. If you begin receiving benefits, you will probably be required to provide evidence that you are actively looking for work in order to continue receiving them.

If you are denied benefits, you may appeal. Your case will be heard at an informal administrative hearing. Witnesses who can substantiate your reasons for receiving unemployment benefits should attend the hearing with you. Also, bring with you any documentation that supports your claim.

If you resign from your job to avoid being fired, you will probably not be eligible for unemployment benefits. If you quit your job because of a problem in the workplace, i.e., sexual harassment or unsafe working conditions, you will be able to collect benefits if you can prove good cause for quitting. However, this often takes time.

Aid to Families with Dependent Children (AFDC) provides cash payments and other assistance to low-income families with dependent children. Dependent children are defined as those who lack the support of one or both parents due to separation, divorce, desertion, death or imprisonment.

AFDC is both a federal and a state program. The federal government gives funds to the states and sets broad guidelines for the use of those funds. The states then set their own eligibility criteria that include the amount of monthly household income a family receives and the dollar value of its assets, excluding a home and an auto. Some states also exclude a certain amount of clothing and furniture as countable assets.

AFDC recipients are required to participate in their state's Job Opportunities and Basic Skills Training (JOBS) program as a condition of eligibility. The program provides job training, work assistance and education opportunities.

The AFDC Unemployed Parent Program was created in 1988 to provide funds to families with children where the primary income earner is unemployed or underemployed.

To find out more about AFDC programs, contact your state's Department of Human Services or Social Services.

The Food Stamp Program gives food stamps or coupons to eligible households to help them supplement the amount of food they are able to buy each month. The program is administered by the U.S. Department of Agriculture, which has established uniform national standards of eligibility for the program. These standards include limits on recipients's monthly income and the dollar value of their assets.

Generally a household's gross monthly income must be at or below 130 percent of federal poverty guidelines in order to qualify, and the net monthly household income must be at or below 100 percent of those guidelines. The total dollar value of the food stamps an eligible household receives is based on the number of persons in the household.

The food stamp program, administered through local or state welfare or social service agencies, also provides employment and training services to food stamp recipients.

Disability Benefits are available to eligible individuals with a physical or mental impairment that is expected to prevent them from doing any *substantial* work for at least one year, as well as to persons with medical conditions that are expected to result in death. These benefits are part of the Social Security program. To qualify, at the time of disability, the individual must have worked for at least five out of the last ten years and been paying into the Social Security system. Family members may also be eligible to receive assistance once the disabled person has begun collecting payments. There is usually a five-month waiting period between the time an application for benefits has been filed and the time that benefits are approved and initiated.

Survivors Benefits under the Social Security program may be payable to members of a family when its breadwinner dies. However, the breadwinner must have been paying into the Social Security system. Benefits are tied to the earnings of the former breadwinner. The more that person earned, the larger the payment, up to a maximum amount.

Supplemental Security Income (SSI) makes monthly payments to individuals who are 65 or over as well as to adults and children who are blind or disabled. To be eligible, the dollar value of an individual's income and assets cannot exceed the limit established by each individual state.

For details and eligibility information about any of these Social Security assistance programs, contact your local Social Security office, or call (800) 772-1213.

The Low-Income Home Energy Assistance Program (HEAP) provides low-income households with heating, cooling and weatherization assistance. Persons participating in the AFDC, Supplemental Security Income or Food Stamps are eligible to participate, as are others who meet the program's eligibility guidelines. HEAP is funded through federal grants to the states. Payments are made directly to eligible households or to home energy suppliers who comply with the program's provisions.

To get details and eligibility criteria for the HEAP in your state, contact your state's Department of Human Services or Social Services.

Conclusion

Keeping your head above water in tough economic times takes a great deal of work. It requires lowering your expectations about the future and a return to *old-fashioned* virtues like thrift and frugality. A prudent approach to financial affairs is called for: pay off your debt, don't take on new debt, save for the future and know your rights as a consumer. Take an active role in solving your problems. Ignoring them or thinking that "things are bound to get better if I just wait long enough" will only lead to disaster.

three

Credit Bureaus

"It does not do to leave a live dragon out of your calculations if you live near him."

J. R. R. Tolkien

A bank asked me to put on a seminar concerning money matters. I invited representatives from Consumer Credit Counseling (CCC), a psychologist who dealt with the emotional and psychological conse-quences of money problems and a representative of a major credit bureau to participate.

Things were going very smoothly; everyone seemed to appreciate the information we were providing, until the credit bureau representative began her presentation. Suddenly, some angry questions were directed at her.

One person said he had been trying to clear up misinformation in his credit record for a year and demanded to know why it was so difficult.

Another said he was delayed in the purchase of a home because of incorrect information in his record.

A third asked how she could make her credit record more attractive to lenders since past financial difficulties had been included in her file.

Every question held a trace of frustration. These people were upset! It was something I had experienced before whenever the issue of credit bureaus came up.

Why do credit bureaus evoke such deep emotions? And why is learning how they work, what your rights are and how to make them responsive so important to everyone? Credit bureaus are the gate consumers must go through to achieve any financial success in America.

If you want to rent an apartment, finance a car or buy a house, it is a credit bureau that determines your ability to do so. A potential employer may use credit bureau information to determine whether or not to hire you. Information in your credit record may even affect your ability to write a check.

Credit bureaus have the power to control your destiny. The information in your credit record literally determines what opportunities you will have or be denied in the future.

Credit bureaus have less influence over you if you can live without credit. However, they always have some impact because they market the information they collect to the government and companies who want to sell you something. It is a fact of life in these complex financial times that some credit is needed to secure proper housing, get transportation and possibly to get a job. Like it or not, credit bureaus are a reality. You cannot deal with them successfully unless you understand how they work and how to make them keep your records straight.

What Is a Credit Bureau?

Credit bureaus, or credit reporting agencies, are in the business of gathering information on individual consumers or users of credit and selling that information to lenders of credit and others. Creditors use this information to make decisions regarding whether or not to extend credit to credit applicants.

There are three national credit bureaus—TRW, Equifax and Trans Union Credit Information Company. Additionally, there are numerous local and regional credit bureaus, many of which are affiliated with one of the nationals.

The information a credit bureau maintains on a consumer in a computerized file is called a *credit history* or *credit record.* Your credit record is essentially a profile of your bill-paying habits—your *track record* as a consumer. It includes information on your debts, on whether you are current or behind on your payments, whether you have defaulted on an account or had one turned over to a collection agency and whether a creditor has closed any of your accounts due to a poor payment history or other related factors. If you have ever applied for a loan or a charge account, at least one credit bureau is maintaining a file on you. When you or someone authorized to review your credit history requests a copy of your credit record, a printed report is made available.

Credit bureaus obtain most of their information from the creditors who subscribe to their credit reporting service. These subscribers include lending institutions, retailers, mortgage companies and credit card companies. Many creditors provide consumer account information to the bureaus they work with on a monthly basis, while others report periodically or only in the case of a default. Some creditors limit their reporting to delinquent accounts or those that have been turned over to a debt collector; others report on all accounts. Figure 3.1 summarizes subscriber reporting activity.

Credit bureaus also collect information, including bankruptcies, foreclosures, tax liens on property, arrests and court judgments, from public records. They also maintain personal statistics on consumers—name and social security number, present and former addresses and employment history.

Who Sees Your Credit Record?

Although lenders of credit are the primary users of credit bureau information, they are not the only ones. The Fair Credit Reporting Act (FCRA), which restricts access to a consumer's credit record and guarantees consumers the right to review and correct their own records, states that prospective landlords, insurance companies for underwriting purposes and potential employers may review a consumer's credit record.

Credit bureaus may also provide identifying information to government agencies, including name, address, former address, place of employment and former place of employment. However, a government agency may review a complete credit file if it needs

Figure 3.1 Frequency of Creditor Reporting

Information on these accounts is generally reported monthly to credit bureaus:

American Express
MasterCard
Visa
Discover
Diners Club
J. C. Penney
Sears
Oil and gas credit cards
Airline charge cards
Department stores and local retailers
Mortgages
Automobile loans
Student loans paid to a bank
Credit union loans

Information on these accounts is generally reported only in the event of collection proceedings, a lawsuit or a judgment:

Utility bills
Telephone bills
Medical bills
Bills from attorneys

to grant credit, review the status of an account, collect on an account or investigate for hiring or insurance purposes. Credit reports are also made available to those evaluating applications for special licenses or security clearances.

The FCRA further states that anyone with a *legitimate business need* may gain access to your credit record. The term *legitimate business need* has been interpreted broadly by credit reporting bureaus, allowing them to justify the sale of repackaged credit bureau data at a considerable profit to direct marketers, retailers and charitable organizations. This is a major loophole in the Act and one that has caused credit bureaus to receive considerable criticism. The House of Representatives is currently considering legislation that would revise the FCRA in the areas of privacy and accuracy.

Reports prepared about a consumer for a potential insurer or employer may contain more information than is found in the traditional credit report. These are *investigative consumer reports* and often include interviews with people familiar with a consumer's lifestyle, character and reputation. If an investigative report is required, you should be notified in writing and will be told how to obtain additional information about the report from the insurer or employer who requested the report.

Why You Should Review Your Credit Record

"Bureaucracy is a giant mechanism operated by pygmies."
Honoré de Balzac

Considering the number of people who can have access to your credit record and the variety of information maintained therein, credit bureaus can have a major impact on your life—affecting your ability to get credit, a job, insurance and a place to live. It is critical to know what information is in your record, review its accuracy and understand how to correct any errors.

A number of independent studies have recently discovered that the files of many credit bureaus are filled with erroneous information as well as with information that should have been deleted from consumers' credit records. A study conducted by Consumers Union, the publisher of *Consumers Report,* revealed that nearly half of the records it studied from the nation's largest bureaus contained errors. Of these, 20 percent had errors serious enough to cause denial of credit.

During 1991 the TRW credit bureau came under fire for the number of inaccuracies in its files and the difficulty consumers experienced trying to correct those errors. In fact, more than 15 state attorney generals filed lawsuits against TRW. Perhaps the most well-publicized example of what can happen when a credit bureau makes a mistake is what happened to many residents of the prosperous town of Norwich, Vermont.

A researcher hired by TRW pulled incorrect information from the town's tax records and inserted it in the credit records of 1,400 people. As a result, the affected parties suddenly found themselves unable to use their credit cards and unable to get mortgages or other types of loans. Not until the local media called attention to the plight of these hapless consumers were they able to get the credit bureau to correct their records.

How To Obtain a Copy of Your Credit Report

Since different credit bureaus get their information from different subscribers, the record one bureau maintains on you may differ from that maintained by another credit reporting agency. First, you'll need to find out which of the national bureaus have you in their files and get a copy of your record from each. Do the same with any local or regional credit reporting agencies not affiliated with one of the nationals.

To do this, look up *credit reporting agencies* or *credit bureaus* in your local Yellow Pages or the Yellow Pages of the city nearest you. Note whether any of the national bureaus are listed. If so, call them, find out if they maintain a file on you, how much it will cost to get a copy of your credit report and how to get the report. In most instances, the cost is between $5 and $15—you can sometimes save money by picking up your report in person.

Next, check with the other credit bureaus in the Yellow Pages and ask each if it is affiliated with one of the nationals. Ask all of them if they maintain a credit record on you. When they say that they do, ask about the process and the cost for getting a copy of your credit report.

To secure a copy of your credit report from one of the national credit bureaus, or to get a question answered about your credit report, write or call your local office or use the following addresses and telephone numbers:

Equifax (Known as CBI in some areas.)
Office of Consumer Affairs
P. O. Box 4081
Atlanta, GA 30302
(800) 685-1111 or (404) 888-3500

TRW Credit Data Division
National Consumer Relations Center
P.O. Box 749029
Dallas, TX 75374-9029
(214) 235-1200, ext. 251

Trans Union Credit Information Company
No national address for assistance. Local offices only.
(800) 521-4019

When submitting a written request for a copy of your credit report, include your full name and social security number, your spouse's full name and social security number (if applicable), your maiden name (if applicable), your current and former address and a check or money order for the appropriate dollar amount. You should obtain a copy of your credit report at least once every six months.

Hot Tip

If you recently applied for credit and were turned down due to information in your credit record, you are entitled to a free report, assuming you make the request in writing within 30 days of the credit denial. Contact the creditor who denied you credit to learn which reporting company to contact. Also, TRW allows consumers one free credit report each year—other credit bureaus may follow suit.

To help you obtain a copy of your credit report, review Letter #1 and Letter #2 in Figure 3.6 and Figure 3.7.

How To Read Your Credit Report

Once you've obtained your credit report, take some time to understand how information is presented and make certain that everything is correct and up-to-date. The Sample Credit Report in Figure 3.2 is similar to the one used by credit bureaus who are members of Associated Credit Bureaus, Inc., a national trade association of credit bureaus and collection agencies. Nonmembers may use a slightly different format but the abbreviations and basic information will generally be the same.

The first section of the sample report provides general background information related to residence, recent employment

Figure 3.2 Sample Credit Report

NAME AND ADDRESS OF CREDIT BUREAU MAKING REPORT

CREDIT BUREAU OF ANYTOWN
1131 MAIN ST.
ANYTOWN, ANYSTATE 12345

☐ SINGLE REFERENCE ☒ IN FILE REPORT ☐ TRADE REPORT
☐ FULL REPORT ☐ EMPLOY & TRADE REPORT ☐ PREVIOUS RESIDENCE REPORT
☐ OTHER ______

FOR FIRST NATIONAL BANK
ANYTOWN, ANYSTATE 12345

Date Received: 4/11/86
Date Mailed: 4/11/86
In File Since: APRIL 1970
Inquired As: JOINT ACCOUNT

CONFIDENTIAL crediscope® REPORT

Member Associated Credit Bureaus, Inc.

REPORT ON: LAST NAME	FIRST NAME	INITIAL	SOCIAL SECURITY NUMBER	SPOUSE'S NAME
CONSUMER	ROBERT	G.	123-45-6789	BETTY R.

ADDRESS:	CITY	STATE:	ZIP CODE	SINCE:	SPOUSE'S SOCIAL SECURITY NO.
1234 ANY ST.	ANYTOWN	ANYSTATE	12333	1973	987-65-4321

COMPLETE TO HERE FOR TRADE REPORT AND SKIP TO CREDIT HISTORY

PRESENT EMPLOYER:	POSITION HELD:	SINCE:	DATE EMPLOY VERIFIED	EST. MONTHLY INCOME
XYZ CORPORATION	ASST. DEPT. MGR.	10/81	12/81	$ 2500

COMPLETE TO HERE FOR EMPLOYMENT AND TRADE REPORT AND SKIP TO CREDIT HISTORY

DATE OF BIRTH	NUMBER OF DEPENDENTS INCLUDING SELF:			OTHER: (EXPLAIN)
5/25/50	4	☒ OWNS OR BUYING HOME	☐ RENTS HOME	☐

FORMER ADDRESS:	CITY:	STATE:	FROM:	TO:
4321 FIRST AVE.	ANYTOWN	ANYSTATE	1970	1973

FORMER EMPLOYER:	POSITION HELD:	FROM:	TO:	EST. MONTHLY INCOME
ABC & ASSOCIATES	SALES PERSON	2/80	9/81	$ 1285

SPOUSE'S EMPLOYER:	POSITION HELD:	SINCE:	DATE EMPLOY VERIFIED	EST. MONTHLY INCOME
BIG CITY DEPT. STORE	CASHIER	4/81	12/81	$ 1200

CREDIT HISTORY (Complete this section for all reports)

						PRESENT STATUS				HISTORICAL STATUS				
							PAST DUE			TIMES PAST DUE				
WHOSE	KIND OF BUSINESS AND ID CODE	DATE REPORTED AND METHOD OF REPORTING	DATE OPENED	DATE OF LAST PAYMENT	HIGHEST CREDIT OR LAST CONTRACT	BALANCE OWING	AMOUNT	NO. OF PAYMENTS	NO. MONTHS HISTORY REVIEWED	30-59 DAYS ONLY	60-89 DAYS ONLY	90 DAYS AND OVER	TYPE & TERMS (MANNER OF PAYMENT)	REMARKS
2	CONSUMER'S BANK B 12-345	2/6/86 AUTOMTD.	12/85	1/86	1200	1100	-0-	-0-	2	-0-	-0-	-0-	INSTALLMENT $100/MO.	
3	BIG CITY DEPT. STORE D 54-321	2/10/86 MANUAL	4/81	1/86	300	100	-0-	-0-	12	-0-	-0-	-0-	REVOLVING $ 25/MO.	
1	SUPER CREDIT CARD N 01-234	12/12/85 AUTOMATD.	7/82	11/85	200	100	100	1	12	1	-0-	-0-	OPEN 30-DAY	

PUBLIC RECORD: SMALL CLAIMS CT. CASE #SC1001 PLAINTIFF: ANYWHERE APPLIANCES
AMOUNT $225 PAID 4/4/82

ADDITIONAL INFORMATION: REF. SMALL CLAIMS CT. CASE #SC1001--5/30/82 SUBJECT SAYS CLAIM PAID
UNDER PROTEST. APPLIANCE DID NOT OPERATE PROPERLY.

This information is furnished in response to an inquiry for the purpose of evaluating credit risks. It has been obtained from sources deemed reliable, the accuracy of which this organization does not guarantee. The inquirer has agreed to indemnify the reporting bureau for any damage arising from misuse of this information, and this report is furnished in reliance upon that indemnity. It must be held in strict confidence, and must not be revealed to the subject reported on, except as required by law.
FORM 2000-5/80

SOURCE: Associated Credit Bureaus, Inc. Reprinted with permission.

history and dependents. The second section presents individual account information and a payment history for each. While most of the account-related information should be fairly easy to understand, there are a few entries that require explanation.

- The numbers **1, 2,** and **3** listed under the heading "**Whose**" (see far left heading under Credit History) indicate who is responsible for payment on an account and who may use the account. "**1**" signifies an individual account. In other words, the person whose name appears on a particular credit record is solely responsible for the account and is the only person who may use the account. "**2**" represents a joint account—responsibility for and use of the account is shared by two persons, usually a husband and wife. "**3**" represents a *user* account—a situation where one person may use the account but a second person is responsible for payment and may also use the account. Parents often arrange this type of account for older children who are college students or who are establishing themselves outside the home.
- The numbers immediately below the account names listed under the heading titled "**Kind of Business and ID Code**" simply represent the numerical system used by the credit bureau to identify a particular creditor.
- Under the heading "**Date Reported and Method of Reporting**" (third heading from the left), the terms "AUTOMTD" or "MANUAL" ("A" or "M" on an actual report) indicate the data source from which account information was compiled.
- The second heading from the right on the sample report is labeled "**Type and Terms.**" Information under this heading indicates the type of payment plan that applies to each account. These payment plans include "**Installment**" ("I" in an actual report), "**Revolving**" ("R") and "**Open 30-day**" ("O"). To the right of the "**Installment**" and "**Revolving**" entries, the amount of each monthly payment is specified.
- There are some other notations and abbreviations not on the sample credit report that you may encounter when reviewing your own report. They include:
- **CURR ACCT**—a current or active account
- **POS**—positive

- **NEG**—negative
- **NON**—not evaluated
- **C**—current or up-to-date on your payments

The bottom section of a credit report is usually where matters of public record are noted. For example, the sample credit report includes some notations regarding a suit in small claims court involving the consumer listed on the report. Although the dispute was settled in favor of the appliance company (plaintiff) in the amount of $225, the consumer protested the decision and was able to include in his credit report a written statement of his side of the dispute as is his legal right under the FCRA.

After receiving your credit report, if you are confused by an entry or don't know how to interpret something, call or visit the credit bureau that prepared the report. All credit bureaus must make trained personnel available to answer questions and provide additional explanations regarding the information in your credit reports.

Common Errors

Review your credit report account by account, notation by notation. As you do, there are a number of common errors to watch for, including:

Accounts That Are Not Yours Credit bureaus frequently confuse the data on people with the same or similar names.

Inaccurate Account Status Information (present status and historical status) This is the heart of your credit report—the part that a creditor will review most closely when evaluating your credit-worthiness. Pay special attention to this section!

Incorrect Dates of Last Activity A *Date of Last Activity*, or DLA, is the last date for which there was some activity on an account. It could be the date the account was turned over to a collection agency, the date a creditor wrote off the account or simply the date final payment was made on the account. It is from this date that information on an account will be maintained for seven years. Obviously you want to make sure that all DLAs in your credit record are correct, especially in the case of an account with negative information.

Outdated Information With few exceptions, credit bureaus are not to report credit information that is more than seven years old. Bankruptcies, however, may be reported for ten years.

Inaccurate Public Record Information

Correcting Your Credit Record

> *"Not everything that is faced can be changed, but nothing can be changed until it is faced."*
>
> ***James Baldwin***

If you discover an error in your credit record, there are a series of steps you must follow to get your record corrected. They are:

- Write (do not call) the credit bureau, explain the error you have noted, ask that it be corrected and request a copy of the corrected report. For an example of the type of letter to write, see Letter #3, Figure 3.8.

Also, send a copy of your letter to the customer service department and the president or CEO of the applicable creditor. If a collection agency reported the incorrect information, send it a copy of your letter as well.

- Contact the creditor involved and find out whether that creditor reports to other credit bureaus. If it does, repeat step #1 with each of the other bureaus.

Once you have contacted the credit bureau about an error, the FCRA requires the bureau to investigate the error and tell you the results of its research within a *reasonable period of time*—generally one month to a month and a half. However, the FCRA does allow a credit reporting agency to refuse to investigate if it feels the dispute is *frivolous* or *irrelevant.*

When researching a possible error, the credit bureau will contact the appropriate creditor and asks it to verify the information in your record. If the credit bureau cannot verify the information in question or if the creditor confirms the error, the erroneous data must be deleted from your record. When this happens, ask the credit bureau to send a corrected report to any creditor who has seen your credit record over the past six months

Figure 3.3 Deleting Information from Credit Reports

Negative account information may be deleted from your credit record when:

- the consumer can prove that the information is in error.
- the creditor can prove the information incorrect.
- the date of last activity (DLA) on the account is more than seven years old.
- the creditor reporting the negative information does not have a record of it.

and to anyone who has reviewed your file for employment purposes over the past two years. If the credit bureau determines that the information you are disputing is correct, it remains in your record.

Hot Tip

When you are trying to get an error corrected, save all your correspondence with the credit bureau, creditor and collection agency. This information could be helpful if you have to go to court over a serious error in your credit record or if you register a complaint with your consumer protection office, attorney general's office or with the FTC.

If the Credit Bureau Won't Correct the Error

"Victory belongs to the most persevering."

Napoleon

Figure 3.3 summarizes the credit bureau's criteria for deleting information. If you don't succeed at getting your record corrected by contacting the credit bureau, take these additional steps:

- Send a letter to the creditor associated with the erroneous information. Explain the error and provide any documentation you may have to support your side of the issue. Such documentation might include a cancelled check, account statements or correspondence between you and the creditor. In your letter, request that the creditor send a correction to you and to all the credit bureaus it reports to. For a sample letter, see Letter #4, Figure 3.9, at the end of this chapter.

- If this resolves your problem, send a follow-up letter to all the credit bureaus involved asking that your credit file be corrected and that a corrected report be sent to you, to anyone who has requested a copy of your credit record over the last six months and to anyone who requested a copy of your record for employment purposes over the past two years. See Letter #5, Figure 3.10, as an example of the type of letter to send.
- If your problem is still not resolved, you may prepare a written statement for your credit record or you may want to consider legal action.

Preparing a Written Statement for Your Credit Record

The FCRA gives you the right to prepare a written statement of up to 100 words, explaining your side of a dispute. You have the right to have that statement made a part of your credit record. If you need help composing this statement, the FCRA states that the credit bureau must provide that help.

Potential creditors, employers, etc. who request a copy of your credit record have the opportunity to review this statement; however, not everyone will necessarily take the time to read it. When you know that someone will be looking at your credit record, it is recommended that you tell that person that you dispute the accuracy of certain information it contains. Indicate why you feel your credit record is in error and if possible, provide information that supports your contention.

How To Deal with Omissions

In reviewing your credit record, you may discover that it omits certain account information that you feel is important to the creation of a full and accurate portrait of you as a potential borrower. You may, for example, have a good mortgage payment history or you may have had excellent credit under another name or in a different part of the country. If you discover important omissions, write the credit bureau and request that the missing information be added to your file. Although credit bureaus are not required to add such information, they may do so for a small fee if the information you want added is verifiable.

If there is anything in your credit report that you feel requires an explanation, ask the credit bureau to allow you to prepare an explanatory statement for inclusion in your file. For example, the plant you worked for may have been shut down leaving you out of work for six months. Or your child may have become seriously ill, saddling you with costly, unexpected medical bills that caused you to fall behind on your financial obligations. Again, while not required to add an explanatory statement to your credit record, credit bureaus may do so if asked.

Hot Tip

If there is negative but correct information in your credit record and you still owe money to the creditor reporting that negative information, consider offering to settle your debt in full in exchange for the creditor changing the way your account is reported. For example, the creditor may agree to report your account as *nonevaluated* rather than as *negative* if you pay your debt in full. Make this request in writing and get your creditor's response in writing before you pay anything.

Women and Credit Histories

Women face unique problems when it comes to credit records. Historically, a woman's credit history was kept in a joint file under her husband's name, which presented her with a serious dilemma if she wanted to obtain credit in her own name or in the event that she became widowed or divorced. In 1974 the federal Equal Credit Opportunity Act (ECOA) was passed to remedy this and other inequities. Among other things, this law says that for all accounts opened jointly after June of 1977, creditors must report account information to credit bureaus in the names of both the husband *and* the wife. (See Chapter 8 for additional details.)

Although passage of the ECOA was a major boon to women, since it made it easier for them to establish their own credit identities, it also poses a potential drawback. If a husband expe-

Figure 3.4 Practical Ways That Married Women Can Prepare for Possible Divorce or Widowhood

- Maintain and manage your own checkbook, whether or not you work outside the home.
- Be sure all credit cards shared by you and your husband are in both of your names.
- Get credit in your own name, if possible.
- Become actively involved in the management of your family's finances.
- Develop good money management skills.

riences credit difficulties, his negative credit information will appear on both his and his wife's credit records. The ECOA dictates that if you can prove that you did not actually use the account in question or were not responsible for the credit difficulties, such negative information may be deleted from your record. Creditors are required to consider any information you may provide toward this end. However, because the ECOA's wording on this issue is quite vague, women usually find it difficult to distance themselves from their husband's financial troubles. Figure 3.4 offers women tips on protecting themselves from future credit difficulties due to divorce or widowhood.

If You Are Married

If you review your credit report and find that the accounts you share with your husband are not included, write to each of the creditors not reporting on you and indicate that you would like all account information reported in both of your names, i.e., Robert Smith and Susan Smith. After doing so, wait a couple of months and recontact the appropriate credit bureaus to confirm that the accounts are now being reported as you had requested.

If you had credit before you were married under a different name or in a different location, make sure that the credit bureaus maintaining a file on you have that information in their files. Also, if you marry and change your name, ask all of your creditors to begin reporting your account information under your new name.

If You Are Widowed or Divorced

If you divorce and decide to change your name, write to all of your creditors asking them to change your name on their account records so that you will continue to build a credit history for yourself under your new name.

If in reviewing your credit record you notice that some of the accounts you shared with your former or deceased husband are not in your record, write the credit bureau and ask it to report them. While the credit bureau is not obligated to do so, it may be willing to include them for a small fee. Prior to adding them, it will probably contact the appropriate creditors to confirm that you did in fact share the account with your husband or were jointly liable for repayment of the debt.

If you were a *user* on your former husband's account (you used and/or paid on the account but were not principally responsible for it), you may also ask the credit bureaus to make those accounts part of your credit history.

Hot Tip

In the event of a separation or divorce, protect your credit record by getting your name removed from all accounts you held jointly with your husband. In doing so, you will no longer be liable for them. This applies to women in all states except the community property states listed below.

Community Property States

Community property states—Arizona, California, Idaho, Louisiana, Nevada, New Mexico, Texas and Washington—present unique obstacles for men and women. In these states, a woman and her husband are legally liable for one another's debts and obligations and have joint control or ownership over all property and income earned during their marriage. Therefore, if a husband defaults on a loan or fails to pay on his credit card, the creditor can take legal action against either the husband or the wife and the credit records of both spouses are equally damaged. The same would apply if a wife defaulted on a loan, etc. Her actions would reflect upon her husband's credit record.

Figure 3.5 Summary of Your Rights under the Fair Credit Reporting Act

- You have the right to a copy of your credit report.
- You have the right to dispute the accuracy and completeness of the information in your credit record.
- You have the right to request that a credit bureau investigate information in your record that you feel is wrong; and you have the right to have that information deleted if it is inaccurate or unverifiable.
- You have the right to have updated information in your credit record sent to any creditors who received a copy of your credit report during the last six months.
- You have the right to place a statement in your credit record if you dispute any of the information in your file.
- You have the right to privacy in terms of who may see your credit record. Access to your credit records is limited to those indicated in the FCRA.
- You have the right to know who has viewed your credit record over the past six months or over the past two years for employment purposes.
- You have the right to have negative information removed from your credit record after seven years, or ten years in the case of a bankruptcy.

Protecting Your Rights under the Fair Credit Reporting Act

Figure 3.5 summarizes your rights under the Fair Credit Reporting Act (FCRA). There are several steps that you should take if you believe that any of your rights under the Act have been violated by a credit bureau or a creditor. First, contact the credit bureau and creditor involved via certified letter. Figure 3.11, Letter #6, at the end of this chapter, provides an example of the type of letter you should write. If sending a letter does not resolve the problem, seek the assistance of your state's consumer protection office or the office of the attorney general. These offices should be able to advise you of your legal rights and of any state laws that may apply to your situation.

You may sue any creditor or credit reporting agency for violating your right to privacy under the FCRA or for not correcting an error in your credit record. You are entitled to sue for actual damages—the financial loss you suffer plus punitive damages—if the court decides that the violation was intentional. You will also be able to recover court costs and attorney fees if you win.

For a more complete discussion of how to protect your rights, refer to Chapter 8.

Small Claims Court

Every state allows consumers to try and settle legal disputes involving small debts and accounts in small claims court assuming the amount of money at issue is under a certain amount. The amount differs from state to state. The advantage of small claims court is that for minimal court costs, you and the other party involved can have an opportunity to state your case in an informal legal setting and have a judge make a decision. You need not have a lawyer in small claims courts, and some states do not even *allow* attorneys to be present. Small claims courts work much like the popular television show *The People's Court.*

To find out how to file a claim in your area's small claims court, look up the court in the city, county or state sections of your telephone directory. When you call, speak with the court clerk and ask about the claims process. If you decide you would like to use small claims court to try and resolve your legal problem, you may want to attend an actual court session ahead of time so you can see the process in action. If you do so, you will probably be less nervous when it is time for your day in court.

Many small claims courts have established mediation or dispute resolution processes that try to resolve a legal dispute before it gets before the judge. A neutral third party listens to both sides of the issue and tries to help the individuals involved work toward a resolution of their problem.

You should also file a complaint with your area's Better Business Bureau and contact the FTC. Although that agency will not intervene on behalf of an individual creditor, it will take action against a credit bureau if it uncovers a pattern of abuse. To register a complaint with the FTC, write: Federal Trade Commission, Bureau of Consumer Protection, Washington, DC 20580. See Letter #7, Figure 3.12 for a sample complaint letter.

Conclusion

It is impossible to know the amount of information credit bureaus gather and how directly that information affects your life. Since their information comes from so many sources, mistakes are inevitable and can prove very costly.

It is essential that all consumers know how credit bureaus work, what their rights are and how to make credit bureaus respect those rights. Unless you understand how to deal with the organizations that influence your life, you risk personal loss as well as the loss of privacy and economic options.

Figure 3.6 Letter Requesting Copy of Your Credit Report

Date

Address of Credit Bureau

Dear Sir or Madam:

Please send me a copy of my credit report.

Full Name ______________________________

Social Security Number ______________________

Date of Birth ____________________________

Current Address __________________________

____

Former Address __________________________

____

(If you have been at your current address for less than ten years)

I've enclosed a check (or money order) in the amount of $________ in payment for the report. Please send the report to me at the following address: (provide complete mailing address).

Thank you for your assistance.

Sincerely,

Signature

Figure 3.7 Letter Requesting Copy of Your Credit Report if You've Been Denied Credit

Date

Address of Credit Bureau

Dear Sir or Madam:

On (date), I was notified by (name of creditor) that I was denied credit due to information in my credit file. I am therefore requesting a copy of my credit report and understand that there will be no fee associated with this request.

Full Name ______________________________

Social Security Number ______________________

Date of Birth ____________________________

Current Address __________________________

____

Former Address ___________________________

____

(If you have been at your current address for less than ten years)

Please send my credit report to the following address: (provide complete mailing address).

Thank you for your assistance.

Sincerely,

Signature

Figure 3.8 Letter Asking To Have an Error Corrected

Date

Address of Credit Bureau

Dear Sir or Madam:

In reviewing a copy of the credit report your company maintains on me, I found the following error(s):

(Succinctly list the errors.)

I request that you investigate these errors, correct them and send me a corrected credit report. Also, please send a copy of the corrected report to any companies and individuals who have requested a copy over the past six months.

Please send my copy to: (provide complete mailing address). If you need to reach me by phone, call (area code/telephone number).

Thank you for your prompt attention to this request.

Sincerely,

Signature

Social Security Number________________________________

Birthdate____

Figure 3.9 Letter to Creditor To Correct an Error

Date

Address of Creditor

Dear Sir or Madam:

I recently received a copy of my credit report from (name of credit bureau). In reviewing it, I noted an error relating to my account with you. I believe this information is in error for the reason(s) listed below and have included documentation that supports this contention.

(Succinctly list your reasons.)

I would appreciate your verifying this error (these errors) and providing the correct information to all the credit bureaus you report to as well as to me. My mailing address is: (provide complete mailing address).

If you need to speak with me I can be reached at: (area code/telephone number).

Thank you for your assistance.

Sincerely,

Signature

Account Number ______________________________

Figure 3.10 Second Letter to Credit Bureau

Date

Address of Credit Bureau

Dear Sir or Madam:

Enclosed is a copy of a letter I received recently from (name of creditor) regarding erroneous information in the credit record you maintain on me. The error relates to my account (give the account number) with (give name of creditor). As you will note, the enclosed letter confirms that the information you have in my file is incorrect.

Please take all necessary steps to correct the error in my record. In addition, please send a corrected copy of my credit report to me as well as to any companies and individuals who have requested a copy of my report over the past six months.

Thank you for your cooperation.

Sincerely,

Signature

Social Security Number ______________________________

Birthdate ____

Figure 3.11 Letter Regarding a Violation of Rights under the FCRA

Date

Address of Credit Bureau

Dear Sir or Madam:

I am writing because I believe that my rights as a consumer under the Fair Credit Reporting Act have been violated. (Note: You may also want to cite any applicable state laws after talking with your state attorney general's office or state office of consumer affairs). My reasons for contending this are: (Succinctly explain what has happened. Include all relevant dates, the actions you have taken to try and resolve the problem, person/s you have spoken with at the company and the actions the company has taken. State what you feel is objectionable about the company's behavior and why you feel it is in violation of the provisions of the FCRA. Enclose copies of all relevant documentation including correspondence, receipts, account statements, etc.).

If we are unable to satisfactorily resolve this problem, I will consider legal action. I am also sending a copy of this letter to the Better Business Bureau, my state's office of the attorney general (or office of consumer affairs) and the Federal Trade Commission (or the appropriate regulatory agency if your problem is with a creditor).

I look forward to hearing from you within seven working days.

Sincerely,

Signature

Figure 3.12 Complaint Letter to the FTC

Date

Address of the FTC

(Washington, D.C. Office or Regional Office)

Dear Sir or Madam:

I am writing to file a formal complaint against__________ ____________________(give complete name of creditor or credit bureau), located at ______________ (give complete mailing address.) My account number is:________ ________________________.

My complaint is as follows: (describe the sequence of events leading up to your problem, include dates, actions you took to resolve the problem, actions the creditor/credit bureau took and state what you feel is objectionable about the company's actions. Enclose copies of any pertinent letters, receipts, account statements, etc.)

I believe that my rights have been violated under the provisions of the Fair Credit Reporting Act.

Sincerely,

Signature

Your Address ____________________________________

Daytime Phone Number ___________________________

four

Rebuilding Credit and Using It Wisely

"There is only one success—to be able to spend your life in your own way."

Christopher Morley

The bankruptcy Gerald and Beth M. went through was unwelcome but gave them an opportunity to start over—a fresh start. They soon discovered, however, that rebuilding their credit would not be easy. Their bankruptcy had been completed more than six months before they came to see me.

Gerald, whose previous unemployment had pushed the couple into bankruptcy, now had a stable job in the management program of a national merchandise store. Tending to three children between the ages of two and six took up most of Beth's time; her earnings were limited to occasional baby-sitting jobs. Although she had tried to work outside the home, the cost of child care for her three young children was so high that her salary barely covered it. She and Gerald felt that it was hardly worth it for her to work considering the small amount of extra money she brought in.

Gerald and Beth asked the same question asked by nearly all of my clients—how to rebuild their credit.

"Are you sure you want to rebuild your credit? I'm familiar with your situation and I don't see how you can afford to take on any new debt," I said.

"We don't want to get in debt again if we can help it," Gerald responded. "We learned our lesson. We once had all the credit cards we could get and discovered they were nothing but trouble."

"Then why do you want to rebuild your credit?"

"We got to talking," Beth answered. "We realized that if we don't rebuild our credit, we're going to have problems in the future. We don't want to limit any chance we might have of improving life for ourselves and our children. Some day we want to buy a house, and we'll need good credit to do that."

Gerald and Beth came to the same conclusion that millions of other people with bad credit have: although living on a cash basis is best, there are times when credit is necessary. For example, the majority of consumers today need credit to finance housing and transportation. It is neither practical nor realistic to think that the average person can save up enough money to buy a new or used car or a home. Everything is too expensive these days.

Another important reason people like Beth and Gerald need to rebuild their credit records has to do with credit bureaus. As discussed in Chapter 3, many employers in both the public and private sectors check a person's credit history before making a hiring decision. In times of high unemployment and fierce competition for jobs, a poor credit history can limit a person's ability to get a good job. See Figure 4.1 for more reasons to rebuild your credit.

Living without credit is the best way to live, but most people simply cannot afford to do that. Credit is a part of the American way of life. You need to have good credit and learn how to use it wisely so it can become a positive financial tool—not something that will get you into financial trouble.

When To Start Rebuilding

"If you do not think about the future, you cannot have one."

John Galsworthy

Once your financial troubles are behind you, it is time to start thinking about building a new credit history for yourself and planning for the future. While you don't want to make the same mistakes with credit that may have gotten you into trouble in the first place, you may need to borrow money from the bank at some point—perhaps to buy a car—and you will probably want a national bankcard for use when traveling or in an emergency.

In general, your bankruptcy must have been concluded or your financial difficulties must have occurred at least two years ago before most creditors will even consider extending credit to you at reasonable terms. Until you reach the two-year mark, therefore, attend to the factors that contributed to your financial troubles, increase your household income as much as possible and start saving—even if it's only a small amount each month. Correct any problems in your credit record so that it looks as good as possible, and keep any active accounts trouble-free.

Rebuilding your credit record takes time, perhaps as long as two or three years. You are creating a new history for yourself as a consumer and need to establish a pattern of responsible credit use over time. As you rebuild, don't get frustrated or discouraged about how slow it's going. Your credit was damaged over time, and it will take time to rebuild it.

Credit Repair Companies

When you are ready to begin rebuilding your credit, do not hire a *credit repair* or *credit fix-it* company to help you. Although they make claims about their ability to "erase bad credit" or "wipe a bankruptcy from your credit record," they can't do anything you can't do for yourself under the terms of the Fair Credit Reporting Act (FCRA), and they can't rebuild your record any faster than you can. They charge between $50 and $1,500—often up front—and their services are generally a waste of money. Credit repair companies *cannot* erase negative information from your credit record—only the credit bureau can do that over time.

If you are victimized by a credit repair company, contact your state attorney general's office or consumer affairs office to learn if you have any legal recourse. In states that have adopted legislation to regulate credit repair companies—including

Figure 4.1 Reasons To Rebuild Your Credit

You will want to rebuild your credit in order to:

- finance the purchase of a home or appropriate, reliable transportation;
- get a job;
- have a credit card for renting a car, reserving a hotel room or using in the event of a serious emergency; or
- help your children go to college.

Key Rules of Thumb When Rebuilding Your Credit

- Build slowly. Do not go out and start applying for a lot of credit. When you apply for new credit, most creditors request a copy of your credit record. Each time they do so, their request shows up on your report as an inquiry. Most creditors take a negative view of credit reports that show many inquiries since they interpret them as an indication that you are trying to get too much credit.
- Keep the amount of credit you get to a minimum. Having a lot of credit can easily lead to abuse and a recurrence of financial difficulty.
- Pay at least the minimum due on all your accounts, pay on time or preferably pay in full each month.
- Steer clear of credit repair or fix-it companies.

Arkansas, California, Connecticut, Florida, Georgia, Louisiana, Maryland, Massachusetts, Nevada, New York, Oklahoma, Texas, Utah, Virginia and Washington—you may be able to get some of your money back.

Also, report your problem to the Federal Trade Commission (FTC). Although the FTC cannot take action on behalf of an individual consumer, it will take action against a company that has shown a pattern of violations. Your complaint may help build a case for such action, and you may be able to save other consumers from being victimized. To lodge a complaint against a credit repair company, contact: Credit Practices Division, Federal Trade Commission, Washington, DC 20580.

What Credit Repair Companies Do

Under the terms of the FCRA, consumers who believe that their credit bureau files contain incorrect information have the right to request that the information be changed. If the credit bureau does not verify the information within a "reasonable period of time," the FCRA stipulates that the unverified information must be dropped from the consumer's credit record. The typical credit repair company inundates credit bureaus with requests for verification of information in a consumer's credit record with the expectation that the bureaus will not be able to check all the requests in a timely manner.

Some credit repair companies advise consumers to bargain with their creditors. Consumers with accounts in collection may be told to pay only part of what is owed, and note on their check for partial payment that in accepting the money the creditor will cease collection activity and erase negative information about the account from the consumer's record. This is generally useless advice since creditors are under no obligation to accept such payment terms.

Be wary of credit repair companies that make *money-back* guarantees. Such claims are simply a way for a company to get a consumer's money and then go out of business before victimized consumers have the chance to get their money refunded.

If you feel that you've actually located a reputable credit repair company, take the following precautions before working with it:

- Check out the company by calling your state attorney general's office or consumer affairs office. Also, contact the Better Business Bureau in your area to see if they have a record of complaints against the company.
- Meet with representatives of the credit repair company, show them a copy of your credit report and ask for a written statement of exactly what they can do for you—what they can get removed from your record and what they will have changed. A formal statement provides you with legal recourse if the company does not live up to its promises. If the

company is not willing to put its promises in writing, take that as a strong indication that it will not be able to do what it has advertised.

The First Step—Getting a Bank Loan

" 'Tain't no use to sit and whine
'Cause the fish ain't on your line
Bait your hook an' keep on tryin',
Keep a-goin."

Frank L. Stanton

Everyone's situation is different, so there is no single guaranteed way to rebuild credit. It is generally a good idea to start by getting a cash-secured loan from a bank in your community. The advantage of rebuilding this way is that you are forced to start saving money, something that many people have difficulty with. Also, by working with a bank, you are developing a positive relationship with a creditor who may be able to make you a car loan or help you buy a house in the future. Other ways to initiate the credit rebuilding process include getting a secured national bankcard or opening a charge account with a local department store and then gradually applying for additional, harder-to-get credit. Figure 4.2 contains five steps for rebuilding credit.

Finding a banker sympathetic to your situation can sometimes be "easier said than done." Unlike most businesses, banks are highly regulated and are required to minimize their risk in order to protect their depositors' money. Federal and state bank examiners regularly review the types of loans a bank is making to ensure that they are not making too many high risk loans—banks that do are in jeopardy of losing their charters. To help minimize their risk, most banks and S & Ls have a written policy of not extending credit to anyone who has filed a Chapter 7 or Chapter 11 bankruptcy. Most banks are also reluctant to loan to consumers who have filed a Chapter 13 bankruptcy or experienced significant financial difficulty.

The professional success of loan officers is strongly influenced by the quality of their loans. If they make a high percentage of good loans that generate money for the bank, they help advance

Figure 4.2 Overview of the Credit Rebuilding Process

Step 1. Find a friendly banker.
Step 2. Get a cash-secured loan.
Step 3. Apply for a national bankcard.
Step 4. Apply for "instant credit."
Step 5. Monitor your credit record.

their careers. If they make a high percentage of bad loans, they jeopardize their careers. Since they are essentially taking a career risk every time they make a loan, loan officers tend to be conservative in their lending decisions. Some banks are more willing than others to work with financially troubled consumers; it is at one of these that you are most apt to find a friendly banker.

Finding a Friendly Banker

> *"A banker is a person who is willing to make you a loan if you present sufficient evidence to show that you don't need it."*
>
> ***Herbert V. Prochnow***

Start your search for a friendly banker with the banks in your community. A bank is usually more open to working with someone from its own area. Note whether any of the banks in your community are promoting consumer-oriented lending programs, such as *debt consolidation programs.* If so, they are sending signals that they are consumer-friendly, and therefore you should put them at the top of your list of banks to contact.

Another approach is to find out where the company you work for does its banking. If your employer is a good bank customer and you are a long-time employee, that bank might be willing to work with you. Ask your employer's financial officer to provide you with a letter of reference to the bank.

Develop a list of banks to contact and call the first bank on your list. Ask to speak with a consumer loan officer. Briefly explain your financial history, the fact that you are trying to rebuild your credit and that you would like to schedule an appointment to talk about the possibility of getting a cash-secured loan. If you get a clear signal that the officer is not interested in meeting, call another consumer loan officer at the same bank. If you have no success at the first bank, go to the next one on your list. Continue this process until you find someone who is willing to meet with you.

If you are unable to find a loan officer to meet with you, or if the ones you meet with won't give you a cash-secured loan, select the bank that seems to be your best bet, open a savings account there and make regular deposits until you've accumulated between $500 and $1,000. By doing this, you demonstrate how serious you are about making a fresh start. Once you've accumulated the money, make an appointment with a loan officer to discuss the possibility of a cash-secured loan. If the officer agrees, the rest of your experience should be similar to what is described elsewhere in this chapter.

If the banker won't give you a cash-secured loan, find out what you need to do to get such a loan. If the terms sound reasonable, you may want to stay at that bank and continue working toward the loan. If they do not, or if the loan officer says that the bank won't ever loan you money on a more normal basis, resume your search for a friendly bank and transfer your funds.

The First Meeting

Once you've found a consumer loan officer willing to talk, request a personal financial statement form from the bank, complete it and bring it with you to your appointment. For your appointment, dress conservatively and neatly, don't wear a lot of expensive jewelry and be on time. Make a good first impression!

At your initial meeting, explain that you are willing to do whatever is necessary to rebuild your credit so that in the future you can borrow money on a more normal basis—e.g., an unsecured loan. Tell the loan officer about your financial goals. For example, you may have children you want to help put through college; you may want to buy a house or remodel the one you are in. Explain what you have been doing to improve your situation since you got into financial trouble—a new or second job, a less expensive place to live, a family budget.

Explain everything that you have done or are doing to address the problems that caused you to get into financial difficulty.

Tell the loan officer of any problems in your credit record that you have had to work out since your efforts will be evidence that you are truly concerned about rebuilding your credit. It is important to do whatever you can to convince the loan officer that your prior financial problems are not likely to recur.

The Second Meeting

If things go well the first time, the loan officer will probably suggest a follow-up meeting. By then, your credit record will have been checked for signs of recurrent trouble and analyzed to determine how long ago your financial troubles occurred.

The loan officer may agree to make you a cash-secured loan, probably for somewhere between $500 and $1,000. You will probably be asked to put the loan proceeds in a certificate of deposit at the bank. You then begin paying off your loan, probably over a year's time. At the end of that year, you will have begun to develop a track record of timely payments with the bank and you will have money in savings!

Getting a Second Loan

Contact the credit bureaus your bank reports to when you've paid off your first loan. Make sure that each one has a record of your payment history on the loan. If they don't, ask your loan officer to report it.

You should then apply for a second loan from the same bank in order to demonstrate a pattern of responsible credit use over time—a new credit history. Good performance on a single loan is not sufficient in most cases.

Manage the second loan the same way you did the first—or you may be able to borrow additional money by collateralizing a loan. Once again, when this second loan is paid off, make sure that your payment history is reflected in your credit record.

Hot Tip

If it has become obvious that the bank that gave you your first loan is happy to have your money in an account but is probably not going to loan you money on a "more normal basis" in the near future, renew your efforts to find a friendly bank.

Shopping for a National Bankcard

When your income has stabilized and your spending habits are under control, your next step in the credit rebuilding process is to apply for a Visa or a MasterCard. Selecting the best one can be tricky given the number of financial institutions and other sources issuing national bankcards these days and the variety of terms available. (See Figure 4.3 for a list of institutions issuing national bankcards.) Take some time to become familiar with the terminology and features you are most likely to encounter when reviewing bankcard offers. And remember, don't take any bankcard offer at face value—read the fine print! Common bankcard terms and features include:

Annual Fee The amount you pay each year for the privilege of having a national bankcard. Annual fees vary widely—usually $15 to $35 for regular bankcards and up to $50 for premium cards.

Some cards do not come with an annual fee. If you find one of these, be sure that the issuing bank is not waiving the fee for the first year only, or substituting a monthly fee for the annual one. Also, check to be sure that the bank is not simply substituting a very high rate of interest for an annual fee.

Interest Rate All bankcard issuers charge interest on an account's unpaid balance. Interest rates vary depending upon the issuer's terms of credit and the laws of the state where the card issuer is located. Different states set different ceilings for the maximum amount of interest that may be charged—usually between 16 percent and 20 percent. If you don't expect to pay your account balance in full each month, finding a card with a low interest rate should be a priority.

Credit Limit Maximum credit limits generally range from $300 to $5,000.

Grace Period This is the approximate amount of time you have to pay your account balance in full each month before finance charges are assessed. Not all bankcards have a grace period, but the longer the grace period the better—especially if you don't expect to be paying your account balance in full each month. In most cases, the grace period is applicable only if the account does not have a previous unpaid balance.

Transaction Fee Some bankcards have a per-use fee for certain card features—cash advances, travelers check transactions, etc.

Late Payment Fee The smaller the fee is the better.

Penalty for Exceeding Your Credit Limit Not all cards have this penalty; if the ones you are considering do, the lower the penalty, the better.

Line of Credit or Credit Limit This is the maximum amount a cardholder can charge on a bankcard, generally between $300 and $6,000.

Special Features These may include personal check cashing, access to money machine networks and travelers check dispensaries, cash advances, etc.

Once you have obtained a national bankcard, do not use it for frivolous purchases just to rebuild your credit; use it for something truly necessary. Also, once you've been making payments on the card for several months, find out which credit bureaus the issuing bank reports to and check with them to make certain that your account payments are now a part of your credit record.

Hot Tip

For practical advice about how to select and use credit cards, read *Credit Card Secrets You Will Surely Profit From* by Howard Strong, Boswell Corporation, 1989.

Secured or Collateralized National Bankcards

If you are turned down for a national bankcard, apply for a secured or collateralized card. These cards, which may be used just like regular bankcards, were devised to help meet the credit needs of the increasing number of consumers with poor credit records. Issuers of secured bankcards require you to collateralize your credit purchases, either by opening a savings account or purchasing a CD from them. If you default on the account or are late with payments, the bank can protect itself by withdrawing an appropriate amount of money from the account. On the other hand, if you make payments on time, the money in the account remains untouched, your credit record gradually improves and you may eventually be able to obtain an unsecured national

Figure 4.3 Sources of a National Bankcard

Don't limit your search for a national bankcard to banks and savings and loans. Other sources of national bankcards, sometimes with excellent terms, include:

- credit unions;
- professional and civic associations;
- labor unions.

Also consider applying for a bankcard from a bank outside your town or state. Financial institutions often solicit out-of-state or regional customers.

bankcard. Deposit requirements and relatively steep interest rates make secured credit cards an expensive form of credit.

For a list of banks that offer secured bankcards, current as of the date of this writing, see the Resources section at the end of this book. This information changes *frequently.* A list of banks offering secured bankcards, updated quarterly, is available for $4 from BankCard Holders of America (BHA). BHA also publishes a list of banks that offer low interest regular bankcards to consumers across the country; this list sells for $1. To order these lists, write: BHA, 560 Herndon Pkwy., Ste. 120, Herndon, VA 22070 or call (800) 638-6407.

Selecting a Secured Bankcard

When shopping for a secured bankcard there are some additional factors to check out besides those that apply to traditional bankcards, including:

- How large a deposit is required? Deposits generally range from a few hundred to a few thousand dollars. Since you may not have access to your deposit while you have the card, the size of the deposit should be a major consideration.
- At what rate will your deposit be earning interest, and will you be earning interest on the entire deposit or only on a portion of it?

- Does the issuing bank require that the deposit go into a savings account, or is a higher yielding certificate of deposit or money market account also an option?
- What percentage of your deposit will your credit line be? It will probably range from 50 percent to 100 percent. In other words, if you deposit $1,000, you will either have a $500 line of credit (50 percent) or a $1,000 line of credit (100 percent).
- Can you increase your credit limit without increasing the deposit, assuming a solid payment history? How soon after getting your card can you increase its limit?
- Can you convert your card to an unsecured bankcard and under what conditions? Some banks permit this after one year, assuming payments have been made on time.
- How soon after an account is past due will the issuing bank apply your deposit to your account balance?
- How long after you close your account can you withdraw your deposit? The typical waiting period is about 45 days. Are there other fees associated with closing the account?
- Are application/processing fees required? How much?

Bankcard Scams

Be wary of two common national card offers—catalog merchandise cards, often marketed as *gold* or *platinum* cards, and *guaranteed* credit cards.

Catalog Merchandise Cards

Marketers of catalog merchandise cards or *gold* or *platinum* cards usually imply that these cards are very similar to regular bankcards; however, the two types of cards have little if anything in common. Catalog merchandise cards are usually good only for the purchase of products from a catalog provided by the card issuer. The variety of merchandise in these catalogs is not only limited but frequently is priced higher than retail.

The company marketing these cards often asks applicants to pay $50 or more just to obtain one and often you incur additional costs after their card has been ordered. In many cases, the application process requires calling a "900" or "976" toll-charge telephone number for which callers are charged by the minute. It is not unusual for the telephone application process alone to cost the applicant as much as $50! Additionally, some card issuers require that card holders put up a cash deposit before ordering any catalog merchandise!

Hot Tip

If you receive a phone call or mail solicitation inviting you to apply for a credit card at terms that sound unbelievably good, call your local Better Business Bureau, attorney general's office and/or your consumer affairs office to find out if there have been any complaints lodged against the company offering the card. Read the fine print in any literature and application forms.

Some of the companies marketing catalog merchandise cards promise access to a MasterCard or Visa once the cardholder has used the catalog merchandise card for a while. In most cases, however, these promised cards are secured, not regular, bankcards, so even more money is involved. In addition, many marketers of catalog merchandise cards imply that cardholders will boost their credit rating by using the card, which is rarely the case. If you are considering using one of these cards to improve your credit record, ask which (if any) credit bureaus the card issuer reports to and call those bureaus to verify the information before you start the card application process.

"Guaranteed" Cards

In most cases, respondents to ads for *guaranteed* credit cards get nothing more than a list of companies that issue secured credit cards. Such lists usually contain information you could easily obtain yourself, for little or no money. According to the Better Business Bureau, one way to identify ads for *guaranteed credit cards* is to note whether the company offering them is *processing* credit cards rather than *issuing* them.

Retailer Cards

After you obtain a national bankcard and have been using it for several months, apply for credit from a retail store in your area. In most cases, retail stores will give you credit simply because you have the bankcard. Again, do not purchase anything frivolous with this additional credit; buy something you truly need and make your payments on time!

After you've made payments on your *instant credit* for several months, contact the appropriate credit bureau(s) to make sure that these payments are reflected in your credit record. If not, take the steps necessary to get this payment information included.

Educating Yourself about Credit

> *"It is possible to fly without motors, but not without knowledge and skill."*
>
> *Wilbur Wright*

To become a smart user of credit, you must become familiar with the basic types of credit and the credit-related terminology that you are most apt to encounter. Figure 4.4 suggests ideas for educating yourself. With this information you will be able to evaluate various loan and bankcard offers and determine whether one credit option has advantages over another. For example, are you better off applying for a bank loan, activating your checking account cash advance or using a bankcard?

Types of Credit

There are three basic types of credit: open-end or revolving, installment or closed-end and 30-day.

Open-End or Revolving Credit Plans

These plans establish a maximum amount or *line* of credit. You may charge up to that maximum, but must pay at least the minimum amount due on the account each month. This minimum will be a percentage of the account's outstanding balance. Examples of this type of credit plan include:

- Bankcards like Visa and MasterCard
- Secured bankcards

Open 30-Day Credit Plans

These plans allow you to charge up to your credit limit or ability to pay but require you to pay your account balance in full each month, or within 30 days of the billing date. This type of credit includes:

Figure 4.4 Ways To Become Credit Smart

- Enroll in a personal finance class at your local community college.
- Read your local paper to find out about low-cost/ no-cost personal finance seminars being offered in your area.
- Ask your friendly banker to recommend courses you might take.
- Ask the librarian at your public library to suggest some books on credit and personal finance.
- Read consumer finance magazines like *Kiplinger's Personal Finance* and *Money*.

- **Retail or Store Charge Cards.** Many retailers also offer open-end charges. The laws of the state where you live govern the terms of retail credit card agreements.
- **Travel and Entertainment Cards.** These cards offer higher credit limits than most bankcards and charge relatively high rates of interest. Interest and penalties are limited by the laws of the state where you live.
- **Oil and Gas Cards.** These easily attainable, convenient to use cards often have higher interest rates. Use with care.

Closed-End or Installment Credit Plans

These plans provide a fixed amount of money to be repaid in predetermined amounts (or installments) over a specific period of time. Credit options that fall under this heading include:

- **Installment Loans.** These are commonly used to finance the purchase of relatively expensive goods and services, such as automobiles, furniture, home improvements and major appliances. Monthly loan payments usually include principal plus interest with interest assessed from the date the loan is made. Depending upon the amount and your credit history, installment loans are often collateralized.
- **Mortgage Loans.** These are essentially large installment loans with very long payback periods, up to 30 years.

Monthly payments often include not only the loan's principal and interest but also insurance and taxes on the property; the mortgaged property serves as collateral. Mortgage loans may sometimes be used to finance home improvements and can represent second and even third loans on a piece of real estate.

- **Home Equity Loans**. See Chapter 2.

The Truth in Lending Act

"'Tis not knowing much but what is useful that makes a man wise."

Thomas Fuller

The task of comparing sources of credit was made significantly easier in 1968 with the passage of the federal *Truth in Lending Act* (TLA). Among other things, the law requires all lenders to fully disclose to potential borrowers the total cost of credit or borrowing. This total cost includes interest plus all fees and must be expressed as both a dollar amount and an annual percentage rate or APR.

The TLA states that this information, in addition to all other TLA-mandated information, must be disclosed in writing—using standard terminology—before a consumer signs for credit. See Figure 4.5 for other provisions of the TLA.

Calculation of Interest

"When money is not a servant, it is a master."

Italian Proverb

As valuable a piece of information as the APR is, don't make credit decisions based on APR alone. It won't tell you all you need to know and relying on it alone can actually be misleading. Other important factors should be considered.

Loans and Other Closed-End Credit

If you are considering getting a loan, it is important that you consider the total amount of interest you will pay over the life of

Figure 4.5 Other Provisions of the Truth in Lending Act

TLA's provisions distinguish between open-end or revolving credit and closed-end or installment credit.

Open-End Credit

Lenders of open-end credit, such as bankcard issuers, must provide information about:

- the length of the grace or free period;
- the method used to calculate finance charges on the account;
- all associated fees, e.g., membership fee, transaction fee, etc.

Closed-End Credit

Lenders of closed-end credit, such as banks making loans, must disclose the:

- amount of any down payment required;
- total amount to be borrowed or financed;
- repayment schedule (This does not apply to housing loans.); the number and amount of payments and the total dollar amount of these payments;
- total amount of finance charges that will be paid over the life of the loan. This total must include all interest payments plus any additional costs such as insurance, service charges, late fees and appraisal fees in the case of a mortgage loan.

the loan. Although loans for the same amount may have the same APRs, their total costs are affected by the method each lender uses to calculate finance charges. When calculating interest, most lenders use one of three basic methods:

Simple Interest Simple interest assumes that you will pay interest only on the original amount of money borrowed—the principal—and that interest will be calculated based on that portion of the original principal you still owe.

Example: Assume you borrow $1,000 at 5 percent for one year. Interest on that loan using the simple interest method will be $50. Therefore, at the end of the year, you will pay $1,050, or the principal plus a year's worth of interest.

Many banks use a variation on simple interest called "interest on the declining balance." With this method, you make periodic loan payments rather than a single payment at the end of the loan period and pay interest on the amount of the original loan principal that has not yet been repaid. The amount of interest paid decreases with each loan payment. At the same time, the amount of the original loan principal that you actually have to use also gets smaller. This interest calculation method is actually more expensive for you than the previous method since you don't have full use of the money borrowed for the entire period of the loan.

Example: Assume you borrow the same $1,000 at 5 percent for one year but will pay off the loan in two payments—the first after having the loan for six months, and the second at the end of the loan period, or the end of the year. The total amount of interest that you pay will be $37.50. The first payment will be $500, or half of the $1,000 plus $25 in interest (5 percent of $1,000 divided by 2, or one-half of a year). Then, at the end of the year, you will pay $512.50 ($500 or the balance of the loan, plus 5 percent of that balance for a half year or $12.50).

Add-on Interest Lenders who use this method calculate interest on the full amount of the principal and then add that amount to the principal. The lender then determines the amount of your payments by dividing the interest plus principal by the number of payments you will make over the life of the loan. When two or more payments are made, this method is quite expensive because you don't have full use of the principal for the total period of the loan. In fact, as the number of loan payments increases, so too does the effective interest rate on the loan since the borrower has increasingly less of the original principal to use. This method is often used by finance companies and is sometimes used by some banks for consumer loans.

Example: Assume the same loan amount and interest rate as in the prior two examples and assume you make two equal loan payments over the one-year period. Using this method, you will pay $525 at the end of the first *six-month period ($1050 divided in half) and the second $525 at the end of the year or loan period. The effective interest rate using this method is 6.6 percent rather than 5 percent, since you don't have the full use of the $1,000 for the full year; instead, $1,000 is available for the first half of the year while only slightly more than $500 is available during the second half of the year.*

Discounted Interest When a creditor uses this method, it calculates the total amount of interest to be paid on the loan, deducts that interest amount from the loan principal and gives you the difference. Generally, this method is used for relatively short-term loans.

Example: Again, making the same assumptions about the amount and terms of the loan as were made in the previous examples, you will actually receive $950 ($1,000 less 5 percent interest on the principal, or $50). If the $1,000 is repaid at the end of the year, the effective rate of interest on the borrowed money will be about 5.3 percent, slightly more than the interest paid using the simple interest calculation. Again, this is because you don't have full use of the borrowed $1,000.

Bankcards and Other Open-End Credit

When considering open-end credit sources, you need to be aware of the method the creditor uses to calculate the balance upon which finance charges are calculated. The method used can significantly affect the amount of interest you pay, even if the APR is the same for every credit source.

Balances for finance charges can be calculated three ways:

Adjusted Daily Balance This is generally your best deal. The balance is calculated by taking an account's opening balance, subtracting all payments made during the grace period and then applying the finance charge to that new or adjusted balance. New purchases made during the billing period are not included in this balance calculation.

Average Daily Balance This method is the one most frequently used by creditors. It monitors an account's balance each day during the billing period, subtracting payments and adding new purchases in some instances. At the end of the billing period, the daily ending balances are totaled up and then divided by the number of days in that period to determine the account's "average daily balance."

Previous Balance This method is generally your worst deal. Finance charges are applied to an account's previous balance without reducing that balance by the amount of payments made during the current billing period; however, new account transactions are not accounted for either.

Hot Tip

From a very practical perspective, the amount of each total monthly payment needs to be an important consideration when shopping for credit since you do not want to have problems making your payments. Two sources of credit may have the same APRs, but different payback periods. The source with the longer payback period costs you less month-to-month, but is the more costly source of credit over the long term since you will pay more in finance charges. However, even if it has a higher APR, this source may be your best option if you need to keep your monthly payment as small as possible.

Home Mortgages

Qualifying for a home mortgage loan after serious financial difficulty may not be easy, but it is not impossible—even in the case of bankruptcy. You may be considered for an FHA loan if you have been out of bankruptcy for at least one year, and considered for a VA loan if you have been out of bankruptcy for two to three years. However, if you were forced into bankruptcy by situations or events beyond your control, you will probably be judged to be a better credit risk at this stage in your recovery than those whose financial troubles were of their own making.

HUD Homes

HUD homes are foreclosed homes that were originally financed with an FHA-insured mortgage. They are an excellent source of well-priced real estate that includes single-family homes, condominiums and town houses. Sold "as is," the average price of a HUD home is $40,000. If you are willing to buy a "fixer-upper," you can get some especially good bargains.

Aside from price, the major advantage of a HUD home to a person recovering from serious financial difficulty is that it will require a lot less money up front than the traditional home. Up-front costs usually include: earnest money or a deposit on the home you want to buy to demonstrate that your offer is a serious one; a down payment; and closing costs. With a HUD home, the typical deposit ranges from $500 to $2,000 and the down payment may be as little as 3 percent of the selling price, compared to a down payment of 10 percent to 20 percent for a traditional home. Additionally, HUD may pay many of the closing costs, which are generally 3 percent to 4 percent of a home's price and, although HUD requires the use of a real estate broker, it will pay the broker's commission.

To find out about the HUD homes for sale in your area, look in your local paper's real estate classified section or call an area realtor. Real estate brokers who sell HUD homes maintain a complete list of available HUD properties.

When you speak with a broker, ask who to contact for loan information. If possible, get prequalified for a loan in order to speed up the loan process after you've found a home. This is important because once you make an offer on a HUD home and your offer is accepted, you have only 60 days to close the sale. Most lenders need three to six weeks after receipt of your application to complete the loan approval process.

Completing an Application for Credit

When completing a credit application, be accurate and thorough; however, present your financial information in as flattering a light as possible. As you list your debts, put those with the best payment history first. Do not omit debts because they have negative histories—the creditor will find out about them when a credit check is run. In fact, omitting such information could actually jeopardize your chance of getting credit by calling into question your honesty and integrity. A better approach involves scheduling a personal meeting with the creditor or attaching an explanatory note to your application.

When listing your assets on the application, be as complete as possible and be sure to value them at their current market value. Some of these assets may be potential collateral.

What Do Creditors Look for When Evaluating a Credit Applicant?

Creditors look at three basics when deciding whether to give you credit:

Capacity Creditors judge ability to repay by looking at your job, income and current obligations. They use this information to calculate how much you have left over each month after bills are paid. A rule of thumb used by many creditors is that your monthly credit payments, including credit cards, should not exceed 10 percent of gross household income or 15 percent of net income, after housing and taxes. Additionally, most creditors do not like to extend credit to anyone whose mortgages exceed 28 percent of their gross income.

Character Creditors evaluate character by reviewing your credit record together with any other information that might be relevant. In general, they believe that past credit handling behavior is indicative of future credit handling behavior, or character. This is why they usually run a credit check on credit applicants.

Collateral Creditors care about collateral because they want to be sure that an applicant has sufficient resources to secure or back up a loan in the event that the consumer defaults. They also care about any sources of income the credit applicant has in addition to regular salary. Collateral can often make the difference between getting and not getting a loan.

The Scoring Process

Most creditors use an internal scoring system to evaluate information in a credit record and on a credit application. They often assign numerical values to particular creditor characteristics or other types of information. For example, a person who owns a home, has a savings and a checking account and has a stable employment history usually scores higher than one who rents, has no savings and has changed jobs frequently.

Larger creditors may feed all relevant information into a computer that will in turn approve or disapprove a credit application. Smaller creditors, or creditors with whom a consumer has an established relationship, may evaluate credit applications more subjectively and be more likely to evaluate loan eligibility on a case-by-case basis rather than according to a rigid formula.

If you are turned down for credit by one creditor, don't lose heart—apply with another. Since different creditors use different scoring systems, a person who is denied credit by one creditor may be granted credit by another.

The sheer number of consumers in serious financial difficulty is causing a growing number of creditors to reevaluate their criteria for granting credit. The emerging trend is for creditors to be more open-minded about extending credit to individuals who have experienced bankruptcy or who have seriously damaged their credit record due to financial trouble. Credit applications are increasingly being evaluated on a case-by-case basis with special attention given to reasons behind financial difficulty and the status of a person's financial situation at the time of application. Creditors like Sears, Citicorp and J.C. Penney are giving special consideration to those consumers who have gone through the Consumer Credit Counseling (CCC) debt management program and paid off all their debt—including their accounts with them. These and other companies will consider extending credit to CCC *graduates,* although working with CCC is not a *guarantee* of credit.

With these changes in mind, it is an excellent idea to accompany each credit application with a letter that explains why you got into financial trouble, discusses what you have done to deal with your finances and the progress you've made. You may also want to include letters of recommendation from your banker and creditors with whom you have a good payment history. Figure 4.6 gives general advice on credit applications.

The Equal Opportunity Act

The Equal Credit Opportunity Act prohibits creditors from discriminating on the basis of sex, age, race, nationality, religion and marital status, among other factors. It also requires that creditors notify you in writing of their acceptance or denial within 30 days of the time they receive the credit application and all information needed to process it. If you are denied credit, the creditor must either state the reason for the denial or inform you of your right to know. You then have 60 days to request in writing the reason for denial of credit.

Conclusion

Despite the difficulties my clients have experienced with credit, the question I am most often asked as a bankruptcy attorney is "How long will it be before I have credit again?" Why are people so anxious to get back in debt, especially after having gone through bankruptcy?

Some people, like Gerald and Beth whose story started this chapter, have good reason to reestablish their credit. They are young and raising a family and do not want to limit any chance they may have of improving life for themselves and their children. And they realize that it will be hard to save enough to pay cash for a home or a car.

To survive in the coming years, the virtues of thrift and savings are essential. Although this chapter tells you how to rebuild your credit, do not do it if your lifestyle will permit you to live without it. DO NOT SPEND MONEY YOU DO NOT HAVE is still the very best advice. However, if like Gerald and Beth, you feel you must have credit, use it wisely. Do not get more credit than you can afford, pay off your debt as quickly as possible and save as much as you can.

Figure 4.6 What To Do before You Sign a Credit Application or Loan Agreement

- Read everything carefully and completely, even the fine print. If you have questions, get them answered to your satisfaction before you sign.
- Do not rely on verbal agreements. Make sure to get them in writing!
- Do not sign any blank forms that the creditor says will be filled out later. If you do, you may discover later that the blanks have been filled in with terms other than what you had agreed to.
- If you need time to think the credit terms over, don't let the creditor talk you into signing the paperwork and calling in your final decision. It is possible that while you're off "mulling it over," the paperwork will be processed, obligating you to the terms of the contract.
- If you discuss changes that will be made to the contract, do not sign until the new paperwork accurately reflects the credit terms you agreed to.
- Make sure that any carbons attached to what you are signing match the actual papers you sign.
- Get a copy of all the documents you sign and file them for safekeeping.

five

Increasing Your Household Income

"I don't have anything against work. I just figure why deprive somebody who really loves it?"

Dobie Gillis

Karla S. was stuck in a merchandise sales job at a large department store. Recently divorced, she knew it was up to her to provide for herself and her 12-year-old son. Her ex-husband sent child support payments on an irregular basis—nothing she could count on.

Because of the debt she and her ex-husband had accumulated, Karla was forced into bankruptcy soon after the divorce. Now she was trying to rebuild her life. As part of that effort, she wanted to find a better paying job. She wanted to become a professional, possibly going back to school to become a nurse. Although Karla was smart and highly motivated, she had no idea how to find a job where she could earn more money, nor did she know how to prepare herself for a professional career.

Since I had helped her with her bankruptcy, Karla made an appointment with me to discuss how she might make these changes in her life and what resources were available to help her. I gave her copies of listings for jobs available through her city and state governments and told her about other sources of employment information that she might use to help her earn more money. We also discussed the sort of professional career she might pursue given her interests and abilities. I told her about a free career development seminar the local women's center sponsored periodically and encouraged her to look into a program offered by the local community college for working women who want to pursue a degree. I also urged her to check into her eligibility for financial assistance.

It takes a lot of effort to find ways to earn extra money, change your career or get more education. It's hard to do the necessary research when you have to earn a living and are exhausted by the time you arrive home each day! However, increasing your household income, whether through a second job, a change of careers or a new job, may be the key to stabilizing your financial situation and ensuring the long-term success of your financial recovery. Use the information in this chapter as a starting point for analyzing your options and planning exactly what you will do to earn more money, now and in the future.

After you decide which options to pursue, set a goal for each one, break the goals into small, achievable steps and establish a time frame for accomplishing each one. This type of planning won't guarantee that you'll successfully achieve your goals, but it will help. Factors such as employment opportunities in your community, the economic conditions in your part of the country and your area's educational resources—not to mention luck—will all play a role in your career change. The process of goal-setting and systematically working toward what you want to achieve will move you toward your goal and increase the likelihood of your success.

There are many ways to make more money. Some are as simple as telling your employer that you would like to work overtime or would like to add a second shift. Locating a better paying job is another obvious option. Another way to make more money is to moonlight—to work a second job. If you choose this option, you will become part of a growing trend. According to the Bureau of Labor Statistics, 6.2 percent of all American workers hold two or more jobs, the highest percentage in 30 years! Of these, 7.9 percent are managers and professionals.

Technological advances have had a dramatic effect on certain industries and have diminished the market value and/or demand for certain types of job skills. If your financial problems are the result of technological change, you probably need to find a new job or get retrained/reeducated for a new career. You may also want to consider learning a new job skill or beginning a new career if you are the victim of a slowed economy and have experienced cutbacks in your hours, suffered temporary layoffs or lost your job entirely.

A full-time or part-time job for a spouse not currently working outside the home is another way to help make ends meet, at least until your finances get stabilized. One alternative is a home-based business, an especially attractive option for mothers who want to work but also want to be at home with their young children. According to the October 1989 issue of *Woman's Enterprise Magazine,* more than 400,000 home-based businesses are started by mothers each year.

How To Find a Better-Paying Job

> *"If you only knock long enough and loud enough at the gate, you are sure to wake up somebody."*
>
> **Henry Wadsworth Longfellow**

Increasing your household income may be a matter of finding a better paying job. If you have good skills and live in a populous area where job opportunities abound, this may be relatively easy to accomplish. Otherwise, landing a better job will require greater effort. Whatever your situation, do not quit your current job until you have a new one.

Here are some hints for finding a new job:

- Tell close friends, family members and professional acquaintances that you are looking for a job and ask them to "keep their eyes and ears open" for any opportunities they feel might be of interest to you. Many jobs are never advertised in the classifieds but are filled through word-of-mouth and networking.

- Ask your professional associates and co-workers if they can suggest people you should meet with—not to talk about a specific job, but to brainstorm about possible job leads.
- Read the employment ads in the classifieds section of your local newspaper and in those of towns and cities within driving distance of your home.
- Track companies moving into your area. They may be looking for people with your job skills and experience.
- Contact companies that interest you even if they don't have a job opening in your area of expertise. Visit these companies to fill out job applications or send a resumé to the head of the division or department you'd like to work for. Attach a cover letter to the resumé expressing your interest in being considered for an appropriate position should one open up. Follow up with a phone call.
- If you belong to a union or professional association, see if they have a job bank or provide other types of job assistance.
- Visit or call your state's Job Service or Public Employment Service office, which maintains information about job vacancies in government and sometimes in the private sector as well. Job counseling and referral services, job search training, resumé development assistance and skills assessment services are also offered. Some state employment offices have specific programs to help laid-off workers, and all give veterans priority treatment.
- Contact your local and/or county Human Resource or Personnel departments to learn about their job placement and referral services.
- Call the Federal Job Information Center about federal government employment (202) 653-8468. You may also be able to find out about specific federal job vacancies in your area from your state Job Service or Public Employment Service office.
- Look in your local Yellow Pages under Employment Services. This listing may include nonprofit agencies, often government-funded, that maintain job banks or offer job placement and referral services at little or no cost.
- Schedule appointments with several of the larger job placement or personnel agencies in your area. They will be listed in the Yellow Pages under Employment or Jobs. Although

they may not have a position that is right for you at the time of your appointment, if you impress them with your attitude, skills and experience, they may call you later when they are trying to fill a job opening.

- If you are a relatively high-paid professional with managerial experience, schedule appointments with executive recruitment or executive search firms. Before you do, be certain you have a well-prepared, up-to-date resumé. See Figure 5.1 for resumé preparation hints. If you need more help, visit your local library to learn how to prepare one.

Outside Help

If you decide you need help finding a job, you should be familiar with the various types of companies and organizations that offer employment-related services so you can select the one best able to help you. Figure 5.2 gives some tips on using outside help, and Figure 5.3 provides advice on job interviews.

Hot Tip

Before you sign an agreement or pay any money to a company offering employment-related services, understand exactly what services the company offers, the cost of those services and whether you or the potential employer will pay for them.

Major sources of employment assistance are:

Employment Agencies and Personnel Placement Services These firms help companies fill specific job vacancies. In some instances, the hiring company pays a placement fee to the employment agency; in others, the fee may be shared by the employer and the new employee or paid entirely by the new employee.

Executive Search Firms or Executive Recruiters Search firms, often referred to as *headhunters,* are used to recruit relatively high-salaried individuals for a specific job. The company hiring a search firm pays all fees.

Public Employment Service or Job Service Offices Operated across the country with federal assistance, these offices are a free source of information—primarily about relatively low-wage,

Figure 5.1 Preparing a Resumé

There is no set format for resumés. In fact, you may want to customize your resumé to reflect the specific type of job you are looking for. When preparing a resumé, it is important to remember the following:

- Keep it as brief as possible.
- Check for misspellings and grammatical errors.
- For a professional look, put your resumé on a neutral-colored paper.
- Attach a separate sheet that lists the names, titles, addresses and phone numbers of your references.
- Include this standard information in your resumé:

  - Your name, address and telephone number

  - Your employment history

List your current or most recent job first. For each position held, include your employer's name and address, dates of employment, your job title and a description of responsibilities and accomplishments.

- Enumerate your educational background, including your degrees or the highest grade you completed, the schools you attended, graduation dates, majors and special awards and recognitions.
- List special skills, achievements, professional or civic organization memberships, awards, etc.
- Attend job fairs. Often an excellent place to learn about companies that are hiring and the types of positions they are filling, they are also good places to gather general background information about the companies that interest you most. Be sure to dress neatly and professionally; company representatives are usually on hand to answer your questions or conduct an initial interview.
- At the library, review reference materials available on job hunting and job opportunities.

unskilled jobs. Job Service offices are mandated to provide special assistance to Vietnam veterans, welfare recipients, the handicapped, older workers, youths and minorities.

Temporary Agencies These agencies find individuals to work for an employer on a temporary basis. The employer pays the agency and the agency pays the temporary worker.

Hot Tip

To help you analyze your strengths and weaknesses in order to determine the jobs for which you are best-suited, read the most recent edition of *What Color Is Your Parachute?* by Richard Nelson Bolles, Ten Speed Press.

Job Scams

"A man who is always ready to believe what he is told will never do well."

Gaius Petronius

In your search for more lucrative employment opportunities, be wary of job scams. Common scams include employment ads that direct you to a "900" telephone number and ads that require you to pay a substantial up-front fee for job-finding assistance.

Often found among more traditional ads in the employment section of the paper, the typical "900" telephone number employment ad promises that with a simple phone call you will gain access to a variety of genuine job possibilities; some ads also imply that you will be guaranteed a job. In reality, the information you receive will be of little or no value. When you call the "900" telephone number, you will be charged a flat fee, a per minute charge or a combination—all are expensive. Be skeptical of ads that advise you to call an "800" toll-free number and once you do, direct you to a "900" number.

"900" ads that require you to pay an up-front fee for job-finding assistance are dangerous because respondents rarely get what they are promised. In some reported instances, consumers have paid as much as $600 to obtain a list of overseas jobs and then been matched with a limited number of prospective employers. Most of these individuals received neither an interview nor a job. Figure 5.4 offers additional job scam protection advice.

Figure 5.2 Three Tips for Getting the Job Help You Need

- Work with an employment assistance company or organization that regularly fills the type of position you are looking for. Your newspaper's classified employment ads, as well as employment ads in relevant trade and professional publications, are good ways to identify the right companies to contact.
- Be very clear about who pays any employment fees. If you have to pay the fees, find out when the fee is due and if you must pay it even if the company is unable to locate a job for you.
- Before signing an agreement, read it carefully and question anything you do not understand.

Changing Careers

"If at first you don't succeed, you are running about average."
M. H. Anderson

Changing careers is a serious and major step, but sometimes a new career is necessary. Your employer may go out of business, leaving no comparable employers in your area; job opportunities in your current field may be declining due to a changing economy; or you may have already reached the maximum earnings potential in your field and you need to earn more money.

When a career change is indicated, try to choose an occupation that offers you job stability, opportunity for advancement and good earnings potential. Determine whether or not the career you are considering is in demand and whether it has application to a number of different industries. Maximize your options.

A number of resources can be used to learn the occupations and industries that are growing or declining. The Department of Labor's Bureau of Labor Statistics publishes an excellent free brochure entitled *Getting Back to Work,* which supplies growth and salary information for a variety of industries and occupations together with general information about the kinds of education

Figure 5.3 How To Have a Good Job Interview

- Prior to your interview, do some background research on the company. Learn as much as you can about the history of the company, where it is heading and any problems it may be having. To get this information, talk to friends or acquaintances who may already work there or go to the library. Also, learn as much as you can about the person who will be interviewing you
- Spend time assessing your strengths, weaknesses and special accomplishments.
- Role play. Ask a friend or professional associate to ask you questions you might be asked during the interview so you can decide how best to phrase your answers.
- Act confident, but don't dominate the interview.
- Don't ask about salary, vacations, sick leave, etc. These are appropriate subjects during a follow-up interview or if you are offered the job.
- Don't act nervous or bored, and do not smoke.

and training these industries typically require. (See Figure 5.5.) It also provides advice about finding a job—including analyzing your job skills, finding job openings, interviewing and preparing a resumé and cover letter. To order, write: Government Printing Office, Publications Service Section, Washington, DC 20402.

Hot Tip

For an in-depth analysis of the training, skills and knowledge necessary for selecting and developing a successful new career in the 90s, read *The 100 Best Jobs for the 1990s & Beyond,* Dearborn Financial Publishing, Inc., 1992. Written by Carol Kleiman, one of the nation's foremost authorities on jobs and the workplace, this book includes information on the fastest-growing job fields, inside tips on finding a job and advice on changing jobs and preparing for the future.

Figure 5.4 How To Protect Yourself from Job Scams

- Don't call an employment ad with a "900" number unless you know how much it will cost.
- If you discover "900" charges on your phone bill as a result of a call to a less than honest employment advertiser, contact your telephone company immediately and request that those charges be deleted. Although not obligated to credit you, many will do so if you ask.
- When a company placing an ad says it can help you but wants you to give it money up front, obtain a written statement of the services it will provide and the guarantees it will make before you pay anything.
- Before any money changes hands, contact your state attorney general's office or office of consumer affairs, the appropriate state licensing agency and the Better Business Bureau in the town where the agency is located to find out about any possible complaints lodged against it. These are the same agencies and offices you should contact if you experience a problem with an employment-related firm.

One of the best ways to learn is to gather information from individuals working in an industry, occupation or at a particular company that interests you. Their experiences can help you find out about specific educational or training requirements, job responsibilities, wages or salaries (starting and potential), advancement opportunities, the future outlook of the industry or occupation and the growth plans of the company.

The assistance of professional career counselors is available through public employment service offices, federally funded job training programs and for-profit companies. See Figure 5.6 for additional sources of career and job hunting information.

Figure 5.5 The Outlook for Selected Occupations

Selected Occupations Projected for Very Fast Rates of Growth Between 1988 and 2000 Include:

- Data processing equipment repairers
- Automotive body repairers
- Taxi drivers and subway operators
- Correction officers and jailers
- Private detectives
- Optical goods workers
- Reservation and travel clerks
- Bread and pastry bakers
- Nurses, medical technicians, home health aids, etc.
- Waiters and waitresses
- Credit checkers and authorizers
- Electrical technicians

Selected Occupations Projected for Slow or Very Slow Rates of Growth Between 1988 and 2000 Include:

- Typists and word processors
- Electronic and electronic equipment assemblers
- Gas and petroleum plant workers
- Data entry keyers
- Telephone and cable TV line installers and repairers
- Farm workers
- Machine operators working in both the metal and plastics fields
- Broadcast operators
- Bank tellers
- Bookkeeping and accounting clerks
- Rail transportation jobs

SOURCE: Information taken from *Getting Back to Work, U.S. Department of Labor, Bureau of Labor Statistics, 1991.*

Job Training and Career Education

"There will never be a system invented that will do away with the necessity of work."

Henry Ford

Private trade, technical or career schools may be one of the first resources you consider if you are contemplating changing your career or learning new job skills. Before you enroll, however, realize that these schools are businesses and exist to make a profit. While there are many reputable trade and technical schools, unscrupulous schools also exist, ready to victimize students through questionable business practices—high pressure sales tactics that lure students with unrealistic promises of high salaries and glamorous jobs upon graduation; failure to properly refund tuition to students; and poor quality instruction. Many of these schools charge exorbitant prices for skills and knowledge that have little marketability or that could be acquired at far less cost at a community college. Also, students at some of these schools show a very high default rate on the federally guaranteed student loans they received to help pay for their education.

Hot Tip

If you borrowed federal funds to help pay for the costs of a trade or technical school, and you believe that the school did not provide the education it promised, overpromised the career possibilities you would have available upon graduation or would not refund your tuition as per your agreement, contact the U.S. Department of Education at (800) 647-8733. In Washington, DC, call 755-2770.

Selecting a Trade or Technical School

To avoid becoming a victim, carefully evaluate the schools you are considering on the basis of the education and training they are offering and all associated costs. Use the following guidelines to select the best school for you.

- Avoid schools that use high pressure tactics to get you to sign a contract and enroll. Many "admissions counselors"

Figure 5.6 Sources of Career and Job Hunting Information

The Department of Labor publishes a number of useful publications including:

- *Occupational Outlook Handbook*
- *Tips for Finding the Right Job*
- *Tomorrow's Jobs*
- *Resumés, Application Forms, Cover Letters and Interviews*

All of these publications are available free or for a nominal fee and can be ordered through the Consumer Information Center. To find out how to order and the costs of each publication, write: *Consumer Information Catalog*, Consumer Information Center, P.O. Box 100, Pueblo, CO 81002.

Merchandising Your Job Talents, another free publication, provides advice about writing resumés, interviewing and taking pre-employment tests. This book can be found at most state-run Public Employment Service offices or can be ordered by calling (202) 783-3238.

are no more than salespeople who earn a commission every time they sign up a student.

- Ask for printed brochures and catalogs that describe programs and costs, and request general background information on the school's history and credentials. Steer clear of any school that doesn't have printed information or will not readily answer your questions.
- Visit the school you are considering and ask to see its classrooms, labs and other teaching-related facilities.
- Ask to sit in on one or more of the classes you would be taking if you enrolled.
- If possible, talk to students currently attending the school you are considering to learn whether they are satisfied with the training and education they are receiving. Also, ask the school for the names and phone numbers of six or more

graduates of the program you are interested in so you can talk with them about how readily they found a job at the salary they wanted after graduation.

- Avoid schools whose administrators act evasive, secretive or make grandiose promises that they won't put in writing.
- Talk to administrators or counselors about their school's academic standards and the training and education they look for before accepting a student into a particular program.
- Contact employers in the field you are considering and ask them to evaluate the curriculum you would be studying. Find out if they would be apt to hire someone who had completed that curriculum.
- Be wary of any school that does not straightforwardly explain the pros and cons of the financial aid you might receive, and fails to convey to you that a student loan is just that—a loan you will have to repay.
- Get written information on tuition and any additional costs. These might include lab fees, equipment, uniforms, books and other classroom materials, meals, etc.
- Find out about the background and experience of the teachers in the program. Do they have the appropriate credentials and skills?
- If you are going to be trained on special equipment, make sure that it is up-to-date and that there is enough of it for everyone in the class to work on.
- Compare the offerings and costs of the school you are considering with community colleges and adult education courses in your area to determine the best value.
- Find out what the school's student loan default rate is. Call (800) 4FED-AID.

Hot Tip

To check out a trade or technical school, contact the National Association of Trade and Technical Schools. This nationally recognized accrediting organization is located at 2251 Wisconsin Avenue, N.W., Washington, DC 20007. You may call the association at (202) 333-1021.

Paying for Job Education and Training

"If you think education is expensive, try ignorance."
Derek Bok

How can you afford the cost of career training and education? The federal government offers a variety of grants, low-interest loans and work-study programs. For specific information, call (800) 333-4636. To find out if the school you are considering participates in any of these programs, contact the school's financial aid office.

Federal Loans

You will be obligated to start repaying your education loan once you complete your education, regardless of whether you actually locate a job in your new field or increase your income. The following federal loans should be investigated.

A Perkins Loan is a 5-percent interest loan available to both undergraduate and graduate students. Students do not have to be full-time to be eligible for a Perkins Loan.

Stafford Loans are low-interest loans for students attending school at least half-time.

Supplemental Loans for Students (SLS) are variable rate loans for both undergraduate and graduate students.

Federal Grants

Grants provide financial assistance that the student does not have to repay. The following are representative examples:

Pell Grants are available to undergraduate students who are attending school at least half-time. Eligibility is based on financial need, and an individual student's need is determined using a complex formula established by Congress.

Supplemental Educational Opportunity Grants (SEOG) are available to undergraduates who can demonstrate an exceptional financial need. Students attending school less than half-time are eligible. Unlike the Pell Grants, SEOG is administered at the individual campus level.

Federal Work-Study

Work-study programs provide jobs to students as a way of helping them pay for their education. The federal College Work-Study program is for both undergraduate and graduate students. It provides on-campus and off-campus jobs to qualifying students.

Hot Tip

The U.S. Department of Education publishes an excellent overview of its education assistance programs—*The Student Guide to Federal Financial Aid Programs.* Updated annually, the guide can be obtained by calling (800) 333-4636 or writing Federal Student Aid Programs, P.O. Box 84, Washington, DC 20044.

Other Sources of Financial Assistance

Your state may fund and administer its own education assistance programs. Call your state Department of Education and talk to the financial aid office at the school you will be attending to learn about possible sources of financial aid. Find out about application deadlines and apply for financial aid as early as possible. Before applying, however, work out a realistic budget so that you borrow as little as possible.

In addition, you may be eligible for a special scholarship or grant due to your ethnicity, sex, religion, academic or professional achievements, artistic abilities or other special characteristics. To find out, talk to a school's financial aid officer, review a directory of scholarships and grants at your local library or get a copy of *Higher Education Opportunities For Minorities and Women.* For price and ordering information, call (202) 783-3238. If you are a veteran, contact your regional Veterans Administration office and your state veterans affairs office to learn if you are eligible for any other assistance.

Federal Job Assistance

A number of federally sponsored programs offer employment assistance and job training. They include:

The Economic Dislocation and Worker Adjustment Assistance Act (EDWAA) provides assistance to individuals who have lost their jobs and are not likely to find new employment in the same industry or occupation. EDWAA covers persons who are the victims of massive layoffs and plant closings, as well as the long-term unemployed, those whose unemployment benefits have run out, farmers and some displaced homemakers.

Services funded by EDWAA and by state matching funds include: skill training, job search assistance, relocation assistance, basic education, English-as-a-second-language classes, and career counseling. Since every state administers its services differently, the best way to learn more about your state's EDWAA policies is to call your Governor's office .

The Job Training Partnership Act (JTPA) provides training and employment assistance to disadvantaged and dislocated workers. Services are planned and delivered locally through partnerships between private and public organizations. The focus of each local service delivery system is the Private Industry Council, or PIC. To find out about the services available in your area and whether or not you might benefit from them, call the Private Industry Council in your area. If you don't see a listing for a PIC in your local phone book, call your Governor's office.

Hot Tip

Veterans should call their nearest U.S. Department of Labor, Veterans's Employment and Training Service office to find out about any special job-related assistance for which they may be eligible.

The Trade Adjustment Assistance Act (TAA) was designed to provide assistance to workers who lose their jobs or become under employed as a direct result of increased foreign imports. Its benefits are similar to those of EDWAA. Unlike EDWAA, however, a single individual cannot apply for TAA assistance. Instead, a group of at least three workers, their union, or some other authorized representative, must file a petition for TAA assistance with the Department of Labor's Office of Trade Adjustment. Upon filing, that office will conduct an investigation to determine whether or not increased imports did contribute significantly to job loss or under-employment. In the case of an affirmative decision, the eligibility of individual workers for

TAA benefits is then determined by individual state unemployment insurance offices.

The Clean Air Transition Assistance Program is specifically targeted toward individuals who were working at or for a facility that had to lay off workers in order to meet the requirements of the Clean Air Act of 1990. To be eligible for assistance, workers must meet EDWAA eligibility criteria. Services provided are the same as those provided through EDWAA.

To learn more about any of these programs, look in your local phone directory under U.S. Government, Labor Department, Employment and Training Administration; write Department of Labor, Employment and Training Administration, RM N-4469, 200 Constitution Avenue, N.W., Washington, DC 20210; or call (202) 523-6871. To find out if your state administers its own job assistance programs, look in the state government section of your telephone book under listings such as Employment Service, Employment Security Commission, Employment and Training, Human Services or Job Service and call the agency listed there.

Moonlighting

"Two men look out through the same bars. One sees the earth, and one sees the stars."

F. Langbridge

The possibilities for moonlighting, or working a second job, are numerous and varied. They include free-lancing, contract work, temporary work and part-time businesses. Some moonlighting jobs develop out of a hobby, a long-time interest or a special skill, while others simply provide a way to earn extra cash during financially tight times. Once your financial pressures are over, the extra job can be dropped. In some instances, however, moonlighting becomes so lucrative and fun that it eventually becomes your main source of income.

Free-Lancing involves selling your skills or services directly to clients. You might become a free-lance writer or graphic artist, a consultant or a free-lance bookkeeper. Free-lancers usually work alone, often out of their homes, although they may get help for an especially big project.

Contract Work involves being hired by a company to accomplish a project that its own employees are either too busy to handle or don't have the expertise to do. Organizing and completing a large mailing, delivering phone books or helping with a telephone survey are all examples of work that is frequently performed on a contract basis.

Often advertised in the employment classifieds section of newspapers under part-time or general work, contract work is also advertised via word-of-mouth. If you would like to work on a contract basis, read your local newspaper and tell your friends and acquaintances about your interest in contract work.

Temporary Work involves working for a company or an organization for a predetermined and relatively short period of time, anywhere from a day to a month or more. Some temporary agencies specialize in workers with specific types of skills such as nursing, clerical or computer knowledge. Others work with day laborers. If you have special training or skills, call the temporary agencies in your area to determine which ones are placing workers like you. It is a good idea to register with several temporary employment agencies in your area.

Hot Tip

Working for a temporary agency can be a good way to figure out the sort of company you want to work for full-time or what sort of work you particularly enjoy. Also, if you work out well as a temporary, you will often have "a foot in the door" if a full-time job opens up at a company you worked for.

Starting a Part-Time Business

"It is the business of the very few to be independent; it is the privilege of the strong."

Friedrich Nietzche

Starting and running a part-time business, whether at home or outside the home, requires more time and energy than the moonlighting opportunities discussed earlier. To succeed you need a good business idea, lots of energy and entrepreneurial and management skills. In most cases, you will also need at least a small amount of seed capital. You will need to do a considerable amount of research and planning in order to maximize your chances for success.

A major drawback of starting your own part-time business is that in most cases, it will not be an immediate additional source of cash. In fact, when just starting out, you should have enough cash on hand to keep your business going for at least three months without any cash income. Depending upon the type of business you start and your own business skills, it may take a couple of years before you start to make money. At least initially, you may even have to reinvest back into the business any money you do make to keep it going. This is particularly true for businesses outside the home since their overhead costs tend to be greater than those of home-based businesses. The next section focuses on the home-based business, however, much of the information applies equally to a part-time business run outside the home.

Before even considering the type of business you might profitably run from your home, spend some time seriously considering whether or not self-employment is really for you. Do you have what it takes to be your own boss, or do you want to have your own business because you think it sounds glamorous and exciting?

Numerous books and magazines can help you determine whether you have the personal characteristics necessary for success as your own boss. (See the Resource section of this book for some suggested titles.) Not everyone does, and it is far better to discover this *before* you have invested your time and energy in a home-based business. As a rule, it takes a unique combination of drive, self-discipline, energy, organizational skills, know-how and luck to turn a good idea into a money-maker, even on a relatively small scale.

Deciding What Your Business Will Be

You may already have a very specific business in mind or you may need to spend some time researching the possibilities. In addition to starting with books and magazines, consider brainstorming with friends and relatives. They can be a good sounding board for ideas and may be able to evaluate potential businesses more objectively than you can.

Hot Tip

Entrepreneur Magazine publishes a biannual *Guide to Home-based Businesses.* The publication offers basic, valuable information for someone considering operating a business at home as well as specific business ideas. Look for it on your local newsstand. If you can't find a copy, call *Entrepreneur* at (714) 261-2325 for assistance. You may also want to invest in *Entrepreneur Magazine's Complete Guide to Owning a Home-based Business,* published by Bantam Books ($12.95).

As you think about the types of businesses you might run from your home, do not overlook your hobbies, activities you enjoy doing or special skills you may have. Perhaps you can turn one of them into a money maker. For example, are you a good cook who enjoys preparing food for large groups of people? If so, you might consider catering. Do you enjoy yard work or gardening; are you a fast typist; do you have a marketable craft; are you good with children? Think about needs that are not being met—you may be able to fill a gap!

Some states have initiated programs to promote crafts native to their area. These programs help craftspeople find markets and teach them how to price their products. Some offer low interest loans. Among the states operating such programs are Kentucky, Texas and North Dakota. To find out if your state runs such a program, call your Governor's office.

Keep your business ideas as simple as possible. The more complicated the idea, the more expensive it usually is and therefore, the more unrealistic it will be given your finances. Try to identify business possibilities that make good use of the resources you already have on hand.

Factors To Consider

"The beginning is the most important part of any business."

Plato

Once you've developed a list of business possibilities, you need to determine the specific space and location requirements of each. During this exercise, you will find that some of your ideas are simply not feasible considering where you live; eliminate them. Among the factors you should consider are:

The Location of Your Home There will be more business opportunities available to someone who lives in a highly populated area than to someone who lives in a more rural setting. Also, if a potential business requires walk-in traffic or generally high visibility in order to attract customers and your home is on a relatively untraveled road, you may want to scratch that business off your list unless you can identify other inexpensive ways to call people's attention to your location.

Your Home's Size If your home is relatively small or its space is already being used, a business that requires room for a staff or inventory or one that will need to accommodate customers may not be feasible.

Parking Do you need parking for customers and if so, how much? Does your municipality have regulations regarding business parking?

Zoning Do the zoning ordinances in your area allow you to operate a business out of your home? Do they limit the kind of business you can operate there? Check with your local planning office or with City Hall.

Factors related to the financing, management and marketing of a business must be addressed. They include:

Up-Front Capital How much money will you need to get a specific business under way? Pad your estimate somewhat because there are always unexpected or overlooked expenses. If a particular business requires a significant investment in equipment, supplies or inventory, you will probably need to eliminate it from your list. The whole point is to make extra money—avoid part-time businesses that are going to put a drain on your wallet.

Estimated Expenses and Sales Revenues You will need to project your expenses and your sales revenues on a month by month basis for at least the first year to determine whether or not a specific business idea is financially feasible.

Competition Are there other businesses offering the same products or services as the business you are considering? If so, is there something unique or different about yours that would attract customers and increase your chance for success?

Staff If you cannot run your business by yourself, how many employees will you need? Will they be part-time or full-time? Will they all need to work out of your home?

Taxes What taxes must you pay and when will they be due?

Permits Will you need to purchase any local, county or state permits? How much will they cost?

Marketing How will you let people know about your business? Advertising, direct mail, promotions, publicity and newsletters are all possibilities. To develop a realistic marketing plan you will need to know who your potential customers are and where they are generally located. You will also need to allocate a certain amount of money each month for marketing. Often overlooked or underbudgeted by first-time business owners, marketing is generally not a one-time effort.

Bookkeeping and Insurance What sort of special insurance will you need, and how will you handle your books? You will need to regularly monitor your cash flow.

Before you start your business, consider enrolling in a basic business management class at a college or university in your area. Contact the local office of the Small Business Administration (SBA). Not only can it provide you with general information and advice about starting and managing a business, it also may offer seminars and free consultations on various aspects of self-employment. If you can't locate an SBA office in your local phone book, call (800) U-ASK-SBA, or write SBA, Office of Consumer Affairs, 409 Third Street, S.W., Washington, DC 20146.

Work-At-Home Schemes

As you review possible work-at-home opportunities, be extremely careful of newspaper classified ads that promise big profits for very little effort. In most cases, the companies placing these ads require you to buy something before you can actually start working. You may have to invest in equipment and supplies, and you may also have to purchase a special permit or pay periodic fees to continue to receive work. Sometimes you will have to work a certain number of hours or produce a certain amount of product before you can get paid. Most work-at-home schemes are for one of two types of work:

Envelope Stuffing is the most common type of work-at-home scheme. Ads for this type of work ask you to send money to learn how to earn "big bucks" stuffing envelopes at home. If you respond, you will receive information advising you to place an ad in your local paper advertising your willingness to stuff envelopes or suggesting that you let your friends and relatives know that you are interested in that sort of work.

Product Assembly or Craft Work such as sewing, usually involves the purchase of equipment or supplies from a company in return for its promise to buy the products you make. Generally, once you've completed your work, the company refuses to buy what you've produced, citing quality problems or substandard work.

Other types of work-at-home schemes include raising animals and clipping articles from newspapers.

A word of warning. Before you send money or purchase supplies or equipment in response to any work-at-home ad, get a written statement from the advertiser describing what it is offering, what your obligations are to the company, how and when you will be paid and who will pay you. This information should be provided free. Also, check with the Better Business Bureau in the town where the advertiser is located and with the state attorney general's office or office of consumer affairs in the state where the company is located. If you have been taken advantage of by one of these companies, see Figure 5.7 for suggestions of where to go for help.

Hot Tip

The U.S. Postal Inspection Service says it "knows of no work-at-home scheme that produces income as alleged."

Part-Time Sales

As you think about the types of businesses you might operate out of your home, don't overlook part-time sales. Not only can this work be very lucrative, it also offers extremely flexible hours. Numerous part-time sales opportunities exist, many with well-established reputable national firms.

These firms offer two different ways of selling products—through at-home parties or one-on-one sales calls. The companies are either multi-level marketing firms or pyramid sales firms. Individuals who work with multi-level marketing firms begin at a basic level and receive promotions to higher levels based on their performance. Those working for pyramid sales firms advance by recruiting new representatives and making sales.

Some of the larger part-time sales companies include:

Amway, (800) 544-7176 This company offers a diverse array of products, including soap powders, legal services and home mortgages. To become an Amway representative, you must be recruited by a distributor in your area. Find one listed in your local phone book, or call the toll-free number listed above.

Tupperware, (800) 858-7221 This is the company most responsible for making home sales parties famous. To get started, Tupperware dealers must purchase a sales kit. They are required to pay their state sales tax up front but may pay for the rest of the kit through their sales. The Tupperware Company provides training for new dealers and organizes an introductory party during which new dealers learn sales techniques by participating in the party. Dealers earn a 35-percent commission on sales and must pay their own expenses, including party hostess gifts.

Discovery Toys, (800) 426-4777 This company also uses parties as a sales tool. Company training for new sales consultants includes a manual, a video and the advice and supervision of a manager. Sales consultants are required to hold five parties, purchase a sales kit and pay an up-front fee of $50 for the kit, tax and shipping. Sales commissions pay the cost of the kit.

Mary Kay Cosmetics, (800) MARY-KAY Sales representatives for this international company sell beauty products through at-home beauty consultations. Representatives are educated about company products and trained in sales techniques through sales aids and periodic meetings.

Avon, (800) 850-8000 As every reader probably knows, Avon sales representatives market cosmetics and other beauty products. These products are sold face-to-face and through a catalogue. A sales representative's up-front investment is relatively small, less than $50, and sales commissions begin at 30 percent.

Figure 5.7 If You Have Been Victimized by a Work-At-Home Scheme

Write the company and ask for your money back. Let the company know that if a refund is not forthcoming, you will inform the proper authorities of the problem. If your letter does not have the desired effect, contact the following:

- Your state attorney general's office, the office of consumer affairs or the equivalent office in the state where the company is located
- Your local Better Business Bureau
- The postmaster in your area (The U. S. Postal Service investigates fraudulent mail practices.)
- The advertising sales manager of the publication running the ad to which you responded
- The Federal Trade Commission

Shaklee, (415) 954-3000 This company sells vitamins and environmentally sound home products. To become a sales representative, a person must be sponsored by a current representative. The company regularly offers *specials* to persons who want to become sales representatives. Some of these specials allow interested persons to begin selling Shaklee products for as little as $5. Sales training and seminars are provided by Shaklee.

Stanley Home Products, (800) 628-9032 Stanley sales representatives sell a variety of personal and household products including vitamins, fragrances and cleaning items. Sales representatives can get started for a relatively small initial investment—as little as $20. New representatives get a 45-percent commission on sales.

Should you decide that you want to pursue part-time sales, find out all you can about the company you want to sell for. Ask questions, read company literature and talk to current sales representatives. Also, call your state attorney general's office or office of consumer affairs to find out if any complaints have been filed or actions taken against the part-time sales company that most interests you.

Conclusion

The American dream is for everyone to earn enough money to live comfortably according to their own standard of comfort and to do enjoyable work. It sounds simple, but it's not.

It takes a lot of work these days to pay for life's necessities—not to mention the extras. And for a growing number of Americans, finding any work at all is becoming increasingly difficult. Hopefully, the information in this chapter has pointed out some new directions for you to take in your job search, as well as some ways that you can make extra money.

Those of you who have employment and may be looking for more lucrative or rewarding work can view your financial crisis as an opportunity to reassess how much money you really need to be happy, how hard you are willing to work to achieve that happiness and what sort of work you want to do. In other words, it can offer you the chance for a meaningful career change.

six

Smart Spending

"Getting money is like digging with a needle. Spending it is like water soaking into sand."

Japanese Proverb

Howard and Jean H., like most of my clients, were facing financial troubles and an uncertain future. Howard sold real estate and had become quite successful during the real estate boom. Jean had stayed home to raise their four children, two of whom were now in college. When the real estate market collapsed, Howard did not have another career to fall back on that could provide the kind of money he and his family had come to expect. With a reduced income and limited job opportunities, his family had to learn to live on less.

Howard and Jean had never really had to watch the way they spent money. They had always managed their money very casually, spending what they made on whatever seemed important—they believed they were living within their means. Both had come from good families but, like most people, were never taught the fundamentals of money management by either their parents or their school system.

Now that things had changed, they realized that they would have to live differently and learn to control their finances. Because they realized this soon enough, they were able to avoid bankruptcy and were trying to work directly with their creditors. Fortunately, theirs was a close-knit family so everyone was willing to do what they could to help the family through its financial crisis.

Sitting across from me, Jean and Howard looked confused and worried. "We know what we need to do to get our financial situation under control," said Howard, "but we're not sure where to start or how to go about it." As we talked about what he meant, it was obvious that Howard and Jean were motivated and willing to work hard to adjust to a new lifestyle based on less money. It was also clear that they recognized the need to manage their money better, but they didn't have the information or tools to do so. I gave them some handouts on creating a budget (or spending plan), and told them about some books I felt would be worthwhile for them to read. I also referred them to several local organizations that had sponsored low-cost money management seminars in the past.

Besides learning new money management skills, Howard and Jean had to realize that survival in tough economic times, when there is little job security and incomes are reduced, requires a change of attitude. I explained that Howard and Jean needed to become constantly concerned about issues related to money and needed to look for ways to reduce their living expenses, especially in view of the fact that they wanted to help send their children through college and prepare for their retirement.

Howard and Jean will need to develop a disciplined approach to money. It is important for them to acquire and use good money management skills, cut costs and stretch the buying power of a dollar. This chapter provides some of the basic information consumers like Howard and Jean will need to successfully reach their goals.

The Importance of a Spending Plan

> *"If you have built castles in the air, your work need not be lost; that is where they should be. Now put the foundations under them."*
>
> **Henry David Thoreau**

A spending plan is an invaluable money management tool and the foundation of a new and healthier financial life. Such a plan helps you live within your means by allocating your household income to cover all of your living expenses, while helping you build your savings and achieve important goals.

Developing and living with a spending plan requires the participation of all household members, even younger children. Involving all household members in a spending plan accomplishes several goals. First, it makes everyone more aware of how much things cost. Second, it makes your household stronger by helping everyone understand that the way they spend money can affect others. Third, it gives household members a regular time—perhaps over dinner—to get together and talk, among other things, about how the spending plan is working. This can be an important benefit of a spending plan. If your lives are like most people's, you are so busy with work, school, activities outside the home and routine day-to-day tasks that it is a rare occasion when all of you get together just to talk. Monthly or bimonthly spending plan meetings provide an excuse for positive interaction.

Another benefit of involving the whole family in a spending plan is the opportunity it allows to teach valuable lessons about money management. Financial difficulty often results when there has been a lack of training in money-management skills. With money, credit cards and bills to pay, the trial-and-error method of learning often results in painful, expensive mistakes.

Hot Tip

Involve your children in the development and management of a spending plan; you can teach them about money using real-life situations. Through your actions as responsible money managers, you'll be positive role models for the next generation of adult consumers.

The involvement of all household members increases the likelihood that everyone will commit to the plan and actively work to make it a success. A team approach is critical since a spending plan necessitates some changes in your lifestyles and some sacrifices as well. If all household members are involved in the plan's development, there is a better chance of successfully making the changes and sacrifices.

Financial Goal Setting

The first step in the development of a spending plan is a brainstorming session to establish your household's short-term and long-term financial goals. This is an opportunity to dream a little bit! Each of you should ask yourself "What do we want to accomplish, or what do we want to be able to afford in six months, one year, two years?" Possible goals might include: get out of debt within the next two years; save $500 over the next year; buy a new washing machine within the next six months; take a family trip to Disneyland two summers from now; or, save $3000 over the next three years as a down payment on a house.

While your session should focus on household financial goals, each of you may also want to develop personal financial goals. These goals need not be discussed with other household members. However, if your ability to achieve a personal goal requires the cooperation of other household members, it should be moved to the list of household goals. For example, you may want to go back to school to get additional job training so you can increase your income. Although this is a personal goal, coming up with the money for your education may require some penny-pinching on the part of others in your family. Also, everyone benefits from your increased income.

Discuss and evaluate the goals proposed during your brainstorming session. Eliminate or revise those that seem unrealistic or have a very low priority. Be prepared to compromise—some household goals will be of obvious importance to everyone, but there may be some differing opinions.

Hot Tip

Post your list of household goals on either your refrigerator or a bulletin board so that all household members can see them regularly. Periodically, indicate your progress in achieving a particular goal—"$200 left to pay on credit card debt," or "As of September 15, $500 is in savings!" Motivate your household and encourage everyone to stick to the spending plan.

Once you have decided on your goals, categorize them as either short-term (six months to two years) or long-term (more than two years). Prioritize them, making the most important or

Figure 6.1 Goal Planning Chart

Short-Term or Immediate Goals

Goal	*Total Cost*	*Monthly Cost*	*Goal Target Date*
Goal #1	$	$	______________
Goal #2	$	$	______________
Goal #3	$	$	______________
Goal #4	$	$	______________

Long -Term Goals

Goal	*Total Cost*	*Monthly Cost*	*Goal Target Date*
Goal #1	$	$	______________
Goal #2	$	$	______________
Goal #3	$	$	______________
Goal #4	$	$	______________

most immediately pressing goal your number one short-term goal. The one that is slightly less important becomes your number two short-term goal, etc. Do the same with your long-term goals. Record each on a goal planning chart like the one in Figure 6.1.

It is probably not possible to work toward all of your goals at once, so prioritizing them can help you to isolate those that should be made a part of your spending plan from the start. Begin with the most important of your short-term goals. As they are accomplished, you can move other short-term goals to the top of your list and onto your spending plan, or you can accelerate your efforts to achieve a high priority long-term goal such as saving for your child's college education or your retirement.

To the right of each high priority goal in both the short-term and long-term categories, record a total cost for each, a monthly cost (total cost of the goal divided by the number of months you have to achieve it) and your goal target date.

Analyze Your Current Spending Patterns

As mentioned earlier, you must change your spending habits to achieve your goals. To pinpoint those changes, you need to develop a detailed picture of your current spending patterns—how you are spending your money. This can be done using your check register, receipts and other household expenditure information for a several-month period. You should also review the previous year's receipts, check registers, etc. to identify total annual costs for one-time or periodic expenses like appliance repairs, medical bills, insurance, clothing, car repairs, taxes, etc. Revise these totals if you feel they are no longer accurate given changes in your current financial situation. Then, divide each total by 12 to calculate a monthly cost for each expense.

As you review your household expenses, organize them into categories: fixed monthly expenses, variable monthly expenses, periodic expenses and "set asides." Fixed monthly expenses are those that occur in the same amount each month. Variable monthly expenses occur each month in different amounts—they are expenses over which you have some discretion or control. Periodic monthly expenses are those that occur throughout the year but not necessarily on a monthly basis; they can be either fixed or variable. Set asides are expenses that are totally discretionary, such as savings or certain goals.

To develop a complete picture of your household's current spending patterns, you should identify all miscellaneous cash expenditures. The best way to do this is for each of the adults and older children in your household to record their daily cash expenditures in a small notebook for several weeks, long enough for everyone to get a clear idea of how they spend the money they carry with them each day. Keep track of everything, even the most incidental expense. You'll be surprised to discover how much you spend on miscellaneous items and how those seemingly minor purchases can add up to a rather significant sum over a period of time. Consider the following: if you spend an average of $5 each working day on lunch, snacks and sodas, that translates into $100 each month, or $1,200 a year!

Don't wait until the end of the day to record your miscellaneous expenditures. Inevitably, you will overlook something or forget entirely to record the information. Use a notebook small enough to fit in your pocket or purse and discipline yourself to record every cash expenditure at the time that you make it.

Spending Plan Worksheet

Using a Spending Plan Worksheet similar to the one in Figure 6.2, record your expenses in the appropriate categories. Total up each category and fill in the line labeled Total Monthly Expenses at the bottom of the worksheet.

Your Household Income

Now, calculate the amount of your net monthly household income (your gross income less all deductions). Include in this total any rental income, child support, retirement benefits, etc. that you receive regularly.

If your income varies due to the type of work you or your spouse do, it is harder to determine your net income. The best solution is to look at your net income for the past two or three years and average those figures together, assuming you feel they are fairly representative of what you will be earning in the immediate future. If not, increase or decrease the averaged amount by however much more or less you expect to be earning. Be sure you do not overestimate your added income. It's always better to be conservative and have an unexpected surplus in your spending plan than to be overly optimistic and end up with a shortfall. Record your Net Monthly Income figure on the Spending Plan Worksheet.

Pinpoint Areas for Reduction

After you've recorded your expense and income figures on the worksheet, subtract total expenses from total income. This will give you either a spending surplus or a deficit. If you have a surplus, it can be allocated toward one or more of your goals. If you have a deficit, however, you don't have enough money to cover all of your expenses much less work toward any of your goals; you will need to identify expenses that you can reduce.

Figure 6.2 Spending Plan Worksheet—Current Income and Expenses*

Fixed Monthly Expenses	*Dollar Amount*
Rent or mortgage	
Car loan	
Other installment loans	
Insurance	
Allowances	
Day care	
Monthly dues	
Newspaper subscriptions	
Cable TV	
Medical, dental and prescriptions (after insurance)	
Transportation	
Total:	$__________

Variable Monthly Expenses	*Dollar Amount*
Groceries and household products	
Utilities	
Telephone	
Gasoline	
Clothing	
Credit card payments	
Cleaning and laundry	
Toiletries and makeup	
Medical, dental and prescriptions (after insurance)	
Magazines and books	
Meals out	
Entertainment and hobbies	
Cigarettes, candy, etc.	
Total:	$__________

Figure 6.2 Spending Plan Worksheet—Current Income and Expenses* (Continued)

Periodic Fixed and Variable Expenses	*Dollar Amount*
(Total annual expense divided by 12 months = monthly cost for each periodic or variable expense)	
Tuition	
Auto registration and license	
Insurance	
Taxes	
Haircuts	
Household repairs	
Clothing	
Birthdays and holidays	
Medical and dental expenses (after insurance)	
Subscriptions	
Total:	$__________
Set Asides	
Savings	
Total:	$__________
Total Monthly Expenses:	$__________
Net Monthly Income:	$__________
Less Total Monthly Expenses:	$__________
Surplus or Deficit:	$__________

*Expenses listed here are not intended to represent an inclusive list of possible household expenses, but rather are examples of common expenses.

Everyone in your household should examine their own spending to identify expenses that they can reduce. Be realistic about where you can cut back; you don't want to develop such a stringent spending plan that you will be unable to live with it. At the same time, remember that the more you reduce, the easier it will be to achieve your goals.

Critically analyze each expense category listed on your Spending Plan Worksheet and go back over your spending notebooks. Your goal should be to get your total monthly expenses below your total net monthly income by the total amount you want to allocate to your goals each month. Figure 6.3 provides tips on saving money. As you think about where you might cut back, here are the kinds of questions you should be asking:

- Do I need to drive to work; could I take public transportation?
- Are there people at work with whom I could car pool?
- Do we fully utilize all the space and the amenities that come with the apartment or home we're renting? If not, perhaps a move is in order.
- Are there things we could do to make more efficient use of our home's heating and air conditioning system? (Call your local utility company for energy saving tips.)
- How can our grocery bill be reduced?
- Can we rent videos rather than seeing first-run movies? Is there a theater that has discount shows? Do we really need a movie channel?
- Can we take lunches from home rather than eating out?

It's human nature to resist change, however change can be a very positive force. It can help you make new discoveries about yourselves, your loved ones and the world around you. Taking public transportation or walking to work each day can help save on gas, tolls, parking and wear and tear on a car—it can also provide a quiet time for contemplation, reading or just watching the world go by. Such times are a rarity—they're worth being open-minded about.

New-Fashioned Holiday Basics

As mentioned in Chapter 1, the holiday season and other gift-giving occasions are especially difficult for those in financial difficulty. During the holidays, intensify your efforts at family meetings in order to reassure each other that the creation of a *new-fashioned* holiday will be a joyful one for all.

Three essentials for creating a *new-fashioned* holiday season are: communication, budgeting and planning. Communication is important because your family and those friends with whom you traditionally exchange gifts or entertain need to understand how and why the holidays are going to change. When you explain the changes you'd like to make, be upbeat and positive. Reassure your younger children that there *will* be presents, but fewer store-bought gifts. Stress the fact that a *new-fashioned* holiday season can be fun for both the gift giver and the gift receiver. See Figure 6.4 for examples of creative gift-giving.

Your Spending Plan

> *"Yesterday is a cancelled check; tomorrow is a promissory note; today is the only cash you have—so spend it wisely."*
>
> **Kay Lyons**

Once you've identified the expenses you can reduce, record the new totals on your worksheet, calculate a new monthly expense total and subtract it from your total monthly household income. If you can now fund at least all of your highest priority short-term goals, you're ready to finalize and begin using your spending plan.

Create a form similar to the chart in Figure 6.5; label it Current Spending Plan; write in your total monthly income; and fill in the amounts you have budgeted to spend each month. In the "set aside" category, record the specific goals you will begin working toward and how much you'll be allocating to them each month. Give each household member a copy of the spending plan.

If you still don't have enough money to fund your highest priority goals, you will have to reduce your spending still more, and may want to identify ways to increase your household income. Your older children may need to get part-time jobs, or you or your spouse may need to find second jobs. For more ideas about increasing your household income, refer to Chapter 5.

Figure 6.3 How To Be a Cheapskate

Here are some cheapskate tips for reducing expenses and keeping your spending within the limits of your spending plan:

- Make your children's school lunches.
- Start a vegetable garden.
- Clean your oven regularly for greater efficiency.
- Change or clean your air conditioner filters once a week during the cooling season.
- Don't go to first-run movies or go only during discount hours.
- Use your town's public library.
- Set your thermostat at 65 degrees during the day.
- Invite your friends over for potluck meals.
- Use your public parks and take advantage of free or low-cost community events.
- If you subscribe to magazines, pass them on to friends when you're finished and ask them to do the same.
- Instead of calling, write friends and relatives who live far away.
- Don't grocery shop when you're hungry and never shop without a list.
- Buy paper products, cleaning supplies and other household items in bulk whenever practical.
- Shop at discount/warehouse stores.
- Use coupons whenever possible. Coupons are available for food and household items as well as for restaurants, carpet cleaning, video rentals, etc.
- Plan your clothing purchases. At the start of every season, look at your clothes and decide what you need to buy. When you do purchase an item of clothing, make sure it will coordinate with as much of your wardrobe as possible. Avoid trendy items.

Figure 6.3 How To Be a Cheapskate (Continued)

- Shop at resale shops, outlets, garage sales and sales whenever possible.
- Swap clothing and jewelry with friends.
- Give up cigarettes.
- Trade services with your neighbors and friends.
- Call your insurance agent to discuss practical ways you can reduce your insurance premiums without jeopardizing your coverage.

Living with a Spending Plan

"Do what you can, with what you have, where you are."

Theodore Roosevelt

Once you've finalized your spending plan, you need to make it work. For that to happen, you must develop a good record keeping system, decide who in your household will be responsible for paying bills each month and hold regular household meetings to monitor the plan and evaluate how well it is working.

Record Keeping

A good record keeping system can help you monitor your household income and expenditures. It can be as simple as a series of manila folders, labeled by category of expense and income and stored in a filing cabinet or box. A second file should be kept for bills to be paid.

Get receipts for all of your expenditures and file them together with account statements and other important documentation at least once a month. Also, at least for the first several months of the spending plan, household members should continue to maintain a record of their miscellaneous cash expenditures.

Figure 6.4 Creative Gift-Giving and Creative Shopping

Experiment with various types of thoughtful, creative gifts for family and friends. Encourage your children to give gifts of time and talent. Ideas for older children include:

- a personalized book of coupons redeemable for special favors—an extra hour of housework, a day's worth of baby-sitting, a week's worth of taking out the garbage, or trips to the movies for a younger sibling;
- an album of photos or a scrapbook of memorabilia;
- homemade potpourri or granola stored in attractive containers;
- handmade ornaments or wreaths;
- a framed drawing or photograph.

Creative Shopping

Before you begin your shopping, make a list of the various retail outlets you want to visit. Evaluate the merchandise at each and buy from those that offer the best quality and price. Experiment—don't limit your gift-buying to traditional retail outlets.

Garage sales, resale shops, vintage clothing stores, used book stores, fashion outlets and warehouse stores can all be great sources of quality gifts that won't break your budget. They can be especially good sources of clothing and toys for younger children who are not yet label and status conscious, and the perfect place to buy gifts for adults who are collectors, have special hobbies or appreciate the unusual.

Figure 6.5 Current Spending Plan

Fixed Monthly Expenses	*Dollar Amount*
Rent or mortgage	
Car loan	
Other installment loans	
Allowances	
Day care	
Monthly dues	
Newspaper subscriptions	
Cable TV	
Medical, dental and prescriptions (after insurance)	
Transportation	
Total:	$__________

Variable Expenses	*Dollar Amount*
Groceries and household expenses	
Utilities	
Telephone	
Gasoline	
Clothing	
Credit card payments	
Cleaning and laundry	
Toiletries	
Medical, dental and prescriptions (after insurance)	
Magazines and books	
Entertainment and hobbies	
Cigarettes and candy, etc.	
Total :	$__________

Figure 6.5 Current Spending Plan (Continued)

Periodic Fixed and Variable Expenses	*Dollar Amount*
School expenses	
Auto registration and license	
Insurance	
Taxes	
Haircuts	
Household repairs	
Clothing	
Birthdays and holidays	
Medical, dental and prescriptions (after insurance)	
Subscriptions	
Total:	$__________

Set Asides	*Dollar Amount*
Savings	
Goal #1	
Goal #2	
Goal #3	
Total:	$__________
Total Monthly Expenses:	$__________
Total Net Monthly Income:	$__________
Less Total Monthly Expenses:	$__________
Surplus or Deficit:	$__________

ATM Machines

Although having easy access to your bank account 24-hours a day through the use of an ATM is convenient, it can also be very dangerous—especially when you are trying to make a spending plan work. The following tips can help you to use ATMs wisely:

Figure 6.6 How To Develop a Spending Plan

Step #1. Establish your goals—what you want your spending plan to help you achieve.

Step #2. Determine how you're spending your money. Where does it go?

Step #3. Compare total monthly household expenses to net monthly household income.

Step #4. If your expenses exceed your income, target areas for reduction.

Step #5. If you have a surplus—you make more than you spend—allocate the excess to your top priority goals.

Step #6. Record your spending plan and give a copy to each member of your household.

Step #7. Monitor your spending and modify your spending plan as necessary.

- Don't use your ATM card to get money that is not budgeted.
- Establish a specific day of the week to use your ATM card and before you go to the machine, determine the exact amount of money you will withdraw based on your spending plan. The rest of the week, leave your ATM card at home.
- Leave your ATM card at home when you go shopping or out for the evening. That way, you won't be tempted to get more money after spending your budgeted allotment.
- Save all ATM receipts. Make a record of each withdrawal and deposit in your checkbook register and make the receipts a part of your monthly spending plan records.

Regular Meetings

At the start of each month, all household members should meet to review how well the plan is working, discuss any problems and make necessary revisions. During these monthly meetings, discuss forthcoming periodic expenses, as well as any unanticipated expenses that have arisen, in order to decide how your spending plan can be adjusted to pay for them. When everyone is comfortable with the plan, budget meetings may only be necessary every other month.

To help you determine how well your plan is working, complete a Monthly Spending Plan Recap form similar to the one in Figure 6.7. The expense categories listed on the recap form should be identical to those on your spending plan. This form can help you compare what you budgeted to what you actually spent.

Don't get upset if you don't initially meet your goals. Instead, figure out *why* you didn't and how you can do better next time.

As your financial plan improves and you begin to have fewer debts and more disposable income, your spending plan should be revised. You may either want to categorize additional goals as high priority and begin actively working toward them, or allocate additional money for the goals you are already working toward.

Teaching Your Children about Money

> *"The object of education is to prepare the young to educate themselves throughout their lives."*
>
> ***Robert Maynard Hutchins***

A spending plan provides parents an ideal opportunity to begin teaching their children how to be smart consumers. By teaching children at an early age about money and money management, parents can instill positive lifelong habits. Children as young as three are able to learn very basic concepts about money and by about five, most children are ready to get a small allowance. Every child is different, so consider your child's abilities and maturity when deciding the best time to begin.

When your child is able to count money and understand how to make change, you can begin an allowance. To be most effective, an allowance is best given at the same time every couple of weeks or every month. Your child should clearly understand what the allowance is to be used for and that once the money is spent, there will be no more until the next allowance date. As your child matures and has more monetary needs, both the size of the allowance and the list of things it can be spent on can increase.

Figure 6.7 Spending Plan—Budgeted versus Actual Month and Year

	Expenses	*Budgeted*	*Actual Difference +/-*
Monthly Fixed Expenses			
List your expenses			
Total: $__________			
Monthly Variable Expenses			
List your expenses			
Total: $__________			
Periodic Fixed and Variable Expenses			
List your expenses			
Total : $__________			

Total Income: $____________________

LessTotal Expenses: $____________________

Net Income: $____________________

You may want to give your child an opportunity to earn extra money by doing chores around the house. Post a chore sheet in the kitchen and assign a monetary value to each job. For example, washing the car may be worth $5 and waxing it worth $7. Let your children sign up for any chore/s they would like. When a task is finished, inspect the work and if it is satisfactory, pay for the job. If the job has not been done well, explain what needs to be done before you will pay. This approach helps your children correlate a well-performed chore with money and helps to prepare them for earning a living as adults.

You can also give your children a specific amount of money to spend on holiday or birthday gifts. Use special days as opportunities to teach children comparison shopping—how to look for good buys and how to determine how much can be spent on a gift before they go out to shop. This helps your children learn how to plan ahead, budget money and maximize their buying power.

A child's first savings account can be a memorable experience. Depositing money in an account, watching it grow and saving it for something special can help your child understand the concept of interest and the value of saving.

Managing Your Checking Account

"Money is something to make bookkeeping convenient."

H.L. Hunt

Knowing how to reconcile your checkbook is an important money management skill, especially when money is tight and every penny counts. If reconciliation is done properly and accurately, you can avoid costly and potentially disastrous mistakes.

Hot Tip

Use cash rather than checks as much as possible. Give yourself a weekly cash allowance based on your spending plan, to pay for groceries, meals out, gasoline, etc. Keep track of how you're doing as the week progresses. If at the end of the week you have money left over, put it toward one of your goals.

Bouncing a Check

A bounced or returned check is one that can't be paid because there is an insufficient amount of money in your account to cover the check. This can happen as the result of a number things:

- You fail to accurately record all the checks you write.
- You do not maintain a running account balance.
- You make an error in calculating your balance.
- You deposit a check in your account that is drawn on a bank other than your own, and you write checks against it before it has had time to clear.

When depositing an out-of-town check, or a local check drawn on a bank other than your own, ask your bank how long it holds the funds before you can write checks against them.

Your bank charges your account for any check you bounce, unless you have overdraft protection. The fee for NSF (not sufficient funds) checks, which generally ranges from $5 to $30, will be deducted immediately from your account's available balance. In addition, the company to which you wrote the check may charge you a fee, which typically averages about $28, to compensate itself for the loss of income and the cost of collection. If the company to which you wrote the check works with a check recovery firm, you may be required to pay as much as $40 per check. Bouncing a check is obviously a very expensive mistake! When you activate your checking account overdraft protection, you are actually borrowing money from the bank at a high interest rate. Although it can be a very convenient feature, when used carelessly, it can also be dangerous and expensive.

After your bank debits your checking account for the first check you bounce, your account balance may be too low to cover checks you wrote before you realized that your balance was insufficient to cover the first check. Therefore, unless you have increased your checking account balance by depositing more money in your account, these checks will bounce as well, resulting in additional charges to your checking account, more check recovery charges, etc. You may soon find that you have a very serious situation on your hands.

If any of the companies to which you wrote a bad check use a check approval service, your name and checking account number will now be in the service's computer system and you'll be unable to write checks to any other business using that same service until you clear up your checks. It is also possible that the businesses to which you wrote bad checks will simply refuse your checks in the future.

Your Checking Account Register

An easy way to avoid problems with your checking account is to record in your check register all transactions as you make them. Record every check you write noting amount, name of the payee (the person or company to whom the check is written), date and check number. Also, record and date all of your deposits.

Throughout the month, as you make these entries in your check register, maintain a running account balance by subtracting each check from your previous balance and adding in each deposit. If you use an ATM card, don't forget to adjust your balance accordingly and do the same for any direct deposits or automatic withdrawals made to your account. This simple routine should help keep you from bouncing checks.

How To Reconcile Your Checkbook

Reconciling your checkbook each month may be a little more time consuming, but it is no more difficult. Every month you receive an account statement from your bank detailing the activity in your account for the previous month. This activity includes deposits, cash withdrawals, checks written and any interest earned. The statement itemizes various miscellaneous charges to your account—automatic debits, fees for new checks, bank service charges, insufficient fund charges, ATM transactions, charges to your account for account research done at your request, etc. It also indicates your ending balance as of the date of the statement, your previous account balance, as well as total deposits, withdrawals and charges for the period covered by the statement.

Hot Tip

You can save money on the monthly cost of your checking account by ordering checks directly from a check printing company rather than from your bank. Two such companies are: Checks in the Mail, P.O. Box 7802, Irwindale CA 91706, (800) 733-443 and Current Inc., Check Printing Department, P.O. Box 19000, Colorado Springs, CO 80935-9000, (800) 426-0822. Contact these companies for a brochure and pricing information.

When you receive your monthly statement, chronologically organize your canceled checks. Do the same with your deposit slips. Then, compare these checks and deposit slips to the entries in your check register, putting a check mark next to each item for which you have a cancelled check or deposit slip. Also, make sure that all ATM transactions noted in your bank statement match those recorded in your register.

In order to have a complete record of all account activities for a given month, record in your checkbook register all account transactions, miscellaneous fees and charges shown on your statement that are not already recorded in your register. Banks do make mistakes, so take note of any transactions you've made that are not reflected in your statement, as well as transactions you didn't make that appear on your statement. If you find something you don't understand, call your bank's customer service office.

Once you have recorded any missing information in your check register and made any necessary corrections, calculate your account balance to arrive at your "adjusted checkbook balance." Next, look on the reverse side of your bank statement for the statement reconciliation work area. Figure 6.8 provides a Sample Reconciliation Worksheet. Total up all deposits you made after the date of the statement. (They will not show up in your current bank statement, but you should have recorded them in your checkbook.) They are called your "deposits outstanding." Write the total for these deposits on the appropriate line of the reconciliation worksheet and then add up all the cash withdrawals, checks, ATM charges, etc., made after the date of your statement. These are your "withdrawals outstanding." Record this total on the worksheet line for "outstanding checks and charges." On the appropriate line of the worksheet, record the ending balance shown on your current bank statement.

The rest of the reconciliation process is simply a matter of adding and subtracting. Add the ending balance to your total "deposits outstanding" and subtract from it your "outstanding checks and charges." This dollar figure is your "adjusted statement balance" and should match the adjusted balance in your checkbook. If it does not, you may have miscalculated, failed to record all account activity or overlooked a deposit or a withdrawal made since the date of your last statement. If you're still having trouble, call or visit your bank's customer service office.

How To Get the Most for Your Medical Dollars

"I got the bill for my surgery. Now I know what those doctors were wearing masks for."

James H. Boren

Figure 6.8 Sample Reconciliation Worksheet

BANK ONE

ACCOUNT RECONCILEMENT

Follow these easy steps to reconcile your checkbook balance with the balance on this statement.

1. Mark off in your checkbook all items shown on this statement, including cleared checks, automatic withdrawals and deposits.
2. Enter any items you may have forgotten to record.
3. Enter in your checkbook any interest earned or bank service charges shown on this statement.
4. List in Section A all deposits shown in your checkbook which are not shown on this statement.
5. List in Section B all checks and automatic withdrawals shown in your checkbook which are not shown on this statement.
6. Enter on this line the "new balance" shown on this statement.
7. On this line add total outstanding deposits (Section A).
8. On this line enter subtotal.
9. On this line subtract total outstanding checks (Section B).
10. On this line record total (should agree with checkbook balance.)

A Outstanding Deposits	
No.	Amount
	.
	.
	.
	.
	.
	.
	.
	.
	.
	.
Total	.
C	.
+	.
	.
–	.
	.

B Outstanding Checks	
No.	Amount
	.
	.
	.
	.
	.
	.
	.
	.
	.
	.
	.
	.
	.
	.
	.
	.
	.
	.
	.
Total	.

SOURCE: Statement courtesy of BANK ONE, TEXAS

The cost of medical care and health insurance is taking an increasingly large bite out of every American's budget and putting good medical care beyond the reach of many people. The average consumer's health insurance costs soared nearly 300 percent between 1980 and 1990, while the cost of prescription drugs increased 152 percent during that same period—an average increase of more than 15 percent a year! And between 1989 and 1990, the Consumer Price Index for medical care increased nearly twice as fast as that for all other items.

Despite rising costs, there are things you can do to help minimize medical expenses while maintaining an adequate level of health care for yourselves and your families.

Prescription Drugs

Before your doctor writes your prescription, ask if there is a generic equivalent. You may save up to 50 percent, and you'll suffer no loss in quality. Some doctors buy medication at cost from a wholesaler or pharmaceutical supplier; if yours does, ask if you can buy directly in order to take advantage of the savings.

Before you get a prescription filled, call drugstores in your area and shop for the best price. Discount pharmacies often offer substantial savings. When you are going to be taking a particular medication for an extended period of time, ask your pharmacist how much you might save by buying in bulk. Some pills or tablets can be split in two—if yours is one of them, buy double the strength and take only half of the medication. If your pill or tablet doesn't split easily, buy a pill splitter at the drug store.

Mail order pharmacies offer excellent prices on prescription drugs, vitamins, first-aid supplies and over-the-counter-medicines. Request catalogues and prices from Action Mail Order Drug Company (800) 452-1976, Prescriptions By Mail (800) 336-7310 and PHARMAIL (800) 237-8927. Also, the American Association of Retired Persons (AARP) has a mail order pharmacy for its members. For membership information, or to learn more about its pharmacy, call (202) 434-2277.

If you are a member of the military, a health professional, or a member of AARP, you are entitled to discounts when you get your prescriptions filled. Members of other professional associations or special groups may also be eligible for a discount. Ask your pharmacist.

Doctors, Lab Tests and Other Medical Procedures

Before choosing a general practitioner or medical specialist, call several doctors to see how much they charge for an office visit and to perform certain routine tests and procedures. Assuming their credentials and abilities are equal, select the least expensive. You can check the backgrounds and reputations of doctors by talking to friends or calling your county medical society or local hospital. A doctor with an in-office lab often provides less expensive lab work—important since insurance companies frequently pay "usual and customary rates" as averaged over a geographic area. Expensive rates come out of *your* pocket!

Read up on your medical problems. Good information allows you to ask your doctor the right questions and may help you avoid needless and expensive treatments and tests.

Let your doctors know how much of a medical bill you, rather than your insurance provider, will be paying. Ask the doctors to be mindful of your out-of-pocket expenses when deciding what tests and procedures to order, drugs to prescribe, etc. Before agreeing to any, ask why they are necessary. If you have recently had the same tests or procedures performed elsewhere, tell your doctor; it may be possible to get copies of those results. Unless your health is in jeopardy or your doctor needs information to diagnose a problem, postpone all elective medical procedures until they will not put a serious strain on your budget.

If you feel that your doctor is over-prescribing or if you question the necessity of the treatments or diagnostic tests prescribed for you, get a second opinion.

Doctors and labs do make mistakes, but the only way you'll know your bill is correct—if you got what you paid for—is to get an itemized bill identifying what you received and what it cost.

Hot Tip

The American Academy of Family Physicians maintains the Medical Information Line. By calling its 900 telephone number, (900) 535-3600, you can get up-to-date information on 352 different medical topics including various diseases, medical tests and operations, pregnancy, substance abuse and children's and women's health issues. The first minute is free, and each additional minute costs $1.35. Topics average five minutes in length.

Hospitals

When you know you must be hospitalized, research your options. Comparison shop room rates in your area, and unless your doctor has a convincing reason for you to do otherwise, choose the hospital with the least expensive rates. Avoid hospital admittance and release fees. Call the hospital before you check in to make certain your doctor is not charging you one of these fees. If so, question your doctor about the purpose of such a fee. Check in on a weekday. Unless you are very ill, it makes no sense to check into a hospital on the weekend or late on a Friday—times when most hospitals offer only the most basic services.

After your hospitalization, review your hospital bill carefully to make sure that you are being charged for services you actually used and medications you took. If you are confused by your bill, ask questions and do not pay for anything you did not receive.

Medical Insurance

You *can* bring your medical insurance costs under control. If you are young and healthy, you may opt for a Health Maintenance Organization (HMO) or Preferred Provider Organization (PPO) where you pay a set fee each month whether you use the organization's services or not. Usually cheaper than traditional medical insurance, many of these organizations offer free annual physicals and blood tests so that you can be assured of regular preventive health care.

With standard health insurance, you can decrease the amount you pay for insurance each year by increasing your deductible. A high deductible can make sense for the individual or family that is in good health and rarely, if ever, sees a doctor. However, if you or someone on your insurance policy has a lot of health problems or takes a lot of medications, you'll want to minimize your out-of-pocket costs by opting for a lower deductible. Preventive health care is ultimately the cheapest kind. The downside of raising your deductible is that you may avoid preventive care since such expenses are rarely reimbursed.

Shop around for a temporary health insurance plan if you are between jobs or will not be covered by a new employer's insurance plan for a few months. A temporary plan can essentially provide you with catastrophic or major medical health coverage until you're covered by your employer's insurance.

Before buying your own medical insurance, talk to an independent agent who sells a variety of health insurance plans. Explain the type of coverage you need and how much you can afford to pay each month and let the agent help you find the best, most affordable coverage.

Some insurance carriers will give a discount on your coverage if you pay your premium annually. Discuss this with your agent.

Shopping at Pawnshops

For many people, the word *pawnshop* probably brings to mind a dark and slightly disreputable store patronized by unsavory individuals. While this type of store still exists, certain segments of the pawnshop industry are spending a considerable amount of money to change that image. Stores are *spiffing up* their interiors, creating more attractive displays for merchandise and hiring service-oriented salespeople to attract shoppers.

Many pawnshops offer excellent bargains on a variety of merchandise, including tools, cameras and electronic items. To get the best bargains possible, it is important to understand some basic rules for pawnshop shopping:

- Negotiate on price. Often the marked price on an item is not the price the shop will actually take. Try bargaining.
- Have a clear idea before you go to a pawnshop to buy a specific item how much you would pay if you bought the item new at a discount retailer in your area.
- Comparison shop. The variety, quality and price of merchandise varies from pawnshop to pawnshop, so visit several to see which one offers the best deal.
- Test all items to see that they work to your satisfaction.
- Make sure that you are not buying an obsolete or discontinued item that will be difficult to find parts for or repair.
- Before you purchase anything, especially a big-ticket item, ask about the store's return and guarantee policies. No deal is a good deal if you get the merchandise home, discover it's defective and you're stuck with it. Policies vary from store to store. Some pawnshops will not guarantee their merchandise once you leave with it; others will guarantee the working condition of the merchandise and take it back if it fails to live up to your expectations.

Traveling Without Credit

Traveling without credit and on a budget, whether for business or pleasure, can be easier than you think. The key is to understand the policies of the hotels, motels and car rental agencies you will be using, to research any discounts you may be able to take advantage of and to plan ahead. In most instances, you will need to make reservations well in advance of your travel date. With proper planning, you will discover that it can be rewarding—and cost-effective—to travel without a stack of credit cards clutched in your hand!

Hotels and Motels

Start planning your trip at least 30 days ahead. If you are a business traveler and know where you will be meeting, try to find a hotel close to your appointment to avoid renting a car.

Since most hotels and motels expect travelers to guarantee their reservations with a credit card, ask about their specific policy regarding "creditless" travel when you make your reservation. Although most hotels and motels prefer that you prepay your stay, they are generally willing to make alternative arrangements if prepayment is impossible or inconvenient.

Hot Tip

Prepaying your hotel stay allows you to travel without having to carry a lot of cash. (When you do travel with large amounts of cash, always use Traveler's Checks.)

Well in advance of the date you plan to travel, call the 800 number of the hotel or motel you will be using. (To get this number, call 800 directory assistance—(800) 555-1212.) The person you speak to when you call the 800 number should be able to tell you about the hotel's creditless policy or refer you to someone who can. In some instances a hotel will have a company-wide policy; in others, policy is decided at the individual locations. The following is a description of how some major hotels and motels handle travelers who need to book a room without credit:

Marriott This hotel chain allows its individual hotels to set their own policy regarding travelers not using credit. In general, however, a Marriott hotel requires a room deposit ranging from the first night's stay to the entire planned stay. The specific amount of the deposit depends somewhat on the season of the year and where you are traveling. You must pay with a money order or company check.

Deposits must be made anywhere from seven to ten days following the date you make your reservation to up to 30 days prior to your arrival. Some Marriots will make late arrival reservations without a deposit by accepting a corporate or company guarantee of payment. For more information, call (800) 228-9290.

Hilton Hilton hotels accept a company or personal check for the first night's stay. The check must be received seven to ten days after you make your reservation. In many cases you can also make arrangements for prepayment of your entire stay, although you should ask the hotel's credit manager for its specific policy. For more information, call (800) 445-8667.

Hyatt Each Hyatt hotel has its own policy, but some will guarantee to a traveler's home address until a deposit for the first night has been received. Company and personal checks are accepted. Travelers who are members of Hyatt's Gold Passport Program can guarantee reservations without a credit card or a deposit. They can enroll in the program over the phone and a bad credit history may not affect their eligibility. For more information, call (800) 233-1234.

Holiday Inn Holiday Inn's corporate policy requires that a deposit for the first night's stay be received at least two days prior to arrival; however, this policy can vary somewhat from hotel to hotel. Ask the Holiday Inn where you will be staying about its specific policy.

Holiday Inn will not accept any personal checks. You can, however, guarantee your room with your account number if your company has a corporate account with Holiday Inn. For details on a corporate account, call (800) 343-5545; if you live in Massachusetts, call (800) 792-5163. For more information on Holiday Inn's policies for travelers not using credit, call (800) 465-4329.

Motel 6 You can either prepay with cash at the Motel 6 closest to you for a stay at the Motel 6 location(s) you will be using during your travels, or you can send a personal check to the motel at which you'll be staying. You must send your check at least 14 days prior to arrival. Motel 6 will not accept personal or company checks at the time of check-in or check-out. For more information, call (505) 891-6161.

Choice Hotels International (Choice Hotels, Quality Inn, Comfort Inn, Sleep Inn, Rodeway Inn, Econolodge and Friendship Inn). Each hotel in the Choice chain has its own policy regarding creditless travelers. In general, however, travelers must get their room deposit to the hotel by the day of arrival if they are paying with a money order, and ten days prior to arrival if they will be using a personal check. No personal or company checks will be accepted at the time of check-in or check-out. Travelers can also go to any hotel in the chain ahead of time, pay a deposit for their first night's hotel stay and get a voucher to take with them for late check-in. For information call (800) 221-2222.

Hotel/Motel Discounts

Many hotels and motels offer substantial discounts on their rooms—for weekend packages, off-season, etc. To learn about discounts, call the hotel directly and ask about packages and discount rates—discount information is *not* something that will be volunteered at the time you make your reservation. Some hotels—Marriott and Days Inn, for example—give discounts for reserving a room well in advance, so ask what is available.

An important drawback of early reservation discount programs is that there is usually a penalty for cancelling your reservation. When getting information about discounts, be sure to find out about the terms of the cancellation policy.

Find out if the hotel you often stay at has a frequent-stay program. Those that do allow you to build up credits to use toward a free room—much like the airlines' frequent flyer programs. Also, request a corporate rate when making reservations—this will usually get you a ten percent discount.

If you are 50 years of age or older, you may be eligible for a senior discount. Ask at the time you make your reservation if the hotel offers such a discount. As a member of the American Association of Retired Persons (AARP), you can get discounts of up to 30 percent at many hotels. For membership information, call (202) 872-4700.

Other professional or association memberships may entitle you to a discount on your accommodations. Call your association headquarters to find out about the benefits of membership.

Hot Tip

Never wait for a hotel reservation clerk to tell you about discounts that may be available to you—they won't tell you unless you ask.

Other tips for getting discounted hotel and motel rooms:

- Join a half price hotel club. For a modest fee, you will get a directory of hotels/motels that give discounts of up to 50 percent on the regular rate for a standard room. Figure 6.9 tells how to get information about some of these clubs as well as other sources of discount hotel accommodations.
- Use the services of a city reservation system. By booking your hotel or motel through one of these systems, you can get hotel discounts of up to 50 percent. Figure 6.10 provides telephone numbers for various city reservation systems.
- Suggest a company subscription to *Frequent,* a newsletter reporting on frequent-stay and frequent-flyer programs.

Rental Cars

If you need a rental car while you are traveling, advance planning will again be essential. Following are the requirements of several major rental car companies for renting a car without using credit.

Avis Avis offers creditless travelers three different options. Its preferred option is a third party charge; in other words, you rent your rental car using someone else's credit card. To do this, you need to obtain a special application from Avis, complete it and get the company's approval.

A second option is to pay with cash. This also requires an application, and you will have to provide bank, personal and employment references. In addition, Avis will want proof of the following: that you are employed and have been with your company for at least one year; that you are at least 25 years old; that you have a phone listed in your name; and that your phone number and address are in your local directory under your name.

If you pay with cash, you will have to provide a $200 deposit at the time of rental and your rental fee will come out of this deposit.

The third option available through Avis involves your company establishing a corporate account. As an employee, you would then be an *authorized rep*, and the rental bill would go to your employer. For more information, call (800) 331-1212.

Hertz Some Hertz locations will accept credit cards only, but specific policies vary from location to location. The following general terms and conditions apply to the locations that will work with creditless travellers: you must pay a cash deposit in advance; the largest vehicle you can rent is a four door, full-size car; you must be at least 25 years old; you must have been employed full-time for at least a year; you must have a phone listed with directory assistance in your or your spouse's name or you must be able to provide a phone bill showing that your number is unlisted; and, you must provide references from a relative and your bank. All of this information must be verifiable during business hours, between 9 AM and 4 PM, Monday through Friday.

At the time of rental, you must also pay a cash deposit in the amount of the estimated rental charges, plus 50 percent of that estimate (for a minimum of $100); and you will also be charged a $10 administrative fee. When you return the car, you will have to pay any balance due over and above the cash deposit. This additional payment can be made with cash, a money order, a personal check or a corporate check. For more information, call (202) 307-2000.

Thrifty Some locations accept credit cards only. Others allow a traveler to "cash qualify." A request to cash qualify must be directed in advance to the particular rental location you will be using. The specific terms and conditions of rental without a credit card vary from location to location. For more information, call (918) 665-3930.

General Travelers may cash qualify at least 48 hours in advance of rental and are required to pay at least a $100 deposit at the time they pick up their car. To cash qualify, you must be at least 25 years old, be able to verify that you have been working full-time for at least one year and provide references from both a relative and your bank. For more information, call (800) 327-7607.

Figure 6.9 Sources for Discount Hotel Accommodations

- *Travel America at Half Price,* Entertainment Publications, $29.95. To order, call (800) 342-0558. Lists 1200 hotels and motels.
- The International Travel Card Program. As a member, one of your benefits will be a copy of *Hotels at Half Price.* Membership is $36 per year. To find out about joining, call (800) 342-1022.
- The Concierge Club specializes in upscale hotels. Membership is $69 per year. To find out about membership, call (800) 767-9484.
- A Privilege card entitles you to discounts of up to 50 percent on rooms at over 3,000 hotels and motels in the U.S., Canada, Mexico and the Caribbean. As a cardholder, you will also get discounts on car rentals. Membership is $49.95 per year. For information, call (800) 359-0066.

Additional Travel Tips

The following information can make traveling without credit easier and less expensive:

- Since hotel food prices tend to be high, try to plan your hotel stay so you are close to various inexpensive restaurants.
- Take tins of food as well as crackers and cheese with you. If your stay is not going to be lengthy, you can actually have a gourmet suitcase feast for a lot less than it would cost to eat out!
- When traveling to a major city, read travel guides and the city's magazines to find out about low-cost, good quality restaurants frequented by the locals. These are often a less expensive alternative to restaurants that rely primarily on travelers and tourists for their business. As a bonus, dining in local eateries gives you a sense of the culture and regional uniqueness of the city you are visiting.
- Use public transportation as much as possible.

Figure 6.10 City Reservation Systems

- Capitol Reservations—(800) 847-4836. Washington, D.C.
- Express Hotel Reservations—(800) 356-1123. New York City and Los Angeles
- Central Reservation Service—(800) 950-0232. Throughout the U.S.

Conclusion

The state of the economy and the increasing complexities of today's world make it vitally important to develop sound money management skills and a regular savings program. A growing number of middle-income Americans are learning that spending money wisely can mean the difference between a comfortable lifestyle and a gradual decline into poverty. In tough economic times, when there is diminishing job security and household income is not keeping pace with rising costs, it is important to make every dollar count.

seven

Arranging for Transportation

"More than any other country, ours is an automotive society"
Lyndon Baines Johnson

Jim and Kathy S. both worked—he as an insurance salesman, she as a part-time teacher. They came to see me because one of their two cars had become so unreliable that they could no longer count on it as a regular source of transportation. They wanted to discuss how they might get a new car.

"I don't know where to turn," Jim told me. "My credit is shot and, we both need dependable cars for work. What do we do?"

There was no simple answer to that question. I talked to them about various options and how to determine if the wisest financial decision might not be to spend money to get the car repaired even though they were both tired of it. We also discussed whether or not Kathy could car-pool with someone from the school where she works or take public transportation. Although I couldn't make a decision for Kathy and Jim, they left with a better idea of their options and how to evaluate them.

Buying a car is the single most significant financial transaction that most Americans make. However, most consumers approach car buying with little or none of the information needed to evaluate their options and make an intelligent buying decision. All too frequently, decisions about personal transportation are based on impulse and emotion.

During your financial recovery you will probably have to make a decision regarding one or more of the following:

- Getting a vehicle repaired
- Deciding whether to keep your current car or get a new one
- Deciding whether to buy a used or a new car
- Deciding whether to lease a new car

When money is tight, decisions about transportation are almost never easy. However, having the right information and knowing how to systematically analyze your options can help.

Should You Keep Your Old Car or Get a New One?

To determine whether you should get another car or keep your current one, compare the costs of owning and maintaining your current car for the additional number of years you would like to keep it with the ownership and maintenance costs of the car you would buy in its place. To do this, list all the costs and considerations discussed in this section on a sheet of paper. Plug in general dollar amounts for your current car and compare them to the general costs of the car you are thinking of replacing it with.

Ownership Costs

In general, the costs of owning a car decrease as the age of your car increases. This is due to several factors including depreciation, insurance, finance charges, taxes and registration.

Depreciation Cars and certain other assets depreciate as they age due to simple wear and tear. Cars usually depreciate the most during the early years of ownership. The more your car depreciates, the lower its resale or trade-in value. Unless you anticipate that your car is going to need some especially costly repairs in the very near future, holding on to it may be a good idea since you will not make much money if you sell it.

Insurance The older your car, the lower your collision and comprehensive insurance costs will be; due to depreciation, your car is not worth as much as it was when it was newer.

When your car is five to six years old, you may want to consider getting rid of collision insurance entirely and retaining only liability coverage.

Finance Charges Auto loans are structured in such a way that the amount of equity you have in your car grows slowly. In the early stages, your payments are primarily applied toward interest on the loan rather than principal, and you will probably owe more on your car than it is worth. Unless your car payments are too high and you simply need to get a car that costs you less each month, it probably won't make a lot of sense to get rid of your car.

At some point in your loan's history, your equity in your car will begin to exceed the amount of your down payment, and a new car becomes a more viable option. To determine when your equity will exceed your down payment and exactly how much equity you have in your car, talk to your banker or the company financing your current vehicle.

If you own your current car outright, and are planning to finance the purchase of a new one, you'll find that the interest charges on a new loan usually add substantially to the costs of owning a new car. This is another reason to hold on to what you've got if at all possible.

To determine your total interest charges, calculate the total dollar value of the car payments you would make over the life of the loan you are considering, and subtract the car's purchase price from that amount.

Taxes and Registration In some states, the cost of registering your car decreases as the age of your car increases. In states where cars are taxed as personal property, the tax rate on your car may decline as your car ages and its market value decreases. To find out about your state's registration and taxation policies, call your state's Department of Motor Vehicles and your insurance agent.

Operating Costs In general, the costs of operating your car—gasoline, maintenance and repairs—increase as the vehicle ages.

Repairs Talk to your auto mechanic and get an estimate of the amount of money you will probably have to spend for repairs over the next several years to keep your car in running order. Ask for an itemization of the things you will have to fix or replace given the age and model of your car, together with a cost estimate for each. Also, ask your mechanic to assess the condition of your car's tires and estimate how soon you will have to replace them given your driving patterns.

Hot Tip

Review the repair frequency information for your car in the most recent edition of *The Complete Car Cost Guide,* published by IntelliChoice.

You can slow the rate at which operating costs increase by giving your car regular care and maintenance. If you have the Owner's Manual, refer to the list of maintenance activities it recommends. If you don't have a manual, talk to your mechanic or a dealer in your area that sells your make of car. Any problem your car is having should be diagnosed and repaired as soon as possible; a delay can result in more costly repairs.

Getting your car repaired can be an expensive and frustrating experience unless you know how to protect yourself from overpriced, incompetent repair shops. Here are some tips for minimizing car repair hassles:

- Check your car's warranty or service contract. Does it place any restrictions on where and how your car is repaired?
- In the case of a major repair, shop around. Ask several repair shops for written estimates. Get in writing each shop's hourly rate and any exceptions to that rate.
- Tell the shops you visit what your car's symptoms are, not what needs to be fixed. Let each shop diagnose the problem.
- Check a shop's complaint record before working with it. Do this by calling your area's Better Business Bureau.

Hot Tip

Many states have *lemon laws* for new cars with recurring problems. Check with your state's attorney general's office or office of consumer affairs.

- Ask if new or rebuilt parts will be used. There are many high quality rebuilt parts available today that can save you a considerable amount of money.
- Find out if a shop offers a warranty. If so, does the warranty cover both parts and labor? Is there a difference for new or rebuilt parts? Get any warranties in writing.
- Before you leave your car at a shop, make sure that the work order reflects what needs to be done.
- Ask that the shop contact you before it makes any repairs not listed on the work order. If it fails to do so, you do not have to pay for the unauthorized work, and you have the right to get your bill adjusted.
- Keep copies of all work orders and receipts.

Maintenance Maintenance activities for your car include things like brake jobs, engine tune-ups and oil changes. Using the same time period as you use for estimating the total cost of future repairs to your car, calculate your probable maintenance costs. Do this by reviewing the maintenance schedule recommended by the manufacturer, getting cost estimates from your auto mechanic and taking your driving conditions into account.

Cost of Gasoline The amount of money you will spend on fuel can be estimated by multiplying the number of miles your car currently gets per gallon by the number of miles per year you expect to drive your car over the additional years you are considering keeping it.

If Getting a New Car Is the Best Option

"If you don't know where you are going, you will probably end up someplace else."

Laurence Peter

When replacing your current car turns out to be your best option, you have a new set of considerations. The most important are your budget, your transportation needs and financing.

Using your spending plan as a guide, you need to determine how much you can afford to spend on another car. Can you afford to make regular monthly payments, or will you need to find a used car that you can buy outright? Do you have money in savings earmarked for a down payment on a car? Are there ways that your spending plan could be revised to accommodate the purchase of a car? What is your car's approximate trade-in or resale value?

You also need to consider how you will use the car you buy and whether you really need one at all. For many people in large cities, public transportation is a viable option; in some communities, a bicycle is a suitable means of transportation. In situations where you absolutely must drive, taking taxis—and even renting a car—can be cheaper than ownership; or perhaps a friend or relative would occasionally be willing to loan you a car. While this approach to transportation may not be something you would want to continue over the long term, it is worth considering while you are getting back on your feet.

If you do need a regular car to drive, consider the following: How many people will it need to carry? Will you be taking clients in it? Do you need something that can carry equipment, supplies or portable baby furniture? Do you travel long distances in your work? Are you in a car pool?

As you consider how best to meet your transportation needs, evaluate the pros and cons of your options if you need a car to drive. They include: buying a new car, buying a used car, leasing a car.

Figure 7.1 presents the pros and cons of each option.

Doing Your Research

Read car buying guides and magazines to determine the makes and models that best fit your transportation needs and budget. Eliminate those that get poor gas mileage or have bad records regarding the frequency and cost of repairs.

Once you've narrowed down your choices, you'll need to get

Figure 7.1 Transportation Pros and Cons

New Car

Pros

- Repairs/servicing covered by warranty in early years
- Generally fewer problems than a used car
- With each loan payment, building equity in an asset that has cash value
- Lower operating costs than a used car

Cons

- Ownership costs higher than a used car
- Higher initial costs than a used or leased car
- Rapid depreciation in early years
- Generally larger monthly payments than a used or leased car

Used Car

Pros

- Lower ownership costs than a new car
- Lower monthly costs than a new or leased car
- Lower initial cost than a new car, if financing

Cons

- Higher operating costs than a new car
- Usually a limited warranty or no warranty at all
- Greater chance of mechanical problems than with a new car

Figure 7.1 Transportation Pros and Cons (Continued)

Leased Car

Pros

- Generally lower initial cost and monthly payments than a new car
- Look and reliability of a new car
- Ease of paperwork, registration and inspection

Cons

- At end of lease period, no car to trade in or sell
- No equity being built

some current price information. When shopping for a new car, you will want to get the manufacturer's suggested retail price and the dealer's invoice price. If you are looking for a used car, you will be interested in the market value of specific cars. This information can help you recognize a good car deal and will make you a better negotiator when you are ready to actually buy a car. A good source of general information on new car prices is *Edmund's New Car Prices,* available in most public libraries. While actual prices vary and need to be determined when you actually visit dealers, this publication is a good place to start.

Hot Tip

If you belong to a credit union, find out if it uses AutoFacts. This free service offers information on a car's price, mileage, repair record, affordability, etc.

Carputer International is another excellent source. This company sells car pricing information on specific cars, including the manufacturer's suggested retail price, the dealer or invoice price, factory options and their costs and any rebate information that might be available. For a small fee, Carputer International will send you a detailed report on a specific make and model of car.

To get pricing information and specific details on what the company has to offer, call (800) 992-7404.

For used car pricing information, the best source is the *Official Used Car Guide*, or *Blue Book*, published by the National Automobile Dealers Association and available at most local libraries and car dealerships. *The Blue Book* provides average trade-in, loan and retail prices for specific used cars. However, *The Blue Book* price is only an approximation since various factors—the region of the country you live in, the time of year, a car's condition and general economic trends—can influence the actual price of a used car. A good way to assess the going price for a used car is to review your area's classifieds for asking prices on used cars identical or comparable to what you are considering. Keep in mind, however, that if you are going to buy a used car from a dealer, the price you can expect to pay will generally be somewhat higher than the classified prices.

If you will be trading or selling a car, you must determine its value. The resources just discussed will be of help. In general, you'll get more money for a car by selling it yourself than by trading it in.

Assessing Your Financing Options

It is best to check with some potential financing sources to learn, in general, what terms they can offer you. You will also want to identify the dealers that offer the most attractive financing packages on the type of car you want to purchase. These calls will help determine the dealers you should visit. Sources of car loans include: banks, savings and loans, credit unions and automobile finance companies such as GMAC and Ford Motor Credit. When you call, be up front if you are recovering from bankruptcy or serious financial difficulty. Such information may affect the terms a creditor will offer as well as their willingness to work with you at all.

A potential creditor will look at the following factors when deciding whether or not to give you a car loan:

- Can you come up with a down payment—either in cash, as a trade-in or a combination?
- Do you have a steady job?

- Are you meeting your current obligations?
- Did you reaffirm your debts if you filed a Chapter 7 bankruptcy? If you filed a Chapter 13, are you meeting the terms of your wage-earner plan?
- What was your history prior to your bankruptcy or severe financial trouble?
- What was the reason for your financial troubles?

Hot Tip

If you are in an active Chapter 13 plan, you must have approval from the courts before incurring any additional debt such as a car loan.

How To Shop for a Car

Once you have a general idea of what you want, the financing options available to you and their likely costs, and how much you can actually afford to spend, it's time to visit some auto dealers. Tell each dealer exactly what you are looking for and listen to what they have to offer. Bring along a notebook and take notes.

Test drive those cars that seem most interesting. Drive the cars on a variety of roads—highways, hills, smooth and bumpy surfaces—in a variety of driving conditions—stop-and-go traffic and at highway speed. Note how well the cars brake, accelerate and steer. Listen to the radios, and see how well the cars heat and cool. With used cars, check the wear on tires and the condition of both the interior and exterior.

Ask for the invoice price of the new cars that most interest you—it's an important piece of information. This is the price the dealer pays for the car before any manufacturer rebates, allowances or discounts. The difference between the manufacturer's suggested retail price for a car and its invoice price represents the dealer's profit margin, and therefore is the area to focus on when you're negotiating a new car purchase price.

Hot Tip

The invoice price always includes freight charges. If you pay invoice price for a car, ask that the freight charge be deducted from it.

When you visit car dealers, also get information about any buyer incentives they may be offering. These might include cash rebates or discounts, special financing and option package discounts. Write all this information in your notebook.

When looking at new cars, note that each vehicle has a *Monroney sticker* in its window. Required by federal law, the sticker provides the following information:

- The car's base price, which is the cost of the car without options, including standard equipment, factory warranty and freight (also known as destination or delivery charges)
- The manufacturer's installed options with the manufacturer's suggested retail price
- The manufacturer's transportation charge

Information about a car's average fuel economy may either be found on the Monroney sticker or on a separate EPA Fuel Economy label.

Some dealers also put a dealer sticker on their new cars. This is a supplemental sticker that states the dealer or Monroney sticker price plus the suggested price of dealer-installed options—additional dealer profit, dealer preparation and undercoating, for example.

New Car Warranties

Several types of warranties are available for new cars, ranging from those that provide basic coverage of all mechanical or other defects for 12 months or 12,000 miles, whichever comes first, to those that provide the same basic coverage for up to four years or 50,000 miles. Some dealers also offer extended warranties for major drivetrain components.

Service contracts and special warranties covering repairs for a longer period of time than basic warranties, or covering repairs that are not usually included in extended drivetrain warranties, are very often available from manufacturers and independent warranty companies.

When evaluating warranties and service contracts, consider the following questions:

- How long does it last and when does it start and end?
- What is covered—problems and parts?
- Will it pay for all repair costs but not for parts or labor?

- Will it pay for parts shipping?
- Will it pay for a loaner car?
- What are your obligations?
- Who will make the repairs?
- How reliable is the company offering the warranty or service contract?
- What sort of cancellation or refund policy does it have?

Hot Tip

Some states offer additional warranty rights for consumers. Check with your state attorney general's office or office of consumer affairs.

Regardless of how much pressure you may feel from a car salesperson or how good a deal you are told that you are getting, do not make a purchase decision in a showroom or a car lot. Instead, after you've finished visiting car dealers, go home, put pencil to paper and analyze your options. Prioritize the cars you are most drawn to in terms of which best suit your needs and fit your budget. Determine how much above the invoice price, if anything, you would be willing to pay for a specific car and what your initial offer would be. Compare the prices and financing packages being offered by dealers. If you've not yet done so, determine the trade-in value of your old car if you are going to make it part of the sale.

After you have finished your analysis and identified your best options, you are ready to start negotiating a purchase price. When you return to a dealer to talk money, start low and negotiate up, but don't go beyond the maximum price you set for a particular car when you were doing your analysis.

When the dealer counters, it is perfectly all right to say that you need to go home and do some more figuring. If you don't feel comfortable or confident doing the negotiating, ask a trusted friend or relative to do it for you.

Buying a Used Car

There are two sources for used cars—dealers and private sellers. If you buy from a private seller, you will probably get a better price than if you buy the same car from a dealer. When you buy from a dealer, you gain the protection of the Federal Trade Commission's Used Car Rule, which requires dealers to post a *Buyers Guide sticker* on their used cars. These stickers provide the following information:

- Whether or not a car comes with a warranty
- The provisions of any warranty
- General information about the problems that any used car may have
- A suggestion that a buyer have the car inspected by an independent mechanic prior to purchase
- A warning to get in writing all dealer promises about the car you wish to purchase

If you negotiate any changes in the warranty coverage, make sure that those changes are written into your *Buyers Guide.* You will receive the original *Buyers Guide,* or an identical copy, when you buy a used car. It will become a part of your sales contract with the dealer.

Buyers Guide Warranties

A used car can come with one of four types of warranty coverages, including:

No Warranty or "As Is" If you buy a used car without a warranty, any problems the car has are yours. The dealer is neither obligated to fix the problem nor pay for the repair. Some states prohibit *as is* sales. Check with your attorney general's office or office of consumer affairs about the law in your state.

Implied Warranties Nearly all used cars come with implied warranties. There are two basic types of implied or unwritten warranties. The most common is the *warranty of merchantability.* Dealers offering this type of warranty promise that the car will do what it is supposed to do—run.

Another common type of implied warranty is a *warranty of fitness.* Dealers offering this type of warranty promise that a vehicle is suitable for a particular purpose.

Dealer Warranties Dealers may offer a written warranty on a used vehicle. When they do, the dealer must fill in the warranty portion of the *Buyers Guide.* The terms and coverage of a used car warranty are often negotiable.

A dealer's warranty may be either full or limited on all or some of a car's components and systems. Full warranties are rare for used cars. Under a limited warranty, the buyer will have to pick up some of the costs of repair, and it is likely that some of the car's components will not be covered.

The *Buyers Guide* must provide the following information on a full or a limited warranty:

- The percentage of the repair costs the dealer will absorb
- The specific parts and systems covered by the warranty
- The duration of the warranty for each covered system
- Applicable deductibles

The Magnuson-Moss Act gives consumers the right to review a copy of a dealer's warranty before purchasing a vehicle. The warranty provides more detailed information than the *Buyers Guide.* Examine it carefully.

When reviewing the warranty on a used car, pay special attention to whether the dealer or a third party will actually fulfill the terms. If it is a third party, check to see if the company is reputable and insured. Find out the name of the insurer, and call the Better Business Bureau to make sure that it has a good record.

Unexpired Manufacturer's Warranties Some used cars come with unexpired manufacturer's warranties—the car is still covered by the original warranty provided by the manufacturer. The dealer may include it in the *systems covered/duration* section of the *Buyers Guide.*

If the used car you are considering has one of these warranties, check with the dealer about what is covered, and find out if you must pay a fee to have it transferred to you.

Independent Inspection Just because a car looks attractive and comes with a warranty, that is no guarantee that it runs well. Therefore, take the car for a test drive, just as you would a new car, and always get it inspected by an independent mechanic. Make your offer to buy a car contingent upon it's either passing inspection or upon the sales price being reduced sufficiently to cover the cost of repairs. Although you will have to pay a fee for an inspection, it is well worth the cost.

Some dealers allow you to take a used car off the lot to get it inspected, while others ask that the mechanic come to the lot. If a dealer discourages you from getting the opinion of an independent mechanic, or tries to get you to use one that he or she recommends, take it as an indication that the car has mechanical problems and look for another car at another dealership.

Buying a Used Car from a Private Seller

If you decide to buy a car from a private seller, there are a number of things you should do to ensure that you are getting a good car. They include:

- Ask to see the car's repair and maintenance records. Check to see if the car has been properly maintained, and review the repair records to identify any problems it may have.
- Ask the owner if the car has ever been in an accident.
- Take the car on a test drive just as you would a new car.
- Take the car to an independent mechanic to have it thoroughly checked out.
- Check the condition of the car's tires.

If the car is relatively new, it may still be covered by the original manufacturer's warranty or by a service contract. Read the terms of each to find out whether or not the benefits will transfer to a new owner and, if they do, whether the transfer will cost you anything.

Hot Tip

Some states require that both dealers and individual sellers of used cars guarantee that the car they are selling pass state inspection. Call your state attorney general's office or office of consumer affairs to learn what your state requires of used car dealers and private sellers.

Financing a Car

"This is the only country that went to the poor house in an automobile."

Will Rogers

An auto loan is an installment loan with your car pledged as collateral. As with other such loans, you will be required to make a series of regular monthly payments in a fixed amount until you have paid off the loan's principal and interest.

Most car loans are made for a period of two to four years. Some banks now make five-year loans—although rarely for used cars. While a longer loan has the advantage of decreasing the amount of each monthly payment, it significantly increases the total amount of interest you pay, and therefore increases a car's total cost.

Two factors affect the total amount of money you need to borrow to purchase a car: the value of the car you are going to trade in, assuming you have one to trade, and the amount of money you have to put down.

Just as you would if you were financing any other purchase, shop around for the financing package with the most advantageous terms. (See Chapter 4 for things to consider when you are shopping for an installment loan.) In most cases, your best source of financing will be a bank, savings and loan or your credit union; however, dealers may be more willing than other creditors to work with people recovering from financial difficulty.

Dealer Financing

Dealer financing usually comes at a relatively high rate of interest because a bank, not the dealer, actually finances the loan. In other words, the dealer borrows money from a bank at one rate of interest and then loans that money to a car buyer at a higher rate of interest. The difference between the dealer's cost of credit and the consumer's cost of credit is profit for the dealer.

A dealer might offer a very competitive financing package but not be willing to negotiate on price, or might require a larger than usual down payment. To determine whether or not a dealer's financing package is a good deal, be sure you understand all the terms and conditions of the package, and compare it to other alternatives. To help you identify your best option, here are some of the questions you need answers to:

- Will you have to pay a higher price for a particular car in order to take advantage of a dealer's financing package?
- Would the car's price be lower if you paid cash or got your financing elsewhere?

- Does the financing package require a larger than usual down payment?
- Are you required to pay the loan in a shorter than usual time, i.e., within two to three years?
- To qualify for the financing, do you have to buy something you wouldn't want otherwise? (This could include rustproofing, an extended warranty or a service contract.)
- Is the financing available for a limited time only?
- Does it only apply to certain cars?
- If there is a manufacturer's rebate, are you required to give it to the dealer in order to get the financing?

If the dealer offers special promotions such as high trade-in allowances or free or low-cost options, make sure they are of real value. Check the following:

- Does the high trade-in allowance apply to all cars regardless of their condition?
- Does the high trade-in allowance end up making the car more expensive than it would be without the trade-in?
- Are you getting a better price from the dealer who is offering the special promotions than you would from one who is not offering such enticements?
- Do the special promotions apply to a car that has to be ordered or only to those on a dealer's lot?

Most creditors will not make a loan to anyone who can't come up with either a cash down payment, a trade-in or a combination. You may, however, be able to find a dealer who will work with you. Such dealers typically have either a lot of money to lend or really want to move their inventory.

Dealers who do their own financing are sometimes willing to carry a separate note for a down payment. However, these loans will usually be made at a very high rate of interest and will come with significant restrictions. Also, some dealers are willing to co-sign the note a consumer gets from a bank.

Service Contracts

When buying either a new or a used car from a dealer, you will probably be offered the opportunity to buy a service contract or an extended warranty. This offer may be made at the time of purchase or at some time after you've bought your car. It may be made by the dealer, the manufacturer or an independent company. Whether or not a contract is worth the additional cost depends upon the answer to a number of key questions, including:

- Do the service contract and the warranty overlap or cover the same things?
- What repairs are covered by the service contract and what are the conditions of the coverage?
- Who will authorize payment of claims if a repair covered by the service contract has to be made? If a dealer or an administrator will, make sure that the company has a solid reputation, and find out how long it has been in business. To do this, call your local Better Business Bureau, your state attorney general's office or office of consumer affairs, or your area's automobile dealers association.
- Is the service contract underwritten by an insurance company? If it is, call your state's Insurance Commission. This office can tell you if the insurance company is in good financial shape and whether any complaints have ever been filed against it.
- Who will make the service contract repairs, and how will payment be made? Be sure that the company making the repairs is convenient to your home or place of employment. Find out whether you will have to pay for the repairs yourself and then get reimbursed for them. If this is the case, be sure that you clearly understand the reimbursement process and how long it generally takes to get reimbursed.

Also, find out whether the service contract is only good within a limited geographic area, whether repair and towing services must be authorized before they are used and the process for such authorization.

- What are your responsibilities under the service contract and the conditions of those responsibilities? Will failure to meet these terms and conditions invalidate the contact?
- How much does the service contract cost, and how long does it last? The up-front cost for a service contract ranges from two or three hundred dollars to $1,000. In many cases,

a deductible or fee must be paid every time the car is brought in for work covered by the service contract. Ask if there is a per-repair or per-visit service fee.

If the duration of the service contract is for longer than you plan on keeping the car, check to see if a shorter contract is available. Also, find out if you can transfer the contract upon sale of the car and if any transfer fees apply.

Leasing a Car

"No man-made device since the shield and lance of the knights quite fulfills a man's ego like an automobile."

William Roberts

Leasing a car has become an attractive option for an increasing number of consumers. To determine whether leasing makes sense for you, compare the initial, ongoing and final costs of leasing to the costs of buying and maintaining the same or an equivalent car. Use the Buy versus Lease Worksheet, in Figure 7.2 to make this comparison.

Hot Tip

If you don't feel comfortable making the comparison yourself, ask your banker, finance company or a dealer to help you compare the costs of buying and leasing after you have gathered all cost information on each option.

There are two basic types of auto leases—closed-end and open-end; the closed-end lease is the most user-friendly.

Closed-End Lease

This type of lease obligates you to pay a fixed amount of money each month for the period of time specified in your lease contract. At the end of the lease, you return the car and have no further responsibility to the lessor unless you put more than the usual amount of wear and tear on the car or drove it more than the number of miles specified in your lease. In other words, the lessor assumes the risk for the value of the car at the end of your lease.

Figure 7.2 Buy versus Lease Worksheet

CHECKLIST FOR COMPARING LEASING AND PURCHASING COSTS

After you have selected a new vehicle, you might wish to use this checklist to help you compare the costs of leasing against the costs of purchasing through a conventional loan. In making such rough comparisons, you will need to consider three categories of costs: initial; continuing; final. However, when deciding whether to lease or purchase, you may not want to base your decision solely on total costs, but also may wish to consider when (or if) any large cash outlays are required.

INITIAL COSTS

Leasing		Purchasing	
Security deposit	______	Downpayment	______
Capitalized cost reduction, if applicable	______		
First periodic payment	______		
Last periodic payment, if applicable	______		
Total amount of fees (license, registration, and taxes)	______	Total amount of fees (license, registration, and taxes)	______
Insurance	______	Insurance	______
Trade-in allowance, if applicable	______	Trade-in allowance, if applicable	______
	$______		$______

CONTINUING COSTS

Leasing		Purchasing	
Periodic payment (expressed as monthly)	______	Monthly payment (including finance charge*)	______
Insurance (expressed as monthly)	______	Insurance (expressed as monthly)	______
Estimated monthly maintenance and repair costs considering warranty coverage	______	Estimated monthly maintenance and repair costs considering warranty coverage	______
	$______		$______

FINAL COSTS

Leasing**		Purchasing	
Maximum end-of-lease payment based on estimated residual value***	______	Balloon payment, if applicable	______
Excessive mileage/wear charges	______		
Disposition charge	______		
Total amount of fees (license, registration, and taxes)	______	Total amount of fees (license, registration, and taxes)	______
Insurance	______	Insurance	______
Trade-in allowance, if applicable	______	Trade-in allowance, if applicable	______
	$______		$______

* Finance charges are deductible if you itemize your tax return. However, beginning in 1987, this benefit will be phased out over four years.

** If you have a purchase option, you may wish to consider the amount of the option price in your comparison.

*** For open-end lease only, see page 5.

SOURCE: Federal Trade Commission, "A Consumer Guide to Vehicle Leasing," 1989

Open-End Lease

Open-end leases tend to be somewhat cheaper than closed-end leases on a month-to-month basis. With an open-end lease, you gamble that at the end of the lease period the car will be worth at least as much as the amount specified in the lease agreement. If, due to factors like wear and tear or excess mileage the car is worth less, you will have to make an "end of lease" payment to the lessor.

An open-end lease will specify a car's *estimated residual value* or what it will be worth once you return it to the lessor. At the end of your lease, the lessor will either sell the car or have it appraised, and will compare the sales price or the appraisal to the car's estimated residual value. If either the sales price or the appraisal is less than the *estimated residual value,* you may have to pay all or a percentage of that difference. If either is higher, you may be able to pocket the difference, depending upon the terms of your lease.

The Consumer Leasing Act (CLA) gives you the right to hire an independent appraiser to provide a second appraisal if you disagree with the one the lessor gets. However, you must pay for the cost of the second appraisal, and the appraiser must be acceptable to the lessor. Both you and the lessor will be bound by the independent appraisal.

The CLA says that in most instances the lessor cannot collect any more than three times the average monthly lease payment if the leased car is appraised at less than its estimated residual value at the end of the lease. There are exceptions:

- If you agree to pay more than what was previously specified in the lease agreement
- If the car suffered unreasonable wear and tear while you had it, or if you drove the car more than the number of miles specified in the contract
- If the lessor takes you to court to collect a larger end-of-lease payment and wins

At the end of the lease period on an open-end lease, the lessor may elect to sell the car you were leasing. If the car is sold for less than its estimated residual value, the CLA says that you can be obligated to pay the lessor up to three times the average monthly lease payment. Although it is unlikely that the lessor will sell the car for less than its estimated residual value, you may want to protect yourself by negotiating a lease agreement that gives you the right to approve the final sales price.

Likely Up-Front Costs

The CLA requires that the lessor indicate to you in writing all the up-front costs you will have to pay before you sign a lease agreement. Usually negotiable, these costs include a security deposit, taxes and title, license fees and insurance.

The Security Deposit protects the lessor in the event that you fail to make your payments, damage the car or exceed the maximum number of miles stated in your lease contract. The deposit could also be applied toward your end-of-lease payment if you sign an open-end lease.

First and Last Lease Payments are usually required at the onset of a lease. Depending upon your credit record and the policies of the lessor, you may be required to pay more than two months rent up front.

Capitalized Cost Reduction is the equivalent of a down payment on a car—the exact amount you pay depends on the lessor's policy and how good a negotiator you are. It is also somewhat dependent upon your credit record—if your record is not strong, you may have to make a larger than average payment. While doing so lowers the amount of your monthly payments, it may make leasing a car less attractive. You may find that the amount of your capitalized cost reduction is close to or more than what you would have paid in a down payment on a car.

Hot Tip

To reduce the size of your capitalized cost reduction, consider trading in a car you own.

Sales Tax, Title and License are all negotiable items so the lessor may be willing to pay a portion of them. Some states allow you to spread these costs out over the period of the lease, including them in your monthly payments. If your state does not explicitly allow this, you may still be able to negotiate a similar arrangement with a lessor.

Insurance Some lessors require that you purchase insurance; others provide it. In either case, the CLA says that the lessor must tell you how much and the type of coverage required.

Ongoing Costs of Leasing If you lease a car, you may not only have to assume responsibility for regular monthly lease payments, but also for regular expenses such as repairs and maintenance on the car. These additional costs are usually negotiable.

Monthly Payments The CLA requires the lessor to disclose certain information about a lease's monthly payment before the lease is signed, including:

- Total number of payments
- Amount of each payment
- Total amount of all payments
- Payment due date or schedule

Repairs and Maintenance

Your lease agreement should state clearly exactly who is responsible for repairs and maintenance, and spell out the standards for these services. If it doesn't, get the lessor to add, before you sign the lease, exactly when and where repairs and maintenance activities must take place. Having this clearly defined should help minimize the potential for end-of-lease disputes regarding what constitutes *excessive wear and tear* on the car.

Hot Tip

Terms like "reasonable wear and tear" or "reasonable maintenance" are too vague and therefore do not provide you with adequate protection. Get these terms defined in your lease agreement.

Final or End-Of-Lease costs are generally negotiable. Since they can significantly affect just how good a deal a lease is, pay careful attention to them. Final costs may include: excessive mileage charges, a default penalty and, in the case of an open-end lease, an end-of-lease payment.

Excessive Wear Charge In most cases, you are responsible for the cost of repair if, at the end of the lease, there has been excessive wear and tear on the car. The amount of the charge or the method used to calculate that charge must be spelled out in your lease.

Excess Mileage Charge Most closed-end leases establish a maximum mileage allowance for the term of a lease. If you exceed that maximum, you must pay an additional fee when you return the car. If you do a lot of driving, be sure that you negotiate a sufficiently high maximum mileage allowance.

Default Penalties Default penalties come into play if you are not able to meet the terms of your lease—you can't make your monthly payments on schedule, or you stop making payments entirely. Your lease should clearly state what will happen in this event. Default penalties might include: losing a security deposit, a demand for payment in full of all your lease obligations, as well as payment of any legal fees and costs the lessor incurs in order to get the vehicle back.

Disposition Charges include cleaning costs, tune-ups and maintenance on a car once it is returned to the lessor and is being prepared for sale. These costs may be charged to you.

Option Rights A lease will typically give you a series of options that you can exercise or not, during or at the end of your lease. These may include: the right to purchase the car you have been leasing, the right to renew or extend your lease and early termination.

Purchase Option If your lease includes a purchase option, the CLA requires that the lessor tell you the estimated residual value of the car and the formula used to calculate the car's purchase price before you sign the lease agreement. Purchase options are most closely associated with open-end leases.

If you would like a purchase option that is not a part of the lease which you are going to sign, ask that it be included. Otherwise, negotiating for a purchase option at the end of your lease will be entirely separate from the lease itself, and purchase terms may not be as advantageous as if they had been negotiated with the lease.

Renewal Option Your lease should include an option to extend or renew. If a lessor knows at the onset that you may want to lease on a month-to-month basis after the term of your lease is up, you will probably be able to negotiate lower monthly payments.

Hot Tip

If you renew your lease for more than four months, or extend it for more than six months, the CLA says that the lessor is required once again to give you all the disclosures you received at the start of the lease.

If You Decide To Lease a Car

Once you have decided to lease, list the cars you are most interested in, and contact local auto leasing companies for leasing information. Many new car dealers also lease cars, and you may want to call them as well. Ask about the types and terms of leases each company offers. Based on what you learn over the phone, select the companies you think are worth visiting.

When you are negotiating a car lease, keep in mind the costs that are generally negotiable so that you can get the best deal possible for yourself. If you don't feel comfortable doing the negotiating, ask a friend or relative to help you.

Contact the National Vehicle Leasing Association at P.O. Box 34028, Los Angeles, CA 90034-0028, (213) 838-3170, as well as your local Better Business Bureau before you do business with a specific auto leasing company to make sure that there have not been a lot of complaints lodged against it.

Early Termination The CLA says that the lessor must tell you before you sign a lease when you can terminate and what the cost is for early termination. In most cases, you cannot end a lease before 12 months.

Hot Tip

For more information about leasing a car, including specific questions to ask a lessor before you sign an agreement and worksheets for comparing the costs of buying and leasing, order *A Consumer Guide to Vehicle Leasing* from the Federal Trade Commission (FTC). This free brochure is available by writing: FTC, 6th and Pennsylvania Avenue, N.W., Washington, DC 20580.

Warranties The lessor is also required by the CLA to disclose in writing information about the warranty for a leased car. The lessor must state whether the standard manufacturer's warranty is in effect and whether the lessor provides additional warranties. You will be required to follow a certain maintenance schedule to keep the warranty in effect.

Many lessors also offer extended service plans or contracts to cover instances where the warranty ends before the term of the lease is up.

Extended Service Plans If a lessor offers an extended service plan for repairs and maintenance at an additional cost to you, carefully compare the car's standard warranty with the extended plan. Compare what each covers to the repairs and maintenance activities you are responsible for. It is possible that you will be able to fulfill your obligation for repairs and maintenance through an extended service plan.

Conclusion

The automobile has had a great impact on the American culture, shaping the way we all live. As a result, proper transportation is a necessity in the United States. The issue of transportation can be an especially problematic one for anyone recovering from serious financial trouble. It's a vicious circle: You need to make money; you need reliable transportation to make that money; and yet you can have difficulty affording reliable transportation.

Carefully consider all of your transportation options. If you, like most people, decide to have an automobile, learn the questions to ask and what to look for when you have to get your car repaired. If you are going to be buying a new or used car, learn everything you can about the ones you are considering so that you make a wise purchase decision.

If you chose not to have an automobile, be sure to consider the impact of that decision on your lifestyle. Although not having a car can relieve you of a significant financial burden, it can also have some important effects on your life: e.g., the sort of job you can have and where you work, how your children get to and from school, your social life, etc.

eight

Protecting Your Rights

"Government is too big and too important to be left to the politicians."

Chester Bowles

Don and Janice W. came to my office visibly upset. Close to tears, Janice sat anxiously on the edge of her chair. "He called me six times at work," she said, referring to a bill collector who was harassing her over a debt. "And every time he calls, he insults me. My boss told me if I don't get my problems worked out, he's going to fire me."

"We tried to get a debt consolidation loan about a year ago," Don said, "when we were able to keep up with what we owed. But we were turned down because of some wrong information in our credit record. Since then we've tried to get the credit bureau to correct the error, but have had no luck."

Like most of my clients, Don and Janice were unaware of their rights as consumers, and didn't know how to make the consumer laws work for them. If Don and Janice had gotten the right information when they first began to experience financial trouble and were denied a loan due to a problem with their credit record, they might never have had to see me about personal bankruptcy.

Most consumers don't know about the laws that can help them protect their rights. Government at all levels does little or nothing to educate the public about consumer protection laws, or provide consumers with the information they need to make those laws work for them. It takes a real effort to know what your legal rights are and how to protect them. The more complicated and troubled your financial affairs, the more you need to educate yourself about federal and state consumer laws and the more worthwhile that effort will be.

To help with this important education process, this chapter discusses what you can do to solve credit-related problems or protect yourselves when, like Don and Janice, you believe your consumer rights are being violated. It also provides an overview of the basic federal consumer protection laws that every American should know.

Direct Contact

"The best way to win an argument is to start by being in the right."

Quenton M. P. Hogg

If you have a problem with a creditor, a credit agency or a collection agency, or if you believe that your legal rights have been violated by one of these companies, you should follow a series of steps to try to resolve your problem. Each step has increasingly serious consequences for the offending party.

Your first step should always be to try to resolve your problem directly with the creditor, credit reporting agency or debt collector. Put your complaint in writing, and send your letter via certified mail to the individual with the authority to resolve the problem—a manager, department head, even the company president. Often you can get better response from the president since company presidents tend to be more attuned to the public relations value of working with consumers.

Keep the tone of your letter polite, not accusatory and include the following information:

- A description of the problem. If you feel that your legal rights have been violated, explain how and why.
- A summary of what you've done to try and resolve the problem and the response you have received. Include all pertinent dates and times and the names of individuals you have spoken with as you have tried to resolve your problem.
- A statement of how you would like the problem resolved.
- Your account number, address and a telephone number where you can be reached during the day.
- The date by which you'd like a response. Two weeks is usually a reasonable timeline.

Be sure to provide copies of pertinent correspondence and other documentation such as receipts, account statements, contracts, etc. Keep a copy of your letter, and send copies to: your state attorney general's office or office of consumer affairs, your Congressman, your local Better Business Bureau or the Better Business Bureau in the city where the company is located, and the federal agency that regulates the company you are having trouble with. See Figure 8.1 for the types of companies regulated by various federal regulatory agencies.

If you don't get a response from the company by the deadline established in your letter, call the person you wrote to and send a follow-up letter.

One sure way to encourage response is to involve the media. Get in touch with the editor of your local newspaper and the news director at TV and radio stations in your community. They may be interested in doing a story on your situation. Unwelcome media attention may put pressure on the company you are having difficulty with and make it more inclined to resolve things with you.

Find out if the company you are having a problem with is a member of a trade or professional association. If so, contact the association to see if it has a dispute resolution program. Many trade and professional organizations have such programs to help consumers resolve problems with their members. These dispute resolution programs typically use one or more of the following techniques: arbitration, conciliation or mediation.

Before you attempt to have your problem resolved through such a program, ask for an explanation of the process involved, whether or not the decision of an arbitrator is binding and whether, in the case of conciliation or mediation, either the consumer or the business must accept the decision. In some programs the decision is only binding on the business; in others it is not binding on either party.

Hot Tip

For a list of trade associations with dispute resolution programs, obtain a copy of the federal *Consumer Resource Handbook*. This handbook is free and can be ordered by writing: Handbook, Consumer Information Center, Pueblo, CO 81009. For trade associations not listed in this handbook, go to your local library and review the National Trade and Professional Associations of the United States. This directory includes the addresses and phone numbers of trade associations throughout the country. Call the association you are interested in, and find out if it has a dispute resolution program.

State Laws

If direct contact, media involvement and alternative dispute resolution programs fail to resolve your problem, contact your state attorney general's office or consumer affairs office to find out if there is a state law that offers you a legal remedy.

Many states have their own consumer legislation that enhances or supplements the protection afforded by federal laws. Unless a state law conflicts with a federal law, the state law usually applies. Your state attorney general's office or office of consumer affairs can tell you about the consumer legislation in your particular state. Get the advice of this office regarding the best course of action for your particular problem. Possible approaches include:

- mediation sessions between you and the company;
- filing a complaint with the appropriate state agency;
- suing the company in small claims court; and
- a civil or criminal lawsuit initiated by the state.

Figure 8.1 Federal Regulatory Agencies To Complain To

- Complain to the Federal Trade Commission about: credit reporting agencies, debt collectors, retail stores, finance companies, charge card and credit card companies, government lending programs, state credit unions, public utility companies and oil and gas companies.
- Complain to the Federal Reserve Board about state-chartered banks and trust companies that are members of the Federal Reserve System.
- Complain to the Federal Deposit Insurance Corporation about banks that are FDIC-insured but not part of the Federal Reserve System.
- Complain to the Comptroller of the Currency about nationally chartered banks. (These banks have *national* in their names or *N.A.* after their names.)
- Complain to the Office of Thrift Supervision, U.S. Treasury Department about savings and loan associations and savings banks.
- Complain to the National Credit Union Administration about federally chartered credit unions.

Federal Regulatory Agencies

When you contact your state attorney general's office or office of consumer affairs, you should also file a formal complaint with the appropriate federal regulatory agency. Although these agencies do not act on behalf of an individual consumer, they will investigate and take action if they receive a sufficient number of complaints about a particular company. Call the appropriate agency to learn the process for filing a formal complaint. See the Resource section at the end of this book for the addresses and phone numbers of these regulatory agencies.

Lawsuits

You may decide that you have a strong legal case against a company and want to take legal action on your own behalf. If your case is a matter for small claims court, you probably won't need an attorney. (See Chapter 3 for a discussion of small claims court.) If your problem is not one for small claims court, however, you will need to find an attorney. Try to find one who will take your case on a *contingency* basis—instead of conventional payment, the attorney agrees to take a percentage of your winnings, and gets no money if you lose.

In most cases, when you file suit in state or federal district court, you may sue to recover actual damages, court costs and attorney fees, as well as punitive damages if the court decides that the violation to your rights was intentional. Punitive damages are usually given to punish defendants for *evil* behavior or to make examples of them.

Your state attorney general's office or office of consumer affairs may decide to initiate a lawsuit on your behalf or on behalf of you and others who have been similarly wronged. This usually happens when the state decides that the wrong is one that is affecting or likely to affect a large number of people. The possibility of such a lawsuit, coupled with the negative publicity and public scrutiny that follow, often encourages the offending company to settle out of court. In other cases, a lawsuit can take months and even years to settle.

The Consumer Credit Protection Act

"'Tis not knowing much, but what is useful, that makes a man wise."

Thomas Fuller

The landmark federal Consumer Credit Protection Act was passed in 1968. This series of laws established a standard regarding how creditors should treat consumers and the types of credit-related information that should be made available to consumers. It also established specific processes and legal mechanisms that consumers can use to protect their rights if they think they have been violated. The Acts comprising this legislation include: Fair Credit Reporting Act, Fair Debt Collection Practices Act, Fair Credit Billing Act, Truth in Lending Act, and Electronic Funds Transfer Act. To get summaries of the key provisions of each of these Acts, contact the Federal Trade Commission (FTC), by writing Consumer and Business Education Division, Washington, DC 20580 or calling (202) 326-3650.

The Fair Credit Reporting Act (FCRA)

The Fair Credit Reporting Act (FCRA) is a fundamental consumer protection law that was covered in detail in Chapter 3. FCRA restricts access to the information in your credit record, gives you the right to review your credit record and allows you to have errors corrected at no charge. Most negative information in your credit record may be reported for up to seven years, with bankruptcies reported for up to ten years.

Senator William Proxmire, the *Father of the FCRA,* reported that the purpose of this legislation is to correct what he believes to be the credit reporting industry's most serious problem—the abuse of "inaccurate and misleading information." Proxmire points out that even if the industry were 99 percent accurate (and recent studies show that it is not), a one percent inaccuracy rate represents more than one million people!

Access to Credit Records FCRA states that, in general, access to a consumer's credit history is only permissible for:

- the extension of credit;
- the issuance of insurance;
- possible employment; or
- a "business purpose related to a business transaction."

FCRA also permits credit bureaus to provide information on a consumer to a government agency and to allow an agency to review a consumer's file under certain circumstances.

Getting a Copy of Your Record If you are denied credit because of information in your credit record, FCRA states that you have the right to obtain a free copy of that record from the credit bureau reporting the negative information, if the copy is requested within 30 days of denial. Otherwise, there will be a fee for the report, typically between $3 and $15.

Errors You may ask a credit reporting agency to verify and correct any information in your credit record that you feel is inaccurate according to FCRA's provisions. The agency must verify the information "within a reasonable period of time." If the reporting agency concludes that there are errors, erroneous information must be deleted from your record. You then have the right to ask that the updated information be sent to anyone who received a copy of your record over the last six months.

In preparing your written statement, be as factual and straightforward as possible. Mention pertinent dates when you have them and, if you have any supporting documentation, indicate that it is available for review.

If the creditor says that the disputed information is correct, it remains in your credit record. However, FCRA gives you the right to prepare a 100-word written statement explaining why you feel your record is in error. The credit bureau must make this statement a permanent part of your credit record.

Your Legal Recourse under FCRA FCRA gives you the right to sue a credit reporting agency or a creditor for violating your rights under the law. You may collect actual and punitive damages if the court rules that the violation was deliberate. You may also collect court costs and attorney fees if you win their lawsuit. Figure 8.2 summarizes some actual legal cases where consumers felt their rights had been violated and successfully prosecuted.

Other Penalties Under FCRA, unauthorized persons who obtain a copy of a credit report, or any credit reporting agency employee who gives a credit report to an unauthorized person, are liable for a fine of up to $5,000, one year in prison or both.

The Fair Debt Collection Practices Act (FDCPA)

FDCPA, discussed in detail in Chapter 2, regulates the behavior of collection agencies and attorneys who collect debts as a regular part of their practice. Figure 8.3 summarizes rights granted by FDCPA; Figure 8.4 summarizes successful lawsuits by consumers using the law.

Your Legal Recourse under FDCPA When a debt collector violates the provisions of FDCPA, you have the right to sue for actual damages plus court costs and attorney fees.

Figure 8.2 Consumer Success Stories

Following are some outcomes in actual cases heard in various state courts regarding credit bureau/ credit record abuse.

- A New York court ordered a company that had secured a consumer's credit report under false pretenses to pay $15,000 in punitive damages to the consumer whose rights had been violated.
- A Michigan court awarded a consumer $50,000 in punitive damages and $21,000 in attorney fees for loss of reputation, embarrassment and humiliation in recognition of the many "subtle and indirect adverse effects upon her personal, social and economic life" caused by a credit bureau.
- In Texas, a consumer was awarded $10,000 in actual damages for humiliation and mental distress and $4,485 in attorney fees at $90 an hour for credit bureau errors that caused the consumer to receive three credit denials.

FDCPA prohibits a variety of specific behaviors on the part of debt collectors, including: repeated phone calls to a debtor; threats of violence, harm, arrest or imprisonment; and making the debtor pay for collect calls or telegrams.

When a creditor violates a provision of FCBA that creditor automatically forfeits the amount in dispute plus applicable finance charges, up to a combined total of $50—even if the court's final conclusion is that there is no problem. In addition, you may sue for actual damages plus twice the amount of the finance charges. This amount can be no less than $100 and no more than $1,000. Court costs and attorney fees can also be collected if the suit is successful, and class action suits are allowed.

The Fair Credit Billing Act (FCBA)

FCBA provides a mechanism for promptly resolving billing problems with open-end credit accounts such as bankcards, retail

Figure 8.3 Consumer Rights under FDCPA

> You have the right to terminate future contacts with bill collectors, and the right to stop contacts at your place of employment if they are inconvenient or prohibited by your employer. Additionally, you have the right to indicate the time of day you want to be contacted by a debt collector, the right to dispute a debt and the right to obtain verification of a debt.

charges or lines of credit. It does not apply to billing problems with closed-end or installment accounts.

Credit Card Billing Problems The following types of billing problems are covered by FCBA:

- Charges you do not understand
- Incorrectly identified charges, charges in the wrong amount or reflecting the wrong date
- Charges you do not believe you or an authorized user made
- Charges for goods/services you did not accept or returned
- Charges for goods different from what you had ordered
- Computational errors
- A creditor's failure to credit an account properly
- A creditor's failure to send your billing statement to your current mailing address provided that, in the event of an address change, you notified the creditor at least 20 days before the billing period ended

The Process for Resolving a Problem To activate the law's protective measures, you must write (*not* call) the creditor about a billing problem within 60 days of the postmark date of the first bill reflecting the problem. Unless the problem has already been resolved by the time the creditor receives your letter, the company must acknowledge its receipt within 30 days. Within 90 days, the creditor must then explain to you why the bill is correct, provide proof if you requested it or correct the problem.

Figure 8.4 FDCPA Consumer Success Stories

Following are actual cases heard in various state courts regarding abuses to consumer rights under FDCPA:

- A New Jersey court awarded a consumer $4,000 for creditor actions that had caused humiliation, emotional distress, injury to reputation and character and extreme nervousness.
- A Pennsylvania court awarded $1,000 in actual damages to an impoverished 70-year old woman who received a letter from a collection agency falsely threatening an imminent lawsuit over a debt. Not only did the letter cause the woman to lose sleep and weight, it also caused her to borrow money and quit her job so that she could cash in her pension to pay off her debt.
- A Florida court awarded two consumers $2,500 in actual damages, $1,000 in statutory damages and $50,000 in punitive damages for a debt collector's late night phone calls, threats of arrest and inappropriate contact of a third party.

In your letter, include your name, account number, date, type and dollar amount of the charge you are disputing and a statement of the problem. It is also a good idea to ask that the creditor provide you proof that there is no problem if that is what the creditor ultimately concludes.

Send your letter via certified mail to the billing inquiries address listed on the bill to increase the likelihood of its timely arrival. Do not send the letter in the same envelope as your payment coupon.

Hot Tip

Many creditors lose their rights under FCBA because they call a company about a billing problem rather than writing. Only writing can activate the law's protective provisions.

While You Are Waiting for a Response When waiting for a response from a creditor regarding a problem with your bill:

- You do not have to pay the amount in question or any related finance charges.
- You must continue to pay on charges that are not in dispute.
- Your creditor may not take legal action to get you to pay the disputed amount.
- Your creditor may not close your account.
- The amount in dispute may be applied against your credit limit.
- Your creditor may not threaten to damage your credit record.

If You Are Told That There Isn't a Problem Once you are notified that there is no problem with your bill, you are expected to make payment. FCBA stipulates that you have at least ten days to pay. If after this time you have not yet paid, the creditor may report your account as delinquent to credit bureaus. If you decide to take further action to get the billing problem corrected, your creditor has the legal right to continue reporting you as delinquent, but must indicate that the delinquent amount is in dispute.

Defective, Damaged or Inferior Quality Merchandise and Services FCBA also allows you to withhold payment on defective, damaged or poor quality merchandise or services purchased with a credit card. However, the law says that you must first make a serious effort to directly resolve the problem with the company selling the product or service.

Your rights regarding defective, damaged or poor quality goods and services are limited when a travel and entertainment card or bankcard has been used to make the purchase rather than a card issued by the company selling the goods or services. For FCBA to apply in such a situation, your purchase must be for more than $50, and must have taken place in your state or within 100 miles of your home address.

The Truth in Lending Act (TLA)

The TLA, which was discussed in Chapter 4, was passed to help you more easily compare the costs of credit options in order to make informed credit decisions. It requires creditors to fully disclose the cost of credit before any credit transaction is finalized. The disclosure must include, among other things, the applicable interest rate or finance charge and the annual percentage rate or APR. The law also requires creditors to provide this information in clear language that can be readily understood.

When Your House Is Used as Collateral Under the provisions of TLA, you have three days to change your mind about certain credit transactions when your house is used as collateral. If you decide to exercise this provision, called *right of rescission,* you must notify the creditor **in writing** that you are cancelling the contract. The three-day period begins when the following has happened:

- You sign the credit contract.
- You receive a Truth in Lending disclosure form.
- You receive two copies of a notice that explains your right to rescind.

The period ends at midnight of the third business day following your credit transaction. (For purposes of rescission, the three days include Saturdays but not Sundays or legal public holidays.)

The right of rescission does not apply in every case where your home is used for loan collateral. Exceptions are as follow:

- You apply for a loan to purchase or build a home.
- You consolidate or refinance a loan already secured by your home and do not borrow additional funds.
- A state agency is the creditor for the loan.

Other provisions in TLA limit your liability in the event that your credit cards are lost or stolen. It stipulates that if you lose a credit card, the most you will have to pay for unauthorized charges is $50. TLA further states that once you have reported a lost or stolen card, you will not have to pay any charges.

Your Legal Recourse under the TLA If a creditor fails to comply with TLA's provisions, the law says that you may sue for actual damages and twice the finance charge in the case of certain credit disclosures. If you win your suit, the court can award you no more than $1,000 and no less than $100. You will also be able to collect court costs and attorney fees. Class action suits are permitted by the TLA.

The Equal Credit Opportunity Act (ECOA)

ECOA gives everyone the right to apply for credit and be evaluated on the basis of their creditworthiness without consideration of age, sex, race, color, national origin or marital status. The legislation also states that you may not be denied credit simply because you are receiving veterans's benefits, welfare payments, social security or child support, or because your income comes from a part-time job. As with other credit applicants, ECOA says that you must be evaluated on the basis of your income and the reliability of that income. A creditor may not discourage you from applying for a loan or deny you credit because you exercised your rights under a federal credit law.

Hot Tip

Anyone over 62 years of age may not be denied credit simply due to age. Also, if you retire and are at least 62, ECOA states that a creditor can neither ask you to reapply for credit nor close your account because of your age. However, the law says that a creditor may take into account your life expectancy or collateral when considering you for credit if you are 62 years old or older.

Acceptance or Denial of Credit According to the ECOA, within 30 days after you complete a credit application and the creditor has all the information needed to process the application, you must be informed as to whether or not you have been approved for credit. If credit has been denied, that information must be provided in writing, and the creditor must either state the reasons for denial at that time or inform you that you are entitled to the information. These same rights apply in the event that a creditor closes an account, refuses to increase a line of credit, makes an unfavorable change in the terms of credit that does not affect the majority of other account holders, or refuses to give you credit with the same or substantially the same terms as when you applied for it.

ECOA states that any accounts that a woman uses with her husband, or for which she is liable, must be reported to credit reporting agencies in both her name and her husband's name. This applies only to accounts opened after June 1, 1977. (See

Chapter 3 for more information about ECOA.) To strengthen her credit record, however, a woman may contact the creditors on accounts that she and her husband opened prior to this date and ask them to report account information in both her name and her husband's. She can also contact credit bureaus and ask that they make the information part of her credit history. While not obligated to do so, most creditors and credit bureaus will comply with this request.

Your Legal Recourse under ECOA If you believe your rights have been violated, ECOA states that you may sue a creditor for actual damages and punitive damages up to $10,000. If you win your lawsuit, you can also recover court costs and attorney fees. Class action suits are permissible under ECOA, and may recover punitive damages of up to $500,000 or one percent of the creditor's net worth, whichever is less.

Electric Funds Transfer Act (EFTA)

EFTA protects consumers who are the victims of automatic teller machine (ATM) fraud. EFTA states that in the event of the unauthorized use of an ATM card, you are only liable for $50 if you notify your financial institution within two business days of discovering the unauthorized use. Otherwise, you are liable for up to $500. EFTA also stipulates that if you fail to report an unauthorized use within 60 days after your bank statement has been mailed to you, you risk losing whatever is in your account as well as any remaining credit you have for overdraft protection. Figure 8.5 describes how to protect yourself from ATM fraud.

EFTA also applies to point-of-sale terminals, telephone fund transfers and computer transactions.

Your Legal Recourse under EFTA If a financial institution violates the provisions of EFTA, you may sue for actual damages plus punitive damages of no less than $100 and no more than $1,000. In certain cases, where the institution fails to correct an error or properly credit an account, you may sue for three times actual damages. Court costs and attorney's fees can be collected if a suit is successful. Class action suits are permitted.

Also, if an institution fails to make an electronic fund transfer or fails to stop payment of a preauthorized transfer after being properly instructed to do so, you may sue for all damages that result from that institution's failure.

Other Important Consumer Laws

There are two more laws that protect you from unsavory credit practices: the Fair Credit and Charge Card Disclosure Act (FCCCDA) and the Consumer Leasing Act (CLA)

Fair Credit and Charge Card Disclosure Act (FCCCDA)

FCCCDA helps ensure that you have adequate information about the costs of a credit card when a company is marketing its card to potential new cardholders. Issuers of credit cards and charge cards are required by FCCCDA to fully disclose the cost of their cards in the solicitations they send by mail. Card issuers must indicate:

- the interest rate on a card and whether it is fixed or variable;
- the card's annual fee;
- the grace period;
- any additional charges; and
- the method used to calculate the balance upon which finance charges are based.

If a credit card solicitation you receive does not contain all this information, it may be a sign that the card offer is actually a consumer scam.

In the case of other types of card solicitations such as applications inserted in printed materials like magazines or newspapers, the law gives card issuers two options. They may disclose all the same information as the FCCCDA requires for mailed solicitations and provide a toll-free number to call for updated information. Or, they may refer consumers to a toll-free number in order to get complete information related to the cost of the card.

Your Legal Recourse under the FCCCDA If a company marketing a credit card violates the provisions of the FCCCDA and you paid a fee for the company's card or used the card, you may sue for actual damages plus twice the amount of the finance charges you incurred. If you win, the court can award you no more than $1,000 and no less than $100. You will also be able to collect court costs and attorney fees.

Figure 8.5 How To Protect Yourself from ATM Fraud

- Do not write your personal identification number (PIN), in your checkbook or carry it in your wallet.
- Select a PIN that is easy to remember and different from other numbers you commonly use such as your social security number or date of birth.
- Memorize your number.
- Check your bank statements promptly.
- Be wary of those standing too close while you are using an ATM. They may be trying to see your PIN.
- Do not lend your ATM card to anyone.

The Consumer Leasing Act (CLA)

CLA applies to long-term leases. It says that all lessors must provide consumers with certain written information that will help them compare the cost and terms of various leases and the cost of leasing versus buying. This law applies to property leased for more than four months for personal, household or family use, including furniture, appliances, and long-term car leases. It does not apply to real estate or to daily car rentals. For a detailed discussion of how the CLA applies to long-term car rentals, refer back to Chapter 7.

According to the CLA, before signing a lease agreement, you must be given a written statement of the costs of leasing, including the amount of any security deposit, the amount of each monthly payment, the cost of taxes, licenses and registration as well as information regarding any maintenance activities you will be responsible for.

You must also be given certain information about the terms of the lease including necessary insurance, guarantees, responsibility for servicing and whether you have an option to purchase the leased property.

Your Legal Recourse under the CLA If your rights under the CLA are violated, you have the right to sue for actual damages and to collect court costs and attorney fees if you win. You may also sue for 25 percent of your total monthly payments. If you win, the court will award you no more than $1,000 and no less than $100. Class action suits are permitted.

Consumer Scams

"Let every eye negotiate for itself, and trust no agent."
William Shakespeare

As you rebuild, be wary of consumer scams. Consumers who are in serious financial trouble and are scrambling to make an extra buck or eager for a money saving deal, can be easy targets for such scams. As a rule of thumb, if a deal sounds too good to be true, it probably is. Although it is impossible to list every existing scam or anticipate those to come, this chapter will highlight the most common consumer scams—those conducted by fraudulent telemarketers—and discuss how to recognize them.

Also, refer to Chapter 5 for specific information about bogus work-at-home schemes, and to learn how to select a reputable trade or technical school.

Phone Fraud

The Federal Trade Commission estimates that fraudulent telemarketers dupe consumers out of more than one billion dollars annually. These companies sell anything and everything—from baldness cures and weight loss plans, to guarantees to sell your home. They usually use a high pressure sales pitch and provide very little information about what they're actually selling. Keep in mind the tips offered in Figure 8.6 when talking to telemarketers.

Fraudulent telemarketers will usually contact you in one of three ways:

By Phone The caller will have gotten your name from either a mailing list or the phone book. When a mailing list is the source, a lot of personal information is often used by the caller in an attempt to build trust and credibility.

A Letter or Postcard This mail often tells you that you have won a prize or a trip and to collect it, you will need to send something back or place a phone call.

TV and Print Ads Some telemarketing companies use advertising to entice consumers to call a phone number–often a costly 900 number–for additional information or in order to complete an application.

How To Protect Yourself from a 900 Scam

Many companies and organizations make legitimate use of 900 numbers by indicating up front what the charge will be for the call and explaining exactly what you will get if you make the call. (Unlike an 800 number, when you call a 900 number, you are charged a flat fee or a per-minute fee for the call.) Fraudulent telemarketers often charge excessively for 900 calls or fail to give you what they led you to expect you would receive.There are a number of things that you can do to avoid being victimized by a 900 scam. They include:

- Know exactly how much the call will cost before you make it. This cost should be stated up front.
- Deal only with companies you are familiar with or that you know have a good reputation. Many very reputable firms use 900 numbers to conduct surveys or provide useful consumer information.
- Avoid making 900 number calls to order a *free* gift or prize since you'll be paying for it with your call.
- Tell your children how 900 numbers work, and ask them not to call a 900 number without your permission.
- Check each phone bill to make sure it does not contain charges for 900 number calls.

Hot Tip

Local 976 and long distance 700 exchanges are often used like 900 numbers. Follow the same advice and warnings with these two exchanges.

If You're a Victim

If you are victimized by a 900 number scam, contact your telephone company and ask that any charges be deleted from your bill. Although phone companies are not obligated to do so, many will delete the charges as a gesture of goodwill.

Another option is to ask the phone company to give you the name and address of the company that charged you for the 900 number call. Write that company, and request that it delete the charge. If it doesn't and you refuse to pay, you risk having your account turned over to a debt collector and negatively affecting your credit record. At this point, you should follow the advice in Chapter 2 about dealing with debt collectors and in Chapter 3 about your credit record.

If you have a problem with a 900 number or with any other type of phone scam, contact the office of your state attorney general or office of consumer affairs, as well as the FTC.

Products and Services Frequently Marketed by Phone

A number of fraudulent products and services are commonly marketed by phone, including:

Partially Developed or Undeveloped Land Telemarketers usually tell you what a wonderful deal you're being offered, how quickly the land is going and that prices will start rising soon.

Travel Packages Usually you learn of a bogus travel package by mail and are referred to a 900 number for more details. On the surface, these packages often sound legitimate and attractive. When you call the 900 number, however, you'll find out that there's a catch—for example, you need to pay a fee to join a travel club in order to take advantage of the offer. If you join, you may later find that when it's time to make your reservation, you have to pay a second fee. Also, if you use the 900 number to join the club and make your reservations, there will be charges on your phone bill for both calls. Many of the people who respond to these ads never get their *free trip* or discount travel package because their reservations are not confirmed or because the conditions of the travel are too restrictive or too expensive.

Investments Gems, oil and gas leases, coins, precious metals and interests in oil wells are investment opportunities frequently sold by fraudulent telemarketers. The caller will usually congratulate you on the fact that you've been selected to participate in a fantastic investment opportunity and then ask you to send money right away.

Figure 8.6 Protecting Yourself from Phone Fraud—General Tips

- Get the offer in writing.
- Physically inspect any property or merchandise before you buy it.
- Hang up on high pressure salespeople.
- Take your time to evaluate any offer; don't be pressured into making your decision on the phone.
- Don't give your credit card number to anyone who calls over the phone trying to sell you something.

Magazines Fraudulent telemarketers often try to trick consumers into purchasing multiple-year subscriptions to magazines they could buy more cheaply through another source or don't really want. Initially, you are led to believe that you've won a sweepstakes or a prize, but the conversation soon switches to magazine subscriptions.

Magazine telemarketers may never identify themselves as magazine salespersons and may avoid stating the total cost for the magazines they're selling. Also, they may indicate that they are regulated or approved by the government. In fact, there is no such regulatory agency.

Art Fraud Typically, you will receive something in the mail discussing a contest or drawing for a free original lithograph by a famous artist. To be eligible for the prize, you are instructed to return the enclosed postcard and are later contacted by telephone for additional information. During this call the telemarketer tries to convince you to spend from $500 to $3,000 to make an investment in art. If you agree, the most you'll probably receive is a poster with a maximum value of $50.

Gold Cards Marketers of *gold* or *platinum* cards imply in their advertising that you will be able to get major national bankcards after using their card, and that their card can help you improve

Figure 8.7 How To Recognize a 900 Number Scam

- You aren't told how much the call will cost.
- You are told the per-minute rate, but no one tells you the number of minutes you will be on the line.
- The recorded message you hear when you call the 900 number runs so quickly that you have to call back several times to understand it all.
- Children and teenagers, who may be more easily taken in by the pitch, are targeted.
- The company is vague about what you'll actually get if you call, or makes grandiose promises about the information, product or service you'll receive.

your credit record. Rarely is this true. Consumers who get a gold or platinum card can usually use it only to order a limited array of merchandise from a catalogue provided by the marketer—and they may have to pay an additional fee to order from the catalogue. Additionally, consumers who apply for one of these cards are often charged a substantial application or initiation fee. For more information about these cards, refer to Chapter 4.

Conclusion

Consumer laws were passed for your protection—however, they have no meaning if you don't understand how to use them to protect your legal rights. Doing so is not always easy, nor will you necessarily get results quickly. Persistence, perseverance and using every resource at your disposal usually pay off. The pursuit of your legal rights is the only way that you can help to get the credit industry to correct the problems that continue to harm so many people!

While staying informed about laws that can protect your interests, you should also be aware of fraudulent marketing efforts. Disreputable companies concentrate on exploiting the financially distressed. Don't be a victim!

epilogue

Toward a New Lifestyle and a Brighter Future

"Success is a process, a quality of mind and way of being, an outgoing affirmation of life."

Alex Noble

The school of hard knocks is one that everyone tries to avoid, but ends up attending nonetheless. What you have gone through has been difficult, and you have learned about the pitfalls you want to avoid in the future. Throughout this book you've learned about a new way of living: frugality, saving and living within your means. This is a lifestyle that will fit comfortably and safely around you.

As you pursue the advice and ideas presented in these pages, think of your efforts at rebuilding your life as opportunities to reorder your priorities. Refocus your energies and create a happier, less stressful, more intrinsically rewarding life for yourself and your family. This book is about recovering from financial difficulty, making a fresh start and creating a brighter future.

Personal sacrifice and hard work are required, but take pride in what you've been able to accomplish so far—creating and living with a spending plan, reducing your debts, finding more rewarding work.

This book advocates self-reliance—realistic expectations, saving for the future and spending money that you have without depending on credit. It is full of information and resources that can help you, and you should take advantage of them. But be wary of becoming too dependent. The most powerful resource you have is yourself. Learn the rewards of doing for yourself and teach your children to do the same. You are fooling yourself if you count on the government or any other institution to take care of you.

When seeking assistance for your problems, be skeptical of anyone who offers you easy chances for new credit, opportunities to wipe your credit history clean or chances to make easy money. People who have gone through financial trouble and are rebuilding their lives are particularly vulnerable to scams that offer to help. Don't let your desire to rebuild your life or the difficulties you have experienced in the past cloud your judgment. There are people in this world who want to make a buck on your misfortunes and hope you are desperate enough not to look too closely at what they are selling. *Caveat emptor*—"let the buyer beware!"

We live in complicated times that require us to know more. Meet the challenge, increase your knowledge and skills. Learn to enjoy what you have. Don't yearn for what used to be or for what you cannot afford. Appreciate the *here and now* with an eye toward what is to come and what you can make happen.

Independence and self-reliance are important, but so is participation in the community at large. Total individualism and self-interest don't work; instead there must be a willingness to share responsibility for the institutions and people around you in order to achieve a brighter future.

Take direction from the many thoughtful observers of society and human nature who lead the way. Here are the words of a few who believe that personal success in the future can result from active participation in your community.

James Michener, Novelist and Historical Observer

James Michener says, *"I still believe that society prospers most when there are laws to bring wealth back into circulation, when there are taxes to provide social services that otherwise might not be available, when there is governmental surveillance to ensure proper business practices and to prevent manipulation of financial markets and when profits are plowed into research and the education of new generations."*

Brenton R. Schlender, Journalist

Brenton R. Schlender, writing in *Fortune* magazine, says the values for the future will be a new view of rugged individualism tempered by civic-minded compassion. He suggests that Americans need to get more involved in the institutions that shape their lives like business, schools and government—but on a local, individual basis. He says we need to find a new sense of community because our well-being in the future may depend more on family, friends and our local community than on the wealth we think we can build.

Buckminster Fuller, Inventor, Scientist and Futurist

Buckminster Fuller said that "We're here for local universe information gathering, local problem solving in support of the integrity of an eternally regenerative universe. . . " "Commit yourself to integrity—whatever the truth may be—and really commit yourself to making all humanity a success."

The Challenge for All of Us

What does this mean to those of you who are starting over, who feel perhaps that taking care of yourself and your loved ones is nearly more than you can handle these days? It means that life is going to require more of you now, that you need to become more caring and more aware of the world around you. Solutions to society's problems require a united effort, one in which everyone must share.

If you want life to be better for yourself and your children, *participate* in your world. Look around you. If you find a problem, don't wait for others to start trying to solve it; start yourself and get others to help you.

Take a more active role in your children's education and in improving the educational system in your town. Join your PTA; meet your child's teachers and the school principal; spend time with your children reviewing their homework and encouraging them to read and to pursue other activities that will expand their minds. Do whatever you can to make sure that your children will be prepared to live in a rapidly changing world economy.

Our Children—The Next Generation of Consumers

Several times in this book I have discussed the importance of teaching your children good money management skills and helping them to develop healthy attitudes toward money. Knowing how to create a spending plan, understanding credit and how to use it, and having an appreciation for the fundamental importance of a regular savings program would be an invaluable legacy for you to leave your children. Such a gift can ensure a brighter future for generations to come.

The Resources section at the end of this book offers many suggestions for books and other publications that can help you educate your children about issues related to personal finance. You may also want to meet with the appropriate school administrators to discuss the possibility of adding instruction about personal finance to your school's curriculum. This education should start in the early elementary grades.

Additional Advice

According to Dr. Martin G. Groder, a psychiatrist and business consultant interviewed in the national newsletter *Bottom Line/ Personal,* Americans have fallen into the habit of drifting through life because the current generation of workers, unlike their parents, has never really had to work hard to get ahead. He believes that to survive and prosper in our increasingly competitive world, we must rediscover the value and rewards of hard work and thrift. Groder also believes that each of us must become committed to learning new skills while updating and renewing existing ones.

Toward this end, Groder suggests:

- Plan your career, even if you are doing fine in your current job. Acquire skills that can help your company during hard times or that will make you employable elsewhere.

- Improve your personal skills—especially in the areas of communication, focus and creativity.
- Recognize that doing well today is not enough. Look to the future, see what will be required to do well and acquire the necessary skills.

Conclusion

> *"The great thing in this world is not so much where we are, but in what direction we are moving."*
>
> ***Oliver Wendell Holmes***

Creating a brighter future, a future not burdened by debt, with decent jobs and happy lives, means taking responsibility for your finances. A brighter, more hopeful future requires hard work, new and better skills and a different attitude toward money. It is a future that is within everyone's reach.

> *" 'Come to the edge,' he said. They said: 'We are afraid.' 'Come to the edge,' he said. They came. He pushed them. . . and they flew."*
>
> ***Guillaumea Pollinaire***

appendix a

Useful Resources

In order to take charge of your financial life and make your fresh start, you must be informed. This appendix refers you to books, periodicals and organizations that can be of assistance in the recovery process. You will find resources listed under the following categories:

- Emotional Recovery and the Psychology of Spending
- Dealing with Debt
- Living on Less
- Medical Expenses
- Money Management
- Children and Money
- Automobiles
- Careers and Job-Hunting
- Self-Employment
- Protecting Your Rights

Emotional Recovery and the Psychology of Spending

Books

Breakthrough Thinking by Gerald Nadler, Prima Publishing, 1990. $22.95.

Couples and Money by Victoria Felton-Collins, Bantam Books, 1990. $17.95.

Creative Visualization by Shakti Gawain, Bantam Books, 1982. $4.50.

The Feeling Good Handbook: Using the New Mood Therapy in Everyday Life by Dr. David Burns, William Morrow Co., 1989. $19.95.

Feeling Good: The New Mood Therapy by Dr. David Burns, Signet Books, 1981. $4.95.

Getting Off the Merry-Go-Round: How To Control Your Destructive Habits in Relationships, Work, Food, Money. . . by Carla Perez, M.D., Simon & Schuster, 1991. $9.95.

How To Get Out of Debt, Stay Out of Debt & Live Prosperously by Jerrold Mundis, Bantam Books, 1988. $17.95.

How To Meditate by Lawrence L. LeShan, Bantam Books, 1974. $4.50.

How To Stop Fighting about Money and Make Some by Adriane Berg, Avon, 1989. $4.50.

Living Through Personal Crisis by Ann Kaiser Stearns, Ballentine Books, 1984. $9.95.

Money Is My Friend by Phil Laut, Trinity Publications, 1978. $7.95.

Necessary Losses by Judith Viorst, Fawcett Gold Medal, 1987. $5.95.

Streamlining Your Life: A Five-Point Plan for Uncomplicated Living by Stephanie Culp, Writers Digest Books, 1991. $11.95.

Who Do You Think You Are? How to Build Self-Esteem by Joel Wells, The Thomas More Press, 1989. $7.95.

Brochures and Pamphlets

Ten Secrets to Successful Problem-Solving. The National Anxiety Center. $2.50. To order, write: National Anxiety Center, Box 40, Maplewood, NJ 07040.

Organizations

Debtors Anonymous (See Dealing with Debt resources).
Lutheran Social Services. Many communities have a Lutheran Social Services office. Among the services provided by this organization is emotional counseling, which is offered on a sliding fee scale and available to anyone regardless of religion.

Dealing with Debt

Books

The Bankruptcy Kit: Understanding the Bankruptcy Process, Knowing Your Options, Making a Fresh Start by John Ventura, Dearborn Financial Publishing, Inc., 1991. $19.95.

Conquer Your Debt by William Kent Brunette, Prentice Hall Press, 1990. $9.95.

Getting to Yes: Negotiating Agreement Without Giving In by Roger Fisher and William Ury of the Harvard Negotiation Project, Penguin, 1991. $8.95.

How Anyone Can Negotiate with the IRS—And Win! by Daniel J. Pila, Winnows Publications, 1988. $12.95.

How To File for Bankruptcy by Stephen Elias, Albin Renauer and Robin Leonard, Nolo Press, 1991. $24.95.

How To Get out of Debt and Live Prosperously by Jerrold Mundis, Bantam Books, 1988. $17.95.

Money Troubles: Legal Strategies To Cope with Your Debt by Robin Leonard, Nolo Press, 1991. $19.95.

Out of Debt: How To Clean up Your Credit and Balance Your Budget While Avoiding Bankruptcy by Robert Steinbeck, Bob Adams, Inc., 1989. $5.95.

Winning the IRS Game: How Anyone Can Beat the IRS by Frederick W. Daily, Dropzone Press, 1990. $19.95.

Brochures and Handbooks

From BankCard Holders of America (BA/A):

Getting out of Debt, 1990. $1.00

Managing Family Debt, 1990. $1.00

To order: write BHA, 560 Herndon Pkwy., #120, Herndon, VA 22070.

Newsletters and Magazines

Fresh Start! A Rebuilding Tool for Survivors of Financial Crisis. A bimonthly newsletter providing practical information and advice about issues related to credit, rebuilding credit, consumer finance, making more money, etc. $20/year (six issues). To order, write: Fresh Start! P.O. Box 10098, Houston, TX 77206-0098.

Organizations

Consumer Credit Counseling (CCC)

A nonprofit organization that provides no-cost/low-cost financial counseling to consumers. It also sponsors seminars on topics related to money management. CCC has nearly 600 offices across the country. For the office nearest you, call (800) 388-2227.

Consumer Fresh Start Association

217 N. Church
Princeton, IL 61356
(800) 352-5353

A national support group for people who have gone bankrupt and others in serious financial trouble. For an annual membership fee of $50, consumers receive a quarterly newsletter and gain access to a number of helpful services.

Debtors Anonymous
General Service Board
P.O. Box 20322
New York, NY 10025-9992
(212) 969-0710

Debtors Anonymous helps consumers overcome problems with overspending and debt using the proven techniques and principles of Alcoholics Anonymous. The organization has chapters across the country. If you cannot find a Debtors Anonymous chapter close to you, contact the organization in New York City.

Other

Westwood Financial Group
1101 Colorado Ave., 2nd Fl.
Santa Monica, CA 90401
(310) 451-0737

This company has produced a Five-Step Financial Program designed for people who want to recover from severe financial difficulty. The program includes five books and five companion audiocassettes covering topics like credit rebuilding, working with banks, long-term financial planning, etc. It also publishes a quarterly newsletter. Because of the cost of the Five-Step Financial Program, $149.95, consider sharing its purchase with several friends.

Living on Less

Books

How To Live within Your Means and Still Finance Your Dreams by Robert A. Ortaldo, Fireside Books, 1990. $9.95.

Living Well or Even Better on Less by Ellen Kunes, Putnam Publishing Company, 1991. $7.95.

Penny Pinching: How To Lower Your Everyday Expenses Without Lowering Your Standard of Living by Lee and Barbara Simmons, Bantam Books, 1991. $4.50.

The Wholesale-By-Mail Catalog by Lowell Miller and Prudence McCullough, The Print Project, Harper & Row Publishers, 1990. $14.95.

Newsletters and Magazines

The Tightwad Gazette. A monthly newsletter full of useful information and ideas for living cheaply. $12/year (12 issues). To subscribe, write: *The Tightwad Gazette*, RR1, Box 3570, Leeds, ME 04263.

Organizations

Catholic Charities. Catholic Charities agencies provide counseling, food and housing to people in need throughout the U.S. Look in your local directory for the Catholic Charities office nearest you.

United Way. Local United Ways publish free directories of social welfare and medical services in their area that could benefit people in financial difficulty. Look in your telephone book for the United Way in your community. Some United Ways cover a multi-community area, so if you don't see a listing in your town's telephone book, look for listings in towns near you.

Medical Expenses

Brochures and Handbooks

From the People's Medical Society:

Health Insurance: How To Evaluate and Select Health Insurance by Michael A. Rooney and the Staff of the People's Medical Society, 1985. $5.95.

150 Ways To Lower Your Medical Costs by Charles B. Inlander and the Staff of the People's Medical Society, 1987. $7.95.

To order, write: People's Medical Society, 462 Walnut St., Allentown, PA 18102.

Taking the Bite out of Insurance. National Insurance Consumer Organization (NICO). $13.95.

To order, write: NICO, 121 N. Payne St., Alexandria, VA 22314.

What You Should Know about Health Insurance. Health Insurance Association of America. Free.

To order, write: Health Insurance Association of America, 1025 Connecticut Ave., N.W., Washington, DC 20030.

Organizations

People's Medical Society
462 Walnut St.
Allentown, PA 18102
(215) 770-1670

A nonprofit citizens' action group that works to achieve better and less expensive medical care for consumers; the People's Medical Society also educates consumers about health care and medical insurance through a variety of publications. Annual membership is $15 and includes a subscription to the *People's Medical Society Newsletter.* Publications are also available to nonmembers.

National Insurance Consumer Organization
121 N. Payne St.
Alexandria, VA 22314
(703) 549-8050

A nonprofit consumer advocacy group that works for reform and greater equity in the insurance industry, the organization publishes a bimonthly consumer newsletter as well as a variety of publications about saving money on insurance and how to buy insurance. Membership is $30/year.

Money Management

Books

The Bank Book: How To Revoke Your Bank's "License to Steal" by Ed Mrkvicka, Jr., Harper Perennial,, 1991. $8.95.

The Easy Family Budget by Jerald W. Mason, Houghton Mifflin Company, 1990. $4.95.

How To Live within Your Means and Still Finance Your Dreams by Robert A. Ortaldo, Fireside Books, 1990. $9.95.

Making the Most of Your Money: A Comprehensive Guide to Financial Planning, by Jane Bryant Quinn, Simon & Schuster, 1991. $14.95.

The Only Investment Guide You'll Ever Need by Andrew Tobias, Bantam Books, 1983. $4.95.

Sylvia Porter's New Money Book for the 80s by Sylvia Porter, Avon Books, 1980. $10.95.

Terry Savage Talks Money: The Common-Sense Guide to Money Matters by Terry Savage, Dearborn Financial Publishing, Inc., 1990. $22.95.

Your Wealth Building Years: Financial Planning for 18 to 34 Year Olds by Adriane Berg, 1990. $18.95.

Brochures and Handbooks

From the U.S. Department of Agriculture:

Financial Tools Used in Money Management, 1987.

The Principles of Managing Your Finances, 1987.

From the U.S. Department of Housing and Urban Development:

A Home of Your Own, 1990.

Wise Homebuying, 1987.

ABCs of Figuring Interest, Federal Reserve Bank of Chicago, 1986.

To order, write: Public Information Center, Federal Reserve Bank of Chicago, Box 834, Chicago, IL 60690.

A Primer on Financial Management for Midlife and Older Women by Wanda Fullner, Association of Retired Persons (AARP), 1988. To order, write: AARP, 601E St., N.W., Washington, DC 20049.

From the American Bankers Association:

Managing Your Checking Account, 1988.

A Guide to Bank Services, 1988.

Both are free. To order, write: American Bankers Association, 1120 Connecticut Ave., N.W., Washington, DC 20036; or call: (202) 663-5087.

Money Management Guide, Bankcard Holders of America, 1990. $5.00.

To order, write: BankCard Holders of America, 560 Herndon Pkwy., Ste. 120, Herndon, VA 22070.

From the Federal Trade Commission:

Getting a Loan: Your Home as Security, 1984.

Home Financing Primer, 1990.

Mortgage Money Guide, 1986.

To order, write: FTC, Office of Consumer and Business Education, Bureau of Consumer Protection, Washington, DC 20580.

Your Child's College Bill: How To Figure It. . . How To Pay for It, The Institute of Certified Planners. Free.

To order, write: The Institute of Certified Planners, 7600 E. Eastman Ave., Ste. 301, Denver, CO 80231.

Newsletters and Magazines

The Banker's Secret Bulletin, Good Advice Press. Covers topics related to consumer finance, $19.95/year (four issues).

To order, write: *The Banker's Secret Bulletin*, Box 78, Elizaville, NY 12523; or call: (914) 758-1400.

Bottom Line/Personal. Published twice monthly, this newsletter is dedicated to helping busy people manage their lives more effectively by providing them information on a variety of important topics including money management, taxes, careers, financial planning and medical care. $49/year (24 issues).

To order, write: *Bottom Line/Personal,* Subscriptions Dept., P.O. Box 58446, Boulder, CO 80322.

Consumer Reports, Consumers Union. This magazine provides information and advice on consumer goods and services, health and personal finance. It accepts no advertising. Published monthly. Single copies are $2.95. $20/year.

To subscribe, write: *Consumer Reports,* Subscription Dept., Box 53017, Boulder, CO 80321-3017.

Inside Financial. Monthly newsletter about financial issues of interest to consumers. Published by Reliance Enterprises, Inc. $39/year (12 issues).

To subscribe, write: Reliance Enterprises, Inc., Box 413, Marengo, IL 60152.

Kiplinger's Personal Finance Magazine, The Kiplinger Washington Editors, Inc. Published monthly. Single copies are $2.50. $18/year.

To subscribe, write: *Kiplinger's,* Subscription Center, Editors Park, MD 20782.

Money. This monthly magazine covers a variety of issues related to money, including jobs, investments, money management and taxes. Single copies are $1.95. $35.95/year.

To subscribe, write: *Money,* P.O. Box 60001, Tampa, FL 33660-0001.

Money Insider, Reliance Enterprises, Inc. Published monthly. $49/year.

To order, write: Reliance Enterprises, Inc., Box 413, Marengo, IL 60152.

Companies, Organizations and Miscellaneous Resources

Consumers Union
101 Truman Ave.
Yonkers, New York 10703-1057
(914) 378-2000

Consumers Union publishes *Consumer Reports* as well as other sources of information on consumer goods and services, health and personal finance.

National Insurance Consumer Organization
121 N. Payne St.
Alexandria, VA 22314
(804) 549-8050

A nonprofit consumer advocacy group. Contact it for a list of its publications.

National Consumers League
815 15th St., N.W., Ste. 928-N
Washington, DC 20005
(202) 639-8140

This nonprofit organization works on behalf of consumers. It publishes a monthly newsletter and a variety of consumer guides and brochures. Annual membership is $20.

American Association of Retired Persons (AARP)
601 E St., N.W.
Washington, DC 20049
(202) 434-2277

AARP is the nation's leading organization for people age 50 and over. In addition to its activities in the areas of legislative advocacy, informative programs and community services, it also publishes a variety of publications related to credit and money management that are of value to people of all ages.

Additionally, AARP sponsors the Women's Financial Information Program (WFIP), a seven-week program designed to assist midlife and older women develop money management skills and decision-making confidence. Offered nationally, the program is sponsored by AARP and local organizations such as YMCAs, community colleges and women's groups.

Children and Money

Books

Children and Money: A Parent's Guide by Grace Weinstein, Signet, 1987. $4.95.

Extra Cash for Kids by Larry Belliston and Kurt Hanks, Wagemirth & Hyatt, 1989. $9.95.

Fast Cash for Kids: 101 Money Making Projects for Young Entrepreneurs by Bonnie Drew, Career Press, Inc., 1991. $13.45.

The Kids Complete Guide to Money by Kathy S. Kyte, Knopf, 1984. $4.95.

Money Matters for Parents and Their Kids by Ron and Judy Blue, Oliver-Nelson Books, 1988. $14.95.

Start Your Own Lemonade Stand by Steve Caney, Workman Publishing, 1991. $12.95.

Teach Your Child the Value of Money by Harold and Sandy Moe, Harsand Financial Press, 1987. $9.95.

Brochures and Handbooks

You and Money: A Learning Unit for Children. Fidelity Investments. Free. (800) 544-6666.

From The Federal Reserve Bank of New York: A series of comic books about finance-related subjects such as inflation, banks, credit and money. Free. To order a set, write: Federal Reserve Bank of New York, Public Information Dept., 33 Liberty St., New York, NY 10045; or call (212) 720-6130.

Magazines

"Teaching Your Kids about Money," *Money* Magazine, March, 1990. For article reprints, call (212) 586-1212.

Zillions, Consumers Union. Published bimonthly. A one-year subscription (six issues) is $13.95. To order, call: (914) 378-2000.

Automobiles

Books

Lemon Rights: Auto Rights for New and Used Cars by Ralph Nader and Clarence Ditlow, Moyer Bell Ltd., 1990. $15.95.

Brochures and Handbooks

From BankCard Holders of America:

Your Next Car: Leasing vs. Buying. What's Best for Consumers, 1990. $1.00.

To order, write: BankCard Holders of America, 560 Herndon Pkwy., Ste. 120, Herndon, VA 22070

From the Federal Trade Commission:

A Consumer Guide to Vehicle Leasing, 1989.

Buying a Used Car, 1989.

New Car Buying Guide, 1988.

Vehicle Repossession.

To order, write: FTC, Public Reference, Washington DC 20580; or call: (202) 326-2650.

Your Money, Your Car, National Automobile Dealers Association. Free. To order, write: NADA, 8400 Westpark Dr., McLean, VA 22102.

Careers and Job Hunting

Books

The Career Finder: Pathways to Over 1500 Entry-Level Jobs by Dr. Lester Schwartz and Irv Brechner, Ballantine Books, 1990. $16.00.

Knock 'em Dead with Great Answers to Tough Interviews by John Yate, Bob Adams, Inc., 1991. $19.95.

The 90 Minute Resumé for Job Hunters Who Want Top-Notch Results—Fast! by Peggy Schmidt, Peterson's Guides, 1990. $5.95.

The 100 Best Jobs for the 1990s & Beyond by Carol Kleiman, Dearborn Financial Publishing, Inc., 1992. $19.95.

The Perfect Resumé by Tom Jackson, Doubleday & Co., 1990. $10.95.

The Resumé Catalog: 200 Damn Good Examples by Yana Parker, Ten Speed Press, 1988. $13.95.

The Resumé Writer's Handbook by Michael Holley Smith, Barnes and Noble Books, 1987. $8.95.

Sweaty Palms: The Neglected Art of Being Interviewed, by H. Anthony Medley, Ten Speed Press, 1991. $8.95.

What Color Is Your Parachute? by Richard Nelson Bolles, Ten Speed Press, 1990. $11.95.

Winning Moves: Coming Out Ahead in a Corporate Shakeup by Jana Ciabattari, Penguin Books, 1989. $8.95.

The Whole Career Sourcebook by Robbie Miller Kaplan, AMACOM, 1991. $16.95.

Newsletters and Magazines

Career Futures Magazine, Career Information Services. Published quarterly. Single copies are $3.50; a one-year subscription is $14. If magazine is not available on your newsstand, write to 21 Charles St., Westport, CT 06880, or call: (203) 227-1775.

Federal Jobs Digest, Break Through Publications. Published biweekly. A comprehensive list of federal job openings. Single copies are $4.50. A three month subscription (six issues) is $29. To order, write: Federal Jobs Digest, 325 Pennsylvania Ave., S.E. Washington, DC 20003; or call: (800) 824-5000.

Self-Employment

Books

Good Idea! Now What? by Howard Bronson, Warner Books, 1990. $6.95.

Home Business Resource Guide by Cheryl Gorder, Blue Bird Publishing, 1989. $11.95

Homebased Businesses, by Beverly Neuer Feldman, Fawcett-Crest, 1990. $3.95.

How To Become Successfully Self-Employed by Brian R. Smith and Bob Adams, Inc., 1991. $15.95.

How To Make Nothing But Money: Discovering Your Hidden Opportunities for Wealth, by Dave Del Dotto, Simon & Schuster, 1990. $19.75.

Marketing for the Home-Based Business, by Jeffrey P. Davidson and Bob Adams, Inc., 1990. $9.95.

The McGraw-Hill Guide to Starting Your Own Business: A Step-by-Step Blueprint for the First-Time Entrepreneur, by Stephen C. Harper, McGraw-Hill Publishing Co., 1991. $22.95.

Moonlighting: 148 Great Ways To Make Money on the Side by Carl Hausman and the Philip Lief Group, Avon Books, 1989. $7.95.

One Hundred Best Home Businesses for the 90s, by Paul and Sarah Edwards, J.P. Tarcher, 1991. $10.95.

184 Businesses Anyone Can Start and Make a Lot of Money by Chase Revel, Bantam Books, 1984. $9.95.

The Start Up Guide: A One-Year Plan for Entrepreneurs by David H. Bangs, Jr., Upstart Publishing Co., 1989. $18.95.

Working from Home: Everything You Need To Know About Living & Working Under the Same Roof by Paul and Sarah Edwards, J.P. Tharcher, 1990. $11.95.

Brochures and Handbooks

Directory of Federal and State Business Assistance: A Guide for New and Growing Companies, U.S. Department of Commerce. To order, write: DOL, National Technical Information Service, Springfield, VA 22161; or, call: (703) 487-4650.

***The U.S. Small Business Administration* (SBA)**
This federal office publishes a variety of publications, videotapes and workbooks about financial management, management, planning and marketing for a small business. For ordering information and a list of publications and tapes, write: The Small Business Directory, SBA, Office of Business Development, 409 Third St., S.W., Washington, DC 20416; or, call: (800) U-ASK-SBA.

Organizations

Mothers' Home-Business Network
P.O. Box 423
East Meadow, NY 11554
(516) 997-7394

A national support/information group for women who want to successfully combine motherhood with a home-based business. A $25/year membership buys a quarterly newsletter as well as several publications.

National Association for the Self-Employed

Member Services
P.O. Box 612067
DFW Airport, TX 75261
(800) 232-6273

A business support group for the self-employed, this organization provides its members with access to group insurance, and discounts on travel and office equipment. It also offers a toll-free business advice hot line. Membership is $48/year.

Protecting Your Rights

Books

Everybody's Guide to Small Claims Court by Ralph Warner, Nolo Press, 1991. $15.95.

Brochures and Handbooks

From BankCard Holders of America:

Consumer Credit Billing, 1990. $1.

Consumer Credit Rights, 1990. $1.

Privacy and Fraud Protection, 1990. $2.

Solving Your Credit Card Billing Questions, 1990. $1.00

Women's Credit Rights, 1990. $1.00

To order, write: BankCard Holders of America, 560 Herndon Pkwy., #120, Herndon, VA 22070.

From the Federal Trade Commission:

Equal Credit Opportunity

Fair Credit Billing

Fair Credit Reporting

Fair Debt Collection

Fix Your Own Credit Problems

Solving Credit Problems

Free. To order, write: Federal Trade Commission, Office of Consumer/ Business Education, Washington, DC 20580.

Consumer Handbook to Credit Protection Laws, the Board of Governors, 1989. Free. To order, write: Board of Governors, Federal Reserve System, Publications Services, MS-138, Washington, DC 20551.

Consumer Rights, Federal Financial Institutions Examination Council, 1990. Free. To order, write: Federal Financial Institutions Examination Council, 1776 G St., N.W., #850B, Washington, DC 20006.

Consumer Resource Handbook, U.S. Office of Consumer Affairs, 1992 edition. To order, write: Handbook, Consumer Information Center, Pueblo, CO 81009.

This is an excellent resource that every consumer should have. It provides the names, addresses and phone numbers of federal, state and local consumer protection agencies, corporate consumer contacts to get in touch with if you have a problem or a complaint, and selected federal agencies, etc.

What To Do if You Are Denied Credit by Emily Park, Ph.D., American Association of Retired Persons (AARP), 1988. Free. To order, write: AARP, 601 E St., N.W., Washington DC 20049.

Newspaper

Nolo News, Nolo Press. Published quarterly, this paper provides practical legal advice and information on consumer issues as well as dates on consumer laws and law changes. A two-year subscription is $12. For free sample, call (800) 922-6656.

appendix b

Information about Credit

One of the first concerns of the financially distressed is rebuilding credit. This appendix contains resources for general information about credit, the bureaus that hold and market credit reports and banks that issue credit cards. It includes sections on:

- Rebuilding Credit and Using It Wisely
- Credit Bureaus and Credit Reports
- Banks offering low interest rate cards. These cards can save you a lot of money, but they are also more difficult to obtain because of a stricter screening process.
- Banks offering Secured Credit Cards. For these cards, as discussed in Chapter 4, you must put up collateral, such as a savings account or CD account at the bank.

Rebuilding Credit and Using It Wisely

Books

Credit Card Secrets You Will Surely Profit From by Howard Strong, Boswell Corporation, 1989. $29.95.

How To Borrow Money and Use Credit by Martin Weiss, Houghton Mifflin Company, 1990. $4.95.

How To Use Credit and Credit Cards by Arnold Corrigan and Phyllis C. Kaufman, Longmeadow Press, 1986. $3.95.

Brochures and Handbooks

From the Federal Trade Commission:

Choosing and Using Credit Cards, 1991.

Credit Repair Schemes, 1991.

Fix Your Own Credit Problems

To order, write: FTC, Office of Consumer Education, Bureau of Consumer Protection, Washington, DC 20580.

From BankCard Holders of America (BHA)

Credit Repair Clinics: Consumers Beware, 1990. $1.00.

How To Choose a Credit Card, 1990. $1.00.

How To Re-establish Good Credit, 1990. $1.00.

Secured Credit Cards: Selecting the Best One for You, 1990. $1.00.

To order, write: BHA, 560 Herndon Pkwy., #120, Herndon, VA 22070.

Newsletters and Magazines

BankCard Consumer News, BankCard Holders of America (BHA). Published six times a year, this newsletter is free to members. (See below.)

Organizations

BankCard Holders of America (BHA)
560 Herndon Pkwy., Ste. 120
Herndon, VA 22070
(800) 638-6407

This nonprofit organization is dedicated to educating consumers about credit. BHA publishes a variety of informative brochures, a bimonthly newsletter and lists of national bankcards and their terms of credit. The publications are free to BHA members and available to nonmembers for a small fee. Membership is $24/year.

Credit Records and Credit Bureaus

Books

Credit Improvement Handbook by James L. Bandy and Robert A. Freiheit, Coastline Associated Enterprises, 1986. $6.95.

Credit Secrets: How To Erase Bad Credit by Bob Hammond, Paladin Press, 1989. $12.00.

Your Credit: A Complete Guide by Emily Card, Ph.D., J.D., American Association of Retired Persons (AARP), 1989. Free. To order, write: AARP, 601 E St., N.W., Washington, DC 20049.

Brochures and Handbooks

From BankCard Holders of America (BHA):

Credit Check-up Kit, 1990. $2.00

Credit Secrets Manual, 1990. $1.00

Understanding Credit Bureaus, 1990. $1.00

To order, write: BHA, 560 Herndon Pkwy., #120, Herndon, VA 22070.

Building a Better Credit Record: What To Do, What To Avoid. Produced by the Federal Trade Commission in cooperation with the Associated Credit Bureaus, Inc., the National Foundation for Consumer Credit, the U.S. Office of Consumer Affairs and the Consumer Information Center, 1988. To order, write FTC, Public Reference, Washington, DC 20580.

Solving Credit Problems, Federal Trade Commission, 1988.

Organizations

Associated Credit Bureaus, Inc.
1090 Vermont Ave., N.W., #200
Washington, DC 20005-4905

This national trade association publishes a variety of brochures related to credit and credit bureaus. Write the Association for a price list.

Banks Offering Low-Interest Bank Cards

Banks Issuing Cards Nationally:

AFBA Industrial Bank
KBC Card Services
909 N. Washington St.
Alexandria, VA 22314
(800) 776-2265
Cards Offered: MasterCard, Visa

Amalgamated Trust and Savings Bank
Card Services Dept.
1 W. Monroe St.
Chicago, IL 60603
(800) 365 6464
Cards Offered: MasterCard, MasterCard Gold

American Express/Centurion Bank
248 Chapman Rd.
Bristol Building
Newark, DE 19702
(800) 678-4628
Card Offered: OPTIMA

Arkansas Federal Savings F.A.
Credit Card Center
P.O. Box 8208
Little Rock, AR 72221
(800) 477-3348
Cards Offered: MasterCard, Visa

Bank of Hawaii
Bank Card Center
P.O. Box 1999
Honolulu, HI 96805
(808) 543-9611
Cards Offered: Visa, Visa Gold

Cowlitz Bank
P.O. Box 1518
927 Commerce Ave.
Longview, WA 98632
(206) 423-9800
Cards Offered: MasterCard, Visa

Crestar Bank
P.O. Box 27172
Richmond, VA 23261
(800) 368-7700
Cards Offered: MasterCard, Visa, Visa Gold

Fidelity National Bank
Credit Card Dept.
P.O. Box 105075
Atlanta, GA 30348
(800) 753-2900
Card Offered: Visa

1st American Bank of Virginia
Bank Card Center
P.O. Box 1307
McLean, VA 22102-8987
(800) 572-4004
Card Offered: Visa

First National Bank
Greatbank Card Services
P.O. Box 403
Chicago Heights, IL 60411
(800) 635-3131
Cards Offered: MasterCard, Visa

First National Bank of Omaha
P.O. Box 3331
Omaha, NE 68103
(800) 688-7070
Cards Offered: MasterCard, Visa

First State Bank
P.O. Box 3550
Austin, TX 78764
(512) 495-1000
Cards Offered: MasterCard, Visa

National Bank of Commerce
P.O. Box 82408
Lincoln, NE 68501
(800) 635-8503
Cards Offered: MasterCard, Visa

Ohio Savings Bank
Credit Card Dept.
P.O. Box 94712
Cleveland, OH 44114
(800) 962-2025
Cards Offered: MasterCard, Visa, MasterCard Gold, Visa Gold

People's Bank of Bridgeport
P.O. Box 637
Bridgeport, CT 06601
(800) 426-1114
Cards Offered: MasterCard, Visa, MasterCard Gold, Visa Gold

Prime Bank
P.O. Box 1343
Elkhart, IN 46515
(800) 627-9159
Cards Offered: MasterCard, Visa

Simmons First National Bank
Bank Card Center
P.O. Box 6609
Pine Bluff, AR 71611
(501) 541-1000 (out-of-state)
(800) 272-2102 (AR)
Cards Offered: MasterCard, Visa

The Abbott Bank
10040 Regency Circle, Ste. 300
Omaha, NE 68114
(800) 999-6977
Cards Offered: MasterCard, Visa

The Bank of New York (Delaware)
P.O. Box 6999
Newark, DE 19714
(800) 942-1977
Card Offered: Consumers Edge MasterCard, Consumers Edge Visa

Union Planters Bank
P.O. Box 3171
Memphis, TN 38173
(800) 628-8946
Cards Offered: Visa, MasterCard Gold

USAA Federal Savings Bank
Bank Card Center
P.O. Box 21658
Tulsa, OK 74121
(800) 922-9092
Cards Offered: MasterCard, Visa

First Wachovia Corporation
Bank Card Services
P.O. Box 12264
Wilmington, DE 19850
(800) 842-3262
Cards Offered: MasterCard, Visa

Banks Issuing Cards Regionally:

Bank of Elmhurst
Credit Card Center
990 N. York Rd.
Elmhurst, IL 60126
(800) 423-7503 (IL only)
Cards Offered: Visa, Visa Gold (Residents of IL only)

Broadway National Bank
Credit Card Center
P.O. Box 17001
San Antonio, TX 78286
(512) 283-6555
Card Offered: Visa (San Antonio area only)

Cumberland Bank, FSB
200 W. Broadway
Louisville, KY 40202
(800) 467-3456
Cards Offered: MasterCard, Visa (Residents of Kentucky and contiguous states only)

First Financial Bank, FSB
1305 Main St.
Stevens Point, WI 54481
(800) 726-0400
Card Offered: MasterCard (Residents IA, IL, IN and MI only)

First Interstate Bank of Billings
401 N. 31st St.
Billings, MT 59101
(406) 255-5000
Cards Offered: MasterCard, Visa, MasterCard Gold, Visa Gold

Firstier Bank Omaha, N.A.
Farnam at Seventeenth
Omaha, NE 68102
(800) 432-3209
Cards Offered: MasterCard, Visa (Residents of WY, ND, SD, MN, MO, KS, IA and NE only)

Indiana National Bank
1 Indiana Square
Indianapolis, IN 46266
(800) 344-1140 accepted).
Card Offered: MasterCard (Midwest residents only)

Manufacturer's Bank—Wilmington
P.O. Box 15147
Wilmington, DE 19885
(800) 635-8350
Cards Offered: MasterCard, Visa (Residents of MI, OH, IL, IN, WI, FL, MN only)

Marine Bank of Springfield
East Old State Capitol Plaza
Springfield, IL 62701
(217) 525-9600
Cards Offered: MasterCard, Visa

Puget Sound National Bank,
P.O. Box 11500
Tacoma, WA 98411
(800) 882-2265, ext. 3877
Card Offered: Banclub Visa, Visa Gold (WA residents only)

Star Bank
Card Services Group
P.O. Box 956
Cincinnati, OH 45201
(800) 999-0619
Cards Offered: MasterCard, Visa (Residents of OH, PA, IN, KY, WV, TN, IL, MI)

The Mid-City National Bank of Chicago
Credit Card Dept.
801 W. Madison St.
Chicago, IL 60607
(312) 421-7600
Cards Offered: Visa, Visa Gold (Residents IL only)

Union Bank and Trust Company
Credit Card Dept.
49th and North May Ave.
Oklahoma City, OK 73112
(405) 949-7200
Cards Offered: Visa, Visa Gold (Residents of OK only)

Union Trust Company
P.O. Box 7023
Bridgeport, CT 06601
(203) 372-2856
Cards Offered: MasterCard, Visa, MasterCard Gold (Residents of CT only)

Wells Fargo Bank, N.A.
P.O. Box 4044
Concord, CA 94524-4044
(800) 642-4720
Cards Offered: MasterCard, Visa (Residents of CA only)

Banks Offering Secured Credit Cards

American National Bank
1890 Palmer Ave., Ste. 403
Larchmont, NY 10538
(914) 833-0560
Card Offered: Visa

American Pacific Bank
P.O. Box 19360
Portland, OR 97280-9360
(800) 879-8745
Card Offered: Visa (Except VT and ME)

Bank One, Lafayette, NA
Credit Card Services
P.O. Box 450
Lafayette, IN 47902
(800) 395-2556
Card Offered: MasterCard, Visa

Budget and Credit Counseling Services, Inc.
Secured Card Program
55 Fifth Ave.

13th Fl.
New York, NY 10003
(212) 675-5070
Card Offered: Visa (Apply in person at the New York office)

Central National Bank
Secured Credit Card Program
Broadway and Charleston at 14th
Mattoon, IL 61938
(800) 876-9119
Cards Offered: Visa, MasterCard

Community Bank
Spirit Visa Card Program
19590 E. Main St.
Parker, CO 80134
(800) 779-8472
Card Offered: Visa

Consumer Fresh Start Association
217 N. Church St.
Princeton, IL 61356
(800) 352-5353
Card Offered: Visa

Dreyfus Thrift and Commerce
P.O. Box 6003
Garden City, NY 11530-9841
(800) 727-3348
Card Offered: MasterCard

First National Bank in Brookings
P.O. Box 6000
Brookings, SD 57006
(605) 692-2680
Cards Offered: Visa, MasterCard

First State Bank
P.O. Box 15414
Wilmington, DE 19850
(302) 322-9111
Cards Offered: Visa, MasterCard

Key Federal Savings Bank
Secured Card Program
P.O. Box 6057
Havre de Grace, MD 21078-9978
(800) 228-2230
Cards Offered: Visa, MasterCard

Pioneer Federal Savings Bank
Secured Visa Program
P.O. Box M
Lynwood, WA 98046
(206) 771-2525
Card Offered: Visa (Residents of WA only)

Service One/Bank of Hoven
Secured Visa and MasterCard Program
Service One Card Center
26660 Agoura Road
Calabasas, CA 91302
(800) 777-7735
Cards Offered: Visa, MasterCard

Signet Bank
P.O. Box C32131
Richmond, VA 23286
(800) 333-7116
Cards Offered: Visa and MasterCard (Residents of DE, DC, KS, ME, VT, WI, MO, NM, NC, OR, MA only)

Texas Bank, N.A.
1845 Precinct Line Rd.
Suite 100
Hurst, TX 76054
(800) 451-0273
Card Offered: Visa

United Savings Bank
Secured Card Program
711 Van Ness Ave.
San Francisco, CA 94102
(415) 928-0700
Cards Offered: Visa and MasterCard (Residents of CA only)

appendix c

Federal Assistance

This appendix, which contains information about how the federal government can assist you during your recovery process, is divided into three categories:

Federal Information Centers. If you have a question about government programs but are not sure what agency to call, you might start with a Federal Information Center (FIC). The FIC can supply you with information about federal services, programs and regulations, as well as the name of the agency you should contact for specific problems.

Federal Government Publications. The federal government produces a vast number of well-written informative publications on a wide variety of topics. Unfortunately, there is no central source that supplies a list of publications. I have supplied a list of agencies to contact for information.

Federal Regulatory Agencies. If you feel you have been treated unfairly and unlawfully by a debt collector, creditor or credit bureau, you will want to report the problem in writing to the appropriate agency.

Federal Information Center

If your area is not listed, call (301) 722-9098. Users of TDD/TTY throughout the U.S. may call (800) 326-2996 (toll-free).

Alabama
Birmingham, Mobile
(800) 366-2998

Alaska
Anchorage
(800) 729-8003

Arizona
Phoenix
(800) 359-3997

Arkansas
Little Rock
(800) 366-2998

California
Los Angeles, San Diego, San Francisco, Santa Ana
(800) 726-4995

Sacramento
(916) 973-1695

Colorado
Colorado Springs, Denver, Pueblo
(800) 359-3997

Connecticut
Hartford, New Haven
(800) 347-1997

Florida
Ft. Lauderdale, Jacksonville, Miami, Orlando, St. Petersburg, Tampa, West Palm Beach
(800) 347-1997

Georgia
Atlanta
(800) 347-1997

Hawaii
Honolulu
(800) 733-5996

Illinois
Chicago
(800) 366-2998

Indiana
Gary
(800) 366-2998
Indianapolis
(800) 347-1997

Iowa
All locations
(800) 735-8004

Kansas
All locations
(800) 735-8004

Kentucky
Louisville
(800) 347-1997

Louisiana
New Orleans
(800) 366-2998

Maryland
Baltimore
(800) 347-1997

Massachusetts
Boston
(800) 347-1997

Michigan
Detroit, Grand Rapids
(800) 347-1997

Minnesota
Minneapolis
(800) 366-2998

Missouri
St. Louis
(800) 366-2998
All other locations
(800) 735-8004

Nebraska
Omaha
(800) 366-2998
All other locations
(800) 735-8004

New Jersey
Newark, Trenton
(800) 347-1997

New Mexico
Albuquerque
(800) 359-3997

New York
Albany, Buffalo, New York, Rochester, Syracuse
(800) 347-1997

North Carolina
Charlotte
(800) 347-1997

Ohio
Akron, Cincinnati, Cleveland, Columbus, Dayton, Toledo
(800) 347-1997

Oklahoma
Oklahoma City, Tulsa
(800) 366-2998

Oregon
Portland
(800) 726-4995

Pennsylvania
Philadelphia, Pittsburgh
(800) 347-1997

Rhode Island
Providence
(800) 347-1997

Tennessee
Chattanooga
(800) 347-1997
Memphis, Nashville
(800) 366-2998

Texas
Austin, Dallas, Fort Worth, Houston, San Antonio
(800) 366-2998

Utah
Salt Lake City
(800) 359-3997

Virginia
Norfolk, Richmond, Roanoke
(800) 347-1997

Washington
Seattle, Tacoma
(800) 726-4995

Wisconsin
Milwaukee
(800) 366-2998

Information was obtained from the *Consumers' Resource Handbook,* 1992 edition, U.S. Office of Consumer Affairs.

General Information Regarding Publications Available from the Federal Government

The federal government produces a vast number of well-written informative publications on a wide variety of topics. Unfortunately, there is no central source for a list of these publications, nor is there a single office from which to order. Federal agencies either fulfill their own publication requests, or rely on other government offices.

The best way to learn about all the publications available from an agency is to send a written request for its list. The list below presents the major sources of federal information of interest to consumers:

Publications
U.S. Department of Agriculture
Cooperative Education Service
Washington, DC 20250
(202) 720-8732

(Also, consult your phone directory for the number of your local Department of Agriculture, Cooperative Extension Service.)

Federal Trade Commission (FTC)
Office of Consumer and Business Education
6th and Pennsylvania Ave., N.W.
Washington, DC 20580
(202) 326-3650

Board of Governors, Federal Reserve Board
Publications Services
Mail Stop 138
Washington, DC 20551
(202) 452-3946

Small Business Administration (SBA)
409 3rd St., S.W.
Washington, DC 20416
(202) 205-6740

(Also, consult your phone directory for the number of your local SBA office.)

Department of Labor (DOL)
Employment and Training Administration
Washington, DC 20210
(202) 523-6871
(Also, consult your phone directory for the number of your local DOL, Employment and Training Office.)

Department of Veterans Affairs
Office of Consumer Affairs
810 Vermont Ave., N.W.
Washington, DC 20420
(202) 535-8962

Department of Energy
Office of Public Affairs
400 Maryland Ave., S.W.
Washington, DC 20202
(202) 401-3020

Department of Housing and Urban Development (HUD)
No central publications office. Contact the HUD office nearest you.

Other Sources of Government Publications

Consumer Information Center
This center distributes over 200 free or nominally priced brochures and handbooks covering a wide variety of topics of interest to consumers. A catalog can be ordered by writing: Catalog, P.O. Box 100, Pueblo, CO 81009.

Note: When reviewing this catalog, it is important to realize that some of the publications listed in it can be obtained free by ordering directly from the federal agency that actually prepared the publication. (The sponsoring agency is indicated in parentheses near the end of each catalog entry.) Therefore, you may want to check with individual agencies before ordering.

Government Printing Office (GPO)
This office is another source of federal publications. Request a catalog of its Consumer Publications by writing: GPO, Publications Service Section, Washington, DC 20402; or call: (202) 275-3050.

Federal Regulatory Agencies

The Federal Trade Commission (FTC)
Office of Credit Practices
Bureau of Consumer Protection
Washington, DC 20580
(202) 326-3175

Regional Offices

Atlanta Regional Office
1718 Peachtree St., N.W., Rm. 1000
Atlanta, GA 30367
(404) 347-4836
(Serves: AL, FL, GA, MS, NC, SC, TN, VA)

Boston Regional Office
Boston, MA 02222-1073
(617) 565-7240
(Serves: CT, ME, MA, NH, RI, VT)

Chicago Regional Office
55 E. Monroe St., Ste. 1437
Chicago, IL 60603
(312) 353-4423
(Serves: IL, IN, IA, MN, MO, WI, KY)

Cleveland Regional Office
668 Euclid Ave., Ste. 520-A
Cleveland, OH 44114
(216) 522-4207
(Serves: MI, OH, PA, WV, DE, MD)

Dallas Regional Office
100 N. Central Expressway, Ste. 500
Dallas, TX 75201
(214) 767-5501
(Serves: AR, LA, NM, OK, TX)

Denver Regional Office
1405 Curtis St., Ste. 2900
Denver, CO 80202-2393
(303) 844-2271
(Serves: CO, KS, MT, NE, ND, SD, UT, WY)

Los Angeles Regional Office
11000 Wilshire Blvd., Ste. 13209
Los Angeles, CA 90024
(310) 575-7575
(Serves: AZ, So. CA)

New York Regional Office
150 William St., Ste. 1300
New York, NY 10038
(212) 264-1207
(Serves: NY, NJ)

San Francisco Regional Office
901 Market St., Ste. 570
San Francisco, CA 94103
(415) 744-7920
(Serves: No. CA, HI, NV)

Seattle Regional Office
2806 Federal Building, 915 Second Ave.
Seattle, WA 98174
(206) 553-4656
(Serves: AK, ID, OR, WA)

The Federal Reserve Board

Board of Governors of the Federal Reserve System
Division of Consumer and Community Affairs
20th & C Sts., N.W.
Washington, DC 20551
(202) 452-3000

Atlanta
P.O. Box 1731
Atlanta, GA 30301-1731
(404) 521-8500

Boston
600 Atlantic Ave.
Boston, MA 02106
(617) 973-3000

Chicago
P.O. Box 834
Chicago, IL 60690-0834
(312) 322-5322

Cleveland
P.O. Box 6387
Cleveland, OH 44101
(216) 579-2000

Dallas
400 South Akard St.
(Station K)
Dallas, TX 75222
(214) 651-6199

Kansas City
925 Grand Ave.
Kansas City, MO 64198

Minneapolis
250 Marquette Ave.
Minneapolis, MN 55480
(612) 340-2345

New York
33 Liberty St.
(Federal Reserve P.O. Station)
New York, NY 10045
(212) 720-5000

Philadelphia
P.O. Box 66
Philadelphia, PA 19105
(215) 574-6000

Richmond
P.O. Box 27622
Richmond, VA 23261
(804) 697-8000

St. Louis
P.O. Box 442
St. Louis, MO 63166
(314) 444-8444

San Francisco
P.O. Box 7702
San Francisco, CA 94120
(415) 974-2000

Office of Thrift Supervision, Community Investment

1700 G St., N.W.
Washington, DC 20552
(202) 906-6000

Northeast Region

Boston
P.O. Box 9020 GMF
Boston, MA 02205-9020
(617) 457-1900

New Jersey
10 Exchange Place Centre, 17th Fl.
Jersey City, NJ 07302
(201) 413-1000

Pittsburgh
One Riverfront Center
Twenty Stanwix Street
Pittsburgh, PA 15222-4893
(412) 338-2500

Southeast Region

Atlanta
P.O. Box 105217
Atlanta, GA 30348-5217
(404) 888-0771

Central Region

Chicago
111 E. Wacker Dr., Ste. 800
Chicago, IL 60601-4360
(312) 565-5300

Cincinnati
P.O. Box 5364
Cincinnati, OH 45201-5364
(513) 762-6100

Indianapolis
P.O. Box 6139
Indianapolis, IN 46206
(317) 465-1600

Midwest Region

Dallas
P.O. Box 619027
Dallas/Ft. Worth, TX 75261-9027
(213) 281-2000

Des Moines
Regency West 2
1401 50th St.
Des Moines, IA 50265-1013
(515) 222-2100

Topeka
P.O. Box 828
Topeka, KS 66601-0828
(913) 233-5300

West Region

San Francisco
P.O. Box 7165
San Francisco, CA 94120
(415) 616-1500

Seattle
2201 Sixth Ave., Ste. 1500
Seattle, WA 98121-1889
(206) 727-5200

Comptroller of the Currency

Administrator of the National Banks
250 E St., S.W.
Washington, DC 20219
(202) 622-2000

Consumer Complaint Specialist
Northeastern District
1114 Avenue of the Americas
Ste. 3900
New York, NY 10036
(212) 819-9860, (212) 790-4040
(Serves: CT, DE, DC, ME, MD, MA, PA, RI, VT, NH, NY, NJ, PR, VI)

Consumer Complaint Specialist
Southeastern District
Marquis One Tower, Ste. 600
245 Peachtree Center Ave., NE
Atlanta, GA 30303
(404) 659-8855
(Serves: AL, FL, GA, MS, NC, SC, TN, VA, WV)

Consumer Complaint Specialist
Central District
One Financial Pl., Ste. 2700
440 S. LaSalle St.
Chicago, IL 60605
(312) 663-8000
(Serves: IL, IN, KY, OH, MI, WI)

Consumer Complaint Specialist
Midwestern District
2345 Grand Ave., Ste. 700
Kansas City, MO 64108
(816) 556-1800
(Serves: ND, SD, MN, IA, KS, MO, NE)

Consumer Complaint Specialist
Southwestern District
1600 Lincoln Plaza
500 North Akard
Dallas, TX 75201-3394
(214) 720-0656
(Serves: AR, LA, NM, OK, TX)

Consumer Complaint Specialist
Western District
50 Fremont St., Ste. 3900
San Francisco, CA 94105
(415) 545-5900
(Serves: AL, AZ, CA, CO, ID, GU, HI, MT, NV, OR, UT, WA, WY)

The National Credit Union Administration

Washington, DC 20456
(202) 682-1900

Region I (Albany)
9 Washington Square
Washington Ave. Extension
Albany, NY 12205
(518) 472-4554
(Serves: CT, ME, MA, NH, NY, PR, RI, VT, VI)

Region II (Capital)
1776 G St., N.W., Ste. 800
Washington, DC 20006
(202) 682-1900
(Serves: DE, DC, MD, NJ, PA, VA, WV)

Region III (Atlanta)
7000 Central Pkwy., Ste. 1600
Atlanta, GA 30328
(404) 396-4042
(Serves: AL, AR, FL, GA, KY, LA, MS, NC, SC, TN)

Region IV (Chicago)
300 Park Blvd., Ste. #155
Itasca, IL 60143
(708) 250-6000
(Serves: IL, IN, MI, MO, OH, WI)

Region V (Austin)
4807 Spicewood Springs Rd., Ste. 5200
Austin, TX 78759
(512) 482-4500
(Serves: AZ, CO, IA, KS, MS, NE, NM, ND, OK, SD, TX, UT, WY)

Region VI (Pacific)
2300 Clayton Rd., Ste. 1350
Concord, CA 94520
(510) 825-6125
(Serves: AK, AS, CA, GU, HI, ID,

appendix d

State and Local Consumer Protection Agencies

Usually the government agencies most responsive to our needs are those at the local and state levels. These agencies have a better understanding of the needs of the people in their area. Following is a list of the state and local government protection agencies that can provide the assistance you need to understand your rights and help you enforce them.

State, County and City Government Consumer Protection Offices

Alabama

State Offices
Consumer Protection Division
Office of Attorney General
11 S. Union St.
Montgomery, AL 36130
(205) 242-7334
(800) 392-5658 (toll-free in AL)

Alaska

The Consumer Protection Section in the Office of the Attorney General has been closed. Consumers with complaints are being referred to the Better Business Bureau, small claims court and private attorneys.

Arizona

State Offices

Consumer Protection
Office of the Attorney General
1275 W. Washington St., Rm. 259
Phoenix, AZ 85007
(602) 542-3702
(602) 542-5763 (consumer information and complaints)
(800) 352-8431 (toll-free in AZ)

Assistant Attorney General
Consumer Protection
Office of the Attorney General
402 W. Congress St., Ste. 315
Tucson, AZ 85701
(602) 628-6504

County Offices

Apache County Attorney's Office
P.O. Box 637
St. Johns, AZ 85936
(602) 337-4364, ext. 240

Cochise County Attorney's Office
P.O. Drawer CA
Bisbee, AZ 85603
(602) 432-9377

Coconino County Attorney's Office
Coconino County Courthouse
100 E. Birch
Flagstaff, AZ 86001
(602) 779-6518

Gila County Attorney's Office
1400 E. Ash St.
Globe, AZ 85501
(602) 425-3231

Graham County Attorney's Office
Graham County Courthouse
800 W. Main
Safford, AZ 85546
(602) 428-3620

Greenlee County Attorney's Office
P.O. Box 1387
Clifton, AZ 85533
(602) 865-3842

LaPaz County Attorney's Office
1200 Arizona Ave.
P.O. Box 709
Parker, AZ 85344
(602) 669-6118

Mohave County Attorney's Office
315 N. 4th St.
Kingman, AZ 86401
(602) 753-0719

Navajo County Attorney's Office
Governmental Complex
Holbrook, AZ 86025
(602) 524-6161

Pima County Attorney's Office
1400 Great American Tower
32 N. Stone
Tucson, AZ 85701
(602) 740-5733

Pinal County Attorney's Office
P.O. Box 887

Florence, AZ 85232
(602) 868-5801

Santa Cruz County Attorney's Office
2100 N. Congress Dr., Ste. 201
Nogales, AZ 85621
(602) 281-4966

Yavapai County Attorney's Office
Yavapai County Courthouse
Prescott, AZ 86301
(602) 771-3344

Yuma County Attorney's Office
168 S. Second Ave.
Yuma, AZ 85364
(602) 329-2270

City Office

Supervising Attorney
Consumer Affairs Division
Tucson City Attorney's Office
220 E. Pennington St., 2nd Fl.
P.O. Box 27210
Tucson, AZ 85726-7210
(602) 791-4886

Arkansas

State Office

Director
Consumer Protection Division
Office of Attorney General
200 Tower Building
323 Center St.
Little Rock, AR 72201
(501) 682-2341 (voice/TDD)
(800) 482-8982
(toll-free voice/TDD in AR)

California

State Offices

Director
Calif. Dept. of Consumer Affairs
400 R St., Ste. 1040
Sacramento, CA 95814
(916) 445-0660 (complaint assistance)
(916) 445-1254 (consumer information)
(916) 522-1700 (TDD)
(800) 344-9940 (toll-free in CA)

Office of Attorney General
Public Inquiry Unit
P.O. Box 944255
Sacramento, CA 94244-2550
(916) 322-3360
(800) 952-5225 (toll-free in CA)
(800) 952-5548 (toll-free TDD in CA)

Bureau of Automotive Repair
Calif. Dept. of Consumer Affairs
10240 Systems Prkwy.
Sacramento, CA 95827
(916) 366-5100
(800) 952-5210
(toll-free in CA–auto repair only)

County Offices

Coordinator, Alameda County Consumer Affairs Commission
4400 MacArthur Blvd.
Oakland, CA 94619
(510) 530-8682

District Attorney
Contra Costa County
District Attorney's Office
725 Court St., 4th Fl.
P.O. Box 670
Martinez, CA 94553
(415) 646-4500

Senior Deputy District Attorney
Business Affairs
Fresno County District Attorney's Office
2220 Tulare St., Ste. 1000
Fresno, CA 93721
(209) 488-3156

District Attorney
Consumer and Major Business Fraud Section
Kern County District Attorney's Office
1215 Truxtun Ave.
Bakersfield, CA 933301
(805) 861-2421

Director, Los Angeles County Dept. of Consumer Affairs
500 W. Temple St., Rm. B-96
Los Angeles, CA 90012
(213) 974-1452

Director, Citizens Service Office
Marin County Mediation Services
Marin County Civic Center
Rm. 412
San Rafael, CA 94903
(415) 499-6190

District Attorney
Marin County District Attorney's Office
Marin County Civic Center
Rm. 112
San Rafael, CA 94903
(415) 499-6482

Deputy District Attorney
Consumer Protection Division
Marin County District Attorney's Office
Hall of Justice, Rm. 183
San Rafael, CA 94903
(415) 499-6450

District Attorney
Mendocino County District Attorney's Office
P.O. Box 1000
Ukiah, CA 95482
(707) 463-4211

Coordinator, Monterey County Office of Consumer Affairs
P.O. Box 1369
Salinas, CA 93902
(408) 755-5073

Deputy District Attorney
Consumer Affairs Division
Napa County District Attorney's Office
931 Parkway Mall
P.O. Box 720
Napa, CA 94559
(707) 253-4059

Deputy District Attorney in Charge
Major Fraud Unit
Orange County District Attor-ney's Office
801 Civic Center Dr. West
Ste. 120
Santa Ana, CA 92702
(714) 541-7600

Deputy District Attorney in Charge
Consumer and Environmental Protection Unit
Orange County District Attorney's Office
801 Civic Center Dr. West
Ste. 120
Santa Ana, CA 92702
(714) 541-7600

Deputy District Attorney
Economic Crime Division
Riverside County District Attorney's Office
4075 Main St.
Riverside, CA 92501
(714) 275-5400

Supervising Deputy District Attorney
Consumer and Environmental Protection Division
Sacramento County District At-torney's Office
P.O. Box 749
Sacramento, CA 95812-0749
(916) 440-6174

Director, Consumer Fraud Division
San Diego County District Attorney's Office
P.O. Box X-1011
San Diego, CA 92112
(619) 531-3507 (fraud complaint line)
(8:30 A.M.–11:30 A.M; at other times, leave a message)

Attorney, Consumer and Environmental Protection Unit
San Francisco County District Attorney's Office
732 Brennan St.
San Francisco, CA 94103
(415) 552-6400 (public inquiries)
(415) 553-1814 (complaints)

Deputy District Attorney
Consumer and Business Affairs Division
San Joaquin County District Attorney's Office
222 E. Weber, Rm. 202
P.O. Box 990
Stockton, CA 95202
(209) 468-2419

Director, Economic Crime Unit
Consumer Fraud Dept.
County Government Center
1050 Monterey St., Rm. 235
San Luis Obispo, CA 93408
(805) 549-5800

Deputy in Charge
Consumer Fraud and Environmental Protection Unit
San Mateo County District Attorney's Office
401 Marshall St.
Hall of Justice and Records
Redwood City, CA 94063
(415) 363-4656

Deputy District Attorney
Consumer Protection Unit
Santa Barbara County District Attorney's Office
1105 Santa Barbara St.
Santa Barbara, CA 93101
(805) 568-2300

Deputy District Attorney
Consumer Fraud Unit
Santa Clara County District Attorney's Office
70 W. Hedding St., West Wing
San Jose, CA 95110
(408) 299-7400

Director, Santa Clara County Dept. of Consumer Affairs
2175 The Alameda
San Jose, CA 95126
(408) 299-4211

Coordinators, Division of Consumer Affairs
Santa Cruz County District Attorney's Office
701 Ocean St., Rm. 200
Santa Cruz, CA 95060
(408) 425-2054

Deputy District Attorney
Consumer Affairs Unit
Solano County District Attorney's Office
600 Union Ave.
Fairfield, CA 94533
(707) 421-6860

Deputy District Attorney
Consumer Fraud Unit
Stanislaus County District Attorney's Office
P.O. Box 442
Modesto, CA 95353
(209) 571-5550

Deputy District Attorney
Consumer and Environmental Protection Division
Ventura County District Attorney's Office
800 S. Victoria Ave.
Ventura, CA 93009
(805) 654-3110

Supervising Deputy District Attorney
Special Services Unit—Consumer/Environmental
Yolo County District Attorney's Office
P.O. Box 245
Woodland, CA 95695
(916) 666-8424

City Offices

Supervising Deputy City Attorney
Consumer Protection Division
Los Angeles City Attorney's Office
200 N. Main St.
1600 City Hall East
Los Angeles, CA 90012
(213) 485-4515

Consumer Affairs Specialist
Consumer Division
Santa Monica City Attorney's Office
1685 Main St., Rm. 310
Santa Monica, CA 90401
(213) 458-8336

Colorado

State Offices

Consumer Protection Unit
Office of Attorney General
110 16th St., 10th Fl.
Denver, CO 80202
(303) 620-4500

Consumer and Food Specialist
Dept. of Agriculture
700 Kipling St., Ste. 4000
Lakewood, CO 80215-5894
(303) 239-4114

County Offices

District Attorney
Archuleta, LaPlata and San Juan Counties
District Attorney's Office
P.O. Drawer 3455
Durango, CO 81302
(303) 247-8850

District Attorney
Boulder County District Attorney's Office
P.O. Box 471
Boulder, CO 80306
(303) 441-3700

Executive Director
Denver County District Attorney's Consumer Fraud Office
303 W. Colfax Ave., Ste. 1300
Denver, CO 80204
(303) 640-3555 (inquiries)
(303) 640-3557 (complaints)

Chief Deputy District Attorney
Economic Crime Division
El Paso and Teller Counties District Attorney's Office
326 S. Tejon
Colorado Springs, CO 80903-2083
(719) 520-6002

District Attorney
Pueblo County District Attorney's Office
Courthouse
215 W. Tenth St.
Pueblo, CO 81003
(719) 546-6030

District Attorney
Consumer Fraud Investigator
Weld County District Attorney's Consumer Office
P.O. Box 1167
Greeley, CO 80632
(303) 356-4000 ext. 4735

Connecticut

State Offices

Commissioner
Dept. of Consumer Protection
State Office Building
165 Capitol Ave.
Hartford, CT 06106
(203) 566-4999
(800) 842-2649

Assistant Attorney General
Antitrust/Consumer Protection
Office of Attorney General
110 Sherman St.
Hartford, CT 06015
(203) 566-5374

City Office

Director, Middletown Office of Consumer Protection
City Hall
Middletown, CT 06457
(203) 344-3492

Delaware

State Offices

Director, Division of Consumer Affairs
Dept. of Community Affairs
820 N. French St., 4th Fl.
Wilmington, DE 19801
(302) 577-3250

Deputy Attorney General for Economic Crime and Consumer Protection
Office of Attorney General
820 N. French St.
Wilmington, DE 19801
(302) 577-3250

District of Columbia

Director, Dept. of Consumer and Regulatory Affairs
614 H St., N.W.
Washington, DC 20001
(202) 727-7000

Florida

State offices

Assistant Director
Dept. of Agriculture and Consumer Services
Division of Consumer Services
218 Mayo Building
Tallahassee, FL 32399
(904) 488-2226
(800) 342-2176 (toll-free TDD in FL)
(800) 327-3382 (toll-free information and education in FL)
(800) 321-5366 (toll-free lemon law in FL)
Chief, Consumer Litigation Section
The Capitol
Tallahassee, FL 32399-1050
(904) 488-9105

Chief, Consumer Division
Office of Attorney General
4000 Hollywood Blvd.
Ste. 505 South
Hollywood, FL 33021
(305) 985-4780

County Offices

Director, Broward County Consumer Affairs Division
115 S. Andrews Ave., Rm. 119
Fort Lauderdale, FL 33301
(305) 357-6030

Consumer Advocate
Metropolitan Dade County
Consumer Protection Division
140 W. Flagler St., Ste. 902
Miami, FL 33130
(305) 375-4222

Chief, Dade County Economic Crime Unit
Office of State Attorney
1469 N.W. 13th Terrace, Rm. 600
Miami, FL 33125
(305) 324-3030

Manager, Hillsborough County Dept. of Consumer Affairs
412 E. Madison St., Rm. 1001
Tampa, FL 33602
(813) 272-6750

Chief, Orange County Consumer Fraud Unit
250 N. Orange Ave.
P.O. Box 1673
Orlando, FL 32802
(407) 836-2490

Citizens Intake
Palm Beach County
Office of State Attorney
P.O. Drawer 2905
West Palm Beach, FL 33402
(407) 355-3560

Director, Palm Beach County Dept. of Consumer Affairs
3111 S. Dixie Hwy., Ste. 128
W. Palm Beach, FL 33405
(407) 355-2670

Administrator, Pasco County Consumer Affairs Division
7530 Little Rd.
New Port Richey, FL 34654
(813) 847-8110

Director, Pinellas County Office of Consumer Affairs
P.O. Box 17268
Clearwater, FL 34622-0268
(813) 530-6200

Coordinator, Seminole Economic Crime Unit
Office of State Attorney
100 E. First St.
Sanford, FL 32771
(407) 322-7534

State Attorney
Consumer Fraud Unit
700 S. Park Ave.
Titusville, FL 32780
(407) 264-5230

City Offices

Chief of Consumer Affairs
City of Jacksonville
Division of Consumer Affairs
421 W. Church St., Ste. 404
Jacksonville, FL 32202
(904) 630-3667

Chairman, Lauderhill Consumer Protection Board
1176 N.W. 42nd Way
Lauderhill, FL 33313
(305) 321-2450

Chairman, Tamarac Board of Consumer Affairs
7525 N.W. 88th Ave.
Tamarac, FL 33321
(305) 722-5900, ext. 389
(Tuesday, Wednesday and Thursday—10 A.M. to Noon)

Georgia

State Office

Administrator
Governors Office of Consumer Affairs
2 Martin Luther King, Jr. Dr., S.E.
Plaza Level—East Tower
Atlanta, GA 30334
(404) 651-8600
(404) 658-3790
(800) 869-1123

Hawaii

State Offices

Director, Office of Consumer Protection
Dept. of Commerce and Consumer Affairs
828 Fort St. Mall, Ste. 600B
P.O. Box 3767
Honolulu, HI 96812-3767
(808) 586-2630

Investigator, Office of Consumer Protection
Dept. of Commerce and Consumer Affairs
75 Aupuni St.
Hilo, HI 96720
(808) 933-4433

Investigator, Office of Consumer Protection
Dept. of Commerce and Consumer Affairs
3060 Eiwa St.
Lihue, HI 96766
(808) 241-3365

Investigator, Office of Consumer Protection
Dept. of Commerce and Consumer Affairs
54 High St.
P.O. Box 3767
Honolulu, HI 96812
(808) 586-2630

Idaho

State Office

Deputy Attorney General
Office of the Attorney General
Consumer Protection Unit
210 Statehouse, Rm. 113A
Boise, ID 83720-1000
(208) 334-2424
(800) 432-3545

Illinois

State Offices

Director, Governors Office of Citizens Assistance
222 S. College
Springfield, IL 62706
(217) 782-0244
(800) 642-3112

Chief, Consumer Protection Division
Office of Attorney General
100 W. Randolph, 12th Fl.
Chicago, IL 60601
(312) 814-3580
(312) 793-2852 (TDD)

Director, Dept. of Citizen Rights
100 W. Randolph, 13th Fl.
Chicago, IL 60601
(312) 814-3589
(312) 814-7123 (TDD)

Regional Offices

Assistant Attorney General
Carbondale Regional Office
Office of Attorney General

626A E. Walnut St.
Carbondale, IL 62901
(618) 457-3505
(618) 457-4421 (TDD)

Assistant Attorney General
Champaign Regional Office
34 E. Main St.
Champaign, IL 61820
(217) 333-7691 (voice/TDD)

Assistant Attorney General
East St. Louis Regional Office
Office of Attorney General
8712 State St.
East St. Louis, IL 62203
(618) 398-1006
(618) 398-1009 (TDD)

Assistant Attorney General
Granite City Regional Office
Office of Attorney General
1314 Niedringhaus
Granite City, IL 62040
(618) 877-0404

Assistant Attorney General
Kankakee Regional Office
Office of Attorney General
1012 N. 5th Ave.
Kankakee, IL 60901
(815) 935-8500

Assistant Attorney General
LaSalle Regional Office
Office of Attorney General
1222 Shooting Park Rd., Ste. 106
Peru, IL 61354
(815) 224-4861
(815) 224-4864 (TDD)

Mt. Vernon Regional Office
Office of Attorney General
3405 Broadway
Mt. Vernon, IL 62864
(618) 242-8200 (voice/TDD)

Assistant Attorney General
Peoria Regional Office
Office of Attorney General
323 Main St.
Peoria, IL 61602
(309) 671-3191
(309) 671-3089 (TDD)

Quincy Regional Office
Office of Attorney General
523 Main St.
Quincy, IL 62301
(217) 223-2221 (voice/TDD)

Assistant Attorney General
Rockford Regional Office
Office of Attorney General
119 N. Church St.
Rockford, IL 61101
(815) 987-7580
(815) 987-7579 (TDD)

Assistant Attorney General
Rock Island Regional Office
Office of Attorney General
1614 2nd Ave.
Rock Island, IL 61201
(309) 793-0950
(309) 793-0956 (TDD)

Assistant Attorney General and Chief
Consumer Protection Division
Office of Attorney General
500 S. Second St.
Springfield, IL 62706
(217) 782-9011
(800) 252-8666

Assistant Attorney General
Waukegan Regional Office
Office of Attorney General
12 S. County St.
Waukegan, IL 60085
(708) 336-2207
(708) 336-2374 (TDD)

Assistant Attorney General
West Frankfort Regional Office
Office of Attorney General
222 E. Main St.
West Frankfort, IL 62896
(618) 937-6453

Assistant Attorney General
West Chicago Regional Office
Office of Attorney General
122A County Farm Rd.
Wheaton, IL 60187
(708) 653-5060 (voice/TDD)

County Offices

Supervisor, Consumer Fraud Division–303
Cook County Office of State's Attorney
303 Daley Center
Chicago, IL 60602
(312) 443-4600

State's Attorney
Madison County Office of State's Attorney
325 E. Vandalia
Edwardsville, IL 62025
(618) 692-6280

Director, Consumer Protect Division
Rock Island County
State's Attorney's Office
County Courthouse
Rock Island, IL 61201
(309) 786-4451, ext. 229

City Offices

Consumer Fraud
Wheeling Township
1616 N. Arlington Heights Rd.
Arlington Heights, IL 60004
(708) 259-7730 (Weds. only)

Commissioner, Chicago Dept. of Consumer Services
121 N. LaSalle St., Rm. 808
Chicago, IL 60602
(312) 744-4090
(312) 744-9385 (TDD)

Administrator, Des Plaines Consumer Protection Commission
1420 Miner St.
Des Plaines, IL 60016
(708) 391-5363

Indiana

State Office

Chief Counsel and Director
Consumer Protection Division
Office of Attorney General
219 State House
Indianapolis, IN 46204
(317) 232-6330
(800) 382-5516 (toll-free in IN)

County Offices

Director, Consumer Protection Division
Lake County Prosecutor's Office
2293 N. Main St.
Crown Point, IN 46307
(219) 755-3720

Marion County Prosecuting Attorney
560 City-County Building
200 E. Washington St.
Indianapolis, IN 46204-3363
(317) 236-3522

Vanderburgh County Prosecuting Attorney
108 Administration Building
Civic Center Complex
Evansville, IN 47708
(812) 426-5150

City Office

Director, Gary Office of Consumer Affairs
Annex E.
1100 Massachusetts St.
Gary, IN 46407
(219) 886-0145

Iowa

State Office

Assistant Attorney General
Consumer Protection Division
Office of Attorney General
1300 E. Walnut St., 2nd Fl.
Des Moines, IA 50319
(515) 281-5926

Kansas

State Office

Deputy Attorney General
Consumer Protection Division
Office of Attorney General
301 W. 10th
Kansas Judicial Center
Topeka, KS 66612-1597
(913) 296-3751
(800) 432-2310 (toll-free in KS)

County Offices

Head, Consumer Fraud Division
Johnson County District
Attorney's Office
Johnson County Courthouse
P.O. Box 728
Olathe, KS 66061
(913) 782-5000

Chief Attorney
Consumer Fraud and Economic
Crime Division
Sedgwick County District
Attorney's Office
Sedgwick County Courthouse
Wichita, KS 67203
(316) 266-7921

Assistant District Attorney
Shawnee County District
Attorney's Office
Shawnee County Courthouse, Rm.
212
Topeka, KS 66603-3922
(913) 291-4330

City Office

Assistant City Attorney
Topeka Consumer Protection
Division
City Attorney's Office
215 E. Seventh St.
Topeka, KS 66603
(913) 295-3883

Kentucky

State Offices

Director, Consumer Protection Division
Office of Attorney General
209 Saint Clair St.
Frankfort, KY 40601-1875
(502) 564-2200
(800) 432-9257 (toll-free in KY)

Administrator, Consumer Protection Division
Office of Attorney General
107 S. 4th St.
Louisville, KY 40202
(502) 588-3262
(800) 432-9257 (toll-free in KY)

Louisiana

State Office

Chief, Consumer Protection Section
Office of Attorney General

State Capitol Building
P.O. Box 94005
Baton Rouge, LA 70804-9005
(504) 342-7373

County Office

Chief, Consumer Protection Division
Jefferson Parish District Attorney's Office
200 Huey P. Long Ave.
Gretna, LA 70053
(504) 364-3644

Maine

State Offices

Superintendent, Bureau of Consumer Credit Protection
State House Station No. 35
Augusta, ME 04333
(207) 582-8718
(800) 332-8529 (toll-free)

Chief, Consumer and Antitrust Division
Office of Attorney General
State House Station No. 6
Augusta, ME 04333
(207) 289-3716 (9 A.M.-1 P.M.)

Maryland

State Offices

Chief, Consumer Protection Division
Office of Attorney General
200 St. Paul Place
Baltimore, MD 21202-2021
(301) 528-8662 (9 A.M.-3 P.M.)
(301) 576-6372 (TDD in Baltimore area)
(301) 565-0451 (TDD in DC metro area)
(800) 969-5766 (toll-free)

Director, Licensing & Consumer Services
Motor Vehicle Administration
6601 Ritchie Hwy., N.E.
Glen Burnie, MD 21062
(301) 768-7420

Consumer Affairs Specialist
Eastern Shore Branch Office
Consumer Protection Division
Office of Attorney General
Salisbury District Court/Multi-service Center
201 Baptist St., Ste. 30
Salisbury, MD 21801-4976
(301) 543-6620

Director, Western Maryland Branch Office
Consumer Protection Division
Office of Attorney General
138 E. Antietam St., Ste. 210
Hagerstown, MD 21740-5684
(301) 791-4780

County Offices

Administrator, Howard County Office of Consumer Affairs
9250 Rumsey Rd.
Columbia, MD 21045
(301) 313-7220
(301) 313-7201, 2323 (TDD)

Executive Director
Montgomery County Office of Consumer Affairs
100 Maryland Ave., 3rd Fl.
Rockville, MD 20850
(301) 217-7373

Executive Director
Prince George's County Consumer Protection Commission
9201 Basil Court
Landover, MD 20785

(301) 925-5100
(301) 925-5167 (TDD)

Massachusetts

State Offices

Chief, Consumer Protection Division
Dept. of Attorney General
131 Tremont St.
Boston, MA 02111
(617) 727-8400
(information and referral to local consumer offices that work in conjunction with the Dept. of Attorney General)

Secretary, Executive Office of Consumer Affairs and Business Regulation
One Ashburton Place, Rm. 1411
Boston, MA 02108
(617) 727-7780
(information and referral only)

Managing Attorney, Western Massachusetts Consumer Protection Division
Dept. of Attorney General
436 Dwight St.
Springfield, MA 01103
(413) 784-1240

County Offices

Complaint Supervisor
Consumer Fraud Prevention
Franklin County District Attorney's Office
238 Main St.
Greenfield, MA 01301
(413) 774-5102

Director, Consumer Fraud Prevention
Hampshire County District Attorney's Office
1 Court Square
Northhampton, MA 01060
(413) 586-9225

Project Coordinator
Worcester County Consumer Rights Project
340 Main St., Rm. 370
Worcester, MA 01608
(508) 754-7420 (9:30 A.M.–4 P.M.)

City Offices

Commissioner, Mayor's Office of Consumer Affairs and Licensing
Boston City Hall, Rm. 613
Boston, MA 02201
(617) 725-3320

Director, Consumer Information Center
Springfield Action Commission
P.O. Box 1449 Main Office
Springfield, MA 01101
(413) 737-4376
(Hampton and Hampshire Counties)

Michigan

State Offices

Assistant in Charge
Consumer Protection Division
Office of Attorney General
P.O. Box 30212
Lansing, MI 48909
(517) 373-1140

Executive Director, Michigan Consumers Council
414 Hollister Building
206 W. Allegan St.
Lansing, MI 48933
(517) 373-0947
(517) 373-0701 (TDD)

Acting Director
Bureau of Automotive Regulation
Michigan Dept. of State
Lansing, MI 48918
(517) 373-7858
(800) 292-4204 (toll-free in MI)

County Offices

Prosecuting Attorney
Bay County Consumer Protection Unit
Bay County Building
Bay City, MI 48708-5994
(517) 893-3594

Director, Consumer Protection Dept.
Macomb County
Office of the Prosecuting Attorney
Macomb Court Building, 6th Fl.
Mt. Clemens, MI 48043
(313) 469-5350

Director, Washtenaw County Consumer Services
4133 Washtenaw St.
P.O. Box 8645
Ann Arbor, MI 48107-8645
(313) 971-6054

City Office

Director, City of Detroit
Dept. of Consumer Affairs
1600 Cadillac Tower
Detroit, MI 48226
(313) 224-3508

Minnesota

State Offices

Director, Office of Consumer Services
Office of Attorney General
117 University Ave.
St. Paul, MN 55155
(612) 296-2331

Consumer Services Division
Office of Attorney General
320 W. Second St.
Duluth, MN 55802
(218) 723-4891

County Office

Citizen Protection Unit
Hennepin County Attorney's Office
C2000 County Government Center
Minneapolis, MN 55487
(612) 348-4528

City Office

Director, Consumer Affairs Division
Minneapolis Dept. of Licenses & Consumer Services
One C City Hall
Minneapolis, MN 55415
(612) 348-2080

Mississippi

State Offices

Special Assistant Attorney General
Chief, Consumer Protection Division
Office of Attorney General
P.O. Box 22947
Jackson, MS 39225-2947
(601) 354-6018

Director, Regulatory Services
Dept. of Agriculture and Commerce
500 Greymont Ave.
P.O. Box 1609
Jackson, MS 39215
(601) 354-7063

Consumer Counselor
Gulf Coast Regional Office of the Attorney General

P.O. Box 1411
Biloxi, MS 39533
(601) 436-6000

Missouri

State Offices

Office of the Attorney General
Consumer Complaints or Problems
P.O. Box 899
Jefferson City, MO 65102
(314) 751-3321
(800) 392-8222 (toll-free in MO)

Chief Counsel, Trade Offense Division
Office of Attorney General
P.O. Box 899
Jefferson City, MO 65102
(314) 751-3321
(800) 392-8222 (toll-free in MO)

Montana

State Office

Consumer Affairs Unit
Dept. of Commerce
1424 Ninth Ave.
Helena, MT 59620
(406) 444-4312

Nebraska

State Office

Assistant Attorney General
Consumer Protection Division
Dept. of Justice
2115 State Capitol
P.O. Box 98920
Lincoln, NE 68509
(402) 471-2682

County Office

Douglas County Attorney
County Attorney's Office
428 Hall of Justice
17th and Farnam
Omaha, NE 68183
(402) 444-7040

Nevada

State Offices

Commissioner of Consumer Affairs
Dept. of Commerce
State Mail Rm. Complex
Las Vegas, NV 89158
(702) 486-7355
(800) 992-0900 (toll-free in NV)

Consumer Services Officer
Consumer Affairs Division
Dept. of Commerce
4600 Kietzke Lane, M-245
Reno, NV 89502
(702) 688-1800
(800) 992-0900 (toll-free in NV)

County Office

Investigator, Consumer Fraud Division
Washoe County District Attorney's Office
P.O. Box 11130
Reno, NV 89520
(702) 328-3456

New Hampshire

State Office

Chief, Consumer Protection and Antitrust Bureau
Office of Attorney General
208 State House Annex

Concord, NH 03301
(603) 271-3641

New Jersey

State Offices

Director, Division of Consumer Affairs
124 Halsey St.
P.O. Box 45027
Newark, NJ 07101
(201) 648-4010

Commissioner, Dept. of the Public Advocate
CN 850, Justice Complex
Trenton, NJ 08625
(609) 292-7087
(800) 792-8600 (toll-free in NJ)

Deputy Attorney General
New Jersey Division of Law
1207 Raymond Blvd.
P.O. Box 45029
Newark, NJ 07101
(201) 648-7579

County Offices

Director, Atlantic County Consumer Affairs
1333 Atlantic Ave., 8th Fl.
Atlantic City, NJ 08401
(609) 345-6700

Director, Bergen County Division of Consumer Affairs
21 Main St., Rm. 101-E
Hackensack, NJ 07601-7000
(201) 646-2650

Director, Burlington County Office of Consumer Affairs
49 Rancocas Rd.
Mount Holly, NJ 08060
(609) 265-5054

Director, Camden County Office of Consumer Affairs
1800 Pavilion W.
2101 Ferry Ave., Ste. 609
Camden, NJ 08104
(609) 757-8397

Director, Cape May County Consumer Affairs
DN-310, Central Mail Rm.
Cape May Court House
Cape May Court House, NJ 08210
(609) 465-1076

Director, Cumberland County Dept. of Consumer Affairs and Weights and Measures
788 E. Commerce St.
Bridgeton, NJ 08302
(609) 453-2203

Director, Essex County Consumer Services
15 Southmunn Ave., 2nd Fl.
E. Orange, NJ 07018
(201) 678-8071
(201) 678-8928

Director, Gloucester County Consumer Affairs
152 N. Broad. St.
Woodbury, NJ 08096
(609) 853-3349
(609) 848-6616 (TDD)

Director, Hudson County Division of Consumer Affairs
595 Newark Ave.
Jersey City, NJ 07306
(201) 795-6295

Director, Hunterdon County Consumer Affairs
P.O. Box 283
Lebanon, NJ 08833
(908) 236-2249

Division Chief
Mercer County Consumer Affairs
640 S. Boad. St., Rm. 229
Trenton, NJ 08650-0068
(609) 989-6671

Director, Middlesex County Consumer Affairs
149 Kearny Ave.
Perth Amboy, NJ 08861
(201) 324-4600

Director, Monmouth County Consumer Affairs
1 E. Main St.
P.O. Box 1255
Freehold, NJ 07728-1255
(908) 431-7900

Director, Morris County Consumer Affairs
P.O. Box 900
Morristown, NJ 07963-0900
(201) 285-6070
(201) 584-9189 (TDD)

Director, Ocean County Consumer Affairs
P.O. Box 2191
County Administration Building
Rm. 130-1
Toms River, NJ 08754-2191
(908) 929-2105

Director, Passaic County Consumer Affairs
County Administration Building
309 Pennsylvania Ave.
Paterson, NJ 07503
(201) 881-4547, 4499

Somerset County Consumer Affairs
County Administration Building
P.O. Box 3000
Somerville, NJ 08876
(908) 231-7000, ext. 7400

Office Manager, Union County Consumer Affairs
300 North. Ave. East.
P.O. Box 186
W.field, NJ 07091
(201) 654-9840

Director, Warren County Consumer Affairs
Dumont Administration Bldg., Route 519
Belvedere, NJ 07823
(908) 475-6500

City Offices

Director, Brick Consumer Affairs
Municipal Building
401 Chambers Bridge Rd.
Brick, NJ 08723
(908) 477-3000, ext. 296

Director, Cinnaminson Consumer Affairs
Municipal Building
1621 Riverton Rd.
Cinnaminson, NJ 08077
(609) 829-6000

Director, Clark Consumer Affairs
430 Westfield Ave.
Clark, NJ 07066
(908) 388-3600

Director, Elizabeth Consumer Affairs
City Hall
60 W. Scott Plaza
Elizabeth, NJ 07203
(908) 820-4183

Director, Fort Lee Consumer Protection Board
Borough Hall
309 Main St.
Fort Lee, NJ 07024
(201) 592-3579

Director, Glen Rock Consumer Affairs
Municipal Building, Harding Plaza
Glen Rock, NJ 07452-2100
(201) 670-3956

Consumer Advocate
City Hall
94 Washington St.
Hoboken, NJ 07030
(201) 420-2038

Director, Livingston Consumer Affairs
357 S. Livingston Ave.
Livingston, NJ 07039
(201) 535-7976

Director, Middlesex Borough Consumer Affairs
1200 Mountain Ave.
Middlesex, NJ 08846
(908) 356-8090

Director, Mountainside Consumer Affairs
1455 Coles Ave.
Mountainside, NJ 07092
(908) 232-6600

Dept. of Community Services
Municipal Building
N. Bergen, NJ 07047
(201) 330-7292, 91

Director, Nutley Consumer Affairs
City Hall
228 Chestnut St.
Nutley, NJ 07110
(201) 284-4936

Director, Parsippany Consumer Affairs
Municipal Building, Rm. 101
1001 Parsippany Blvd.
Parsippany, NJ 07054
(201) 263-7011

Director, Perth Amboy Consumer Affairs
City Hall
260 High St.
Perth Amboy, NJ 08861
(908) 826-0290, ext. 61, 62

Director, Plainfield Action Services
510 Watchtung Ave.
Plainfield, NJ 07060
(908) 753-3519

Director, Secaucus Dept. of Consumer Affairs
Municipal Government Center
Secaucus, NJ 07094
(201) 330-2019

Director, Union Township Consumer Affairs
Municipal Building
1976 Morris Ave.
Union, NJ 07083
(908) 688-6763

***Director, Wayne Township Consumer* Affairs**
475 Valley Rd.
Wayne, NJ 07470
(201) 694-1800, ext. 290

Director, Weehawken Consumer Affairs
400 Park Ave.
Weehawken, NJ 07087
(201) 319-6005

Director, W. New York Consumer Affairs
428 60th St.
West New York, NJ 07093
(201) 861-2522

New Mexico

State Office

Consumer Protection Division
Office of Attorney General
P.O. Drawer 1508

Santa Fe, NM 87504
(505) 827-6060
(800) 432-2070 (toll-free in NM)

New York

State Offices

Chairperson and Executive Director
New York State Consumer Protection Board
99 Washington Ave.
Albany, NY 12210-2891
(518) 474-8583

Assistant Attorney General
Bureau of Consumer Frauds and Protection
Office of Attorney General
State Capitol
Albany, NY 12224
(518) 474-5481

Chairperson and Executive Director
New York State Consumer Protection Board
250 Broadway, 17th Fl.
New York, NY 10007-2593
(212) 417-4908 (complaints)
(212) 417-4482 (main office)

Assistant Attorney General
Bureau of Consumer Frauds and Protection
Office of Attorney General
120 Broadway
New York, NY 10271
(212) 416-8345

Regional Offices

Assistant Attorney General in Charge
Binghamton Regional Office
Office of Attorney General
59-61 Court St., 7th Fl.
Binghamton, NY 13901
(607) 773-7877

Assistant Attorney General in Charge
Buffalo Regional Office
Office of Attorney General
65 Court St.
Buffalo, NY 14202
(716) 847-7184

Assistant Attorney General in Charge
Plattsburgh Regional Office
Office of Attorney General
70 Clinton St.
Plattsburgh, NY 12901
(518) 563-8012

Assistant Attorney General in Charge
Poughkeepsie Regional Office
Office of Attorney General
235 Main St.
Poughkeepsie, NY 12601
(914) 485-3920

Assistant Attorney General in Charge
Rochester Regional Office
Office of Attorney General
144 Exchange Blvd.
Rochester, NY 14614
(716) 546-7430

Assistant Attorney General in Charge
Suffolk Regional Office
Office of Attorney General
300 Motor Prkwy.
Hauppauge, NY 11788
(516) 231-2400

Assistant Attorney General in Charge
Syracuse Regional Office
Office of Attorney General
615 Erie Blvd. West
Syracuse, NY 13204-2465
(315) 448-4848

Assistant Attorney General in Charge
Utica Regional Office
Office of Attorney General
207 Genesee St.
Utica, NY 13501
(315) 793-2225

County Offices

Deputy Director of General Services
Broome County Bureau of Consumer Affairs
Government Plaza, P.O. Box 1766
Binghamton, NY 13902
(607) 778-2168

Director, Dutchess County Dept. of Consumer Affairs
38-A Dutchess Turnpike
Poughkeepsie, NY 12603
(914) 471-6322

Assistant District Attorney
Consumer Fraud Bureau
Erie County District Attorney's Office
25 Delaware Ave.
Buffalo, NY 14202
(716) 858-2424

Commissioner, Nassau County Office of Consumer Affairs
160 Old Country Rd.
Mineola, NY 11501
(516) 535-2600

Executive Director
New Justice Conflict Resolution Services Inc.
210 E. Fayette St., Ste. 700
Syracuse, NY 13202
(315) 471-4676

Commissioner, Orange County Dept. of Consumer Affairs and Weights and Measures
99 Main St.
Goshen, NY 10924
(914) 294-5151, ext. 1762

District Attorney
Orange County District Attorney's Office
255 Main St.
County Government Center
Goshen, NY 10924
(914) 294-5471

Putnam County Office Facility
Dept. of Consumer Affairs
Myrtle Ave.
Mahopac Falls, NY 10542-0368
(914) 621-2317

Director/Coordinator
Rockland County Office of Consumer Protection
County Office Building
18 New Hempstead Rd.
New City, NY 10956
(914) 638-5282

Director, Steuben County Dept. of Weights, Measures and Consumer Affairs
3 E. Pulteney Square
Bath, NY 14810
(607) 776-9631
(607) 776-9631, ext. 2101 (voice/TDD)

Commissioner, Suffolk County Dept. of Consumer Affairs
Suffolk County Center
Hauppauge, NY 11788
(516) 360-4600

Director, Ulster County Consumer Fraud Bureau
285 Wall St.
Kingston, NY 12401
(914) 339-5680, ext. 240

Chief, Frauds Bureau
Westchester County
District Attorney's Office
111 Grove St.
White Plains, NY 10601
(914) 285-3303

Director, Westchester County Dept. of Consumer Affairs
Rm. 104, Michaelian Office Building
White Plains, NY 10601
(914) 285-2155

City Offices

Director, Babylon Consumer Protection Board
Town Hall Office Annex
281 Phelps Lane
N. Babylon, NY 11703
(516) 422-7636

Town of Colonie Consumer Protection
Memorial Town Hall
Newtonville, NY 12128
(518) 783-2790

Commissioner, Mt. Vernon Office of Consumer Affairs
City Hall
Mt. Vernon, NY 10550
(914) 665-2433

Commissioner, New York City Dept. of Consumer Affairs
42 Broadway
New York, NY 10004
(212) 487-4444

Bronx Neighborhood Office
New York City Dept. of Consumer Affairs
1932 Arthur Ave., Rm. 104-A
Bronx, NY 10457
(212) 579-6766

Brooklyn Neighborhood Office
New York City Dept. of Consumer Affairs
1360 Fulton St., Rm. 320
Brooklyn, NY 11216
(718) 636-7092

Director, Queens Neighborhood Office
New York City Dept. of Consumer Affairs
120-55 Queens Blvd., Rm. 301A
Kew Gardens, NY 11424
(718) 261-2922

Director, Staten Island Neighborhood Office
New York City Dept. of Consumer Affairs
Staten Island Borough Hall, Rm. 422
Staten Island, NY 10301
(718) 390-5154

Director, City of Oswego Office of Consumer Affairs
City Hall
West Oneida St.
Oswego, NY 13126
(315) 342-8150

Chairwoman, Ramapo Consumer Protection Board
Ramapo Town Hall
237 Rte 59
Suffern, NY 10901-5399
(914) 357-5100

Schenectady Bureau of Consumer Protection
City Hall, Rm. 22
Jay St.
Schenectady, NY 12305
(518) 382-5061

Director, White Plains Dept. of Weights and Measures
77 S. Lexington Ave.
White Plains, NY 10601-2512
(914) 422-6359

Director, Yonkers Office of Consumer Protection, Weights and Measures
201 Palisade Ave.

Yonkers, NY 10703
(914) 377-76807

N. Carolina

State Office

Special Deputy Attorney General
Consumer Protection Section
Office of Attorney General
Raney Building
P.O. Box 629
Raleigh, NC 27602
(919) 733-7741

N. Dakota

State Offices

Office of Attorney General
600 E. Blvd. Ave.
Bismarck, ND 58505
(701) 224-2210
(800) 472-2600 (toll-free in ND)

Director, Consumer Fraud Section
Office of Attorney General
600 E. Blvd. Ave.
Bismarck, ND 58505
(701) 224-3404
(800) 472-2600 (toll-free in ND)

County Office

Executive Director
Quad County Community Action Agency
27 1/2 S. Third St.
Grand Forks, ND 58201
(701) 746-5431

Ohio

State Offices

Consumer Frauds and Crimes Section
Office of Attorney General
30 E. Broad. St.
State Office Tower, 25th Fl.
Columbus, OH 43266-0410
(614) 466-4986 (complaints)
(614) 466-1393 (TDD)
1 (800) 282-0515 (toll-free in OH)

Office of Consumers' Counsel
77 S. High St., 15th Fl.
Columbus, OH 43266-0550
(614) 466-9605 (voice/TDD)
(800) 282-9448 (toll-free in OH)

County Offices

Director, Economic Crime Division
Franklin County Office of Prosecuting Attorney
369 S. High St.
Columbus, OH 43215
(614) 462-3555

County Prosecutor
Consumer Protection Division
Lake County Office of Prosecuting Attorney
Lake County Court House
Painesville, OH 44077
(216) 357-2683
(800) 899-5253 (toll-free in OH)

Assistant Prosecuting Attorney
Montgomery County Fraud Section
301 W. 3rd St.
Dayton Montgomery County Courts Building
Dayton, OH 45402
(513) 225-5757

Prosecuting Attorney
Portage County Office of Prosecuting Attorney
466 S. Chestnut St.
Ravenna, OH 44266-0671
(216) 296-4593

Prosecuting Attorney
Summit County Office of Prosecuting Attorney

53 University Ave.
Akron, OH 44308-1680
(216) 379-2800

City Offices

Chief, Cincinnati Office of Consumer Services
Division of Human Services
City Hall, Rm. 126
Cincinnati, OH 45202
(513) 352-3971

Director, Youngstown Office of Consumer Affairs and Weights and Measures
26 S. Phelps St.
City Hall
Youngstown, OH 44503-1318
(216) 742-8884

Oklahoma

State Offices

Assistant Attorney General
Office of Attorney General
420 W. Main, Ste. 550
Oklahoma City, OK 73102
(405) 521-4274

Administrator, Dept. of Consumer Credit
4545 Lincoln Blvd., Ste. 104
Oklahoma City, OK 73105-3408
(405) 521-3653

Oregon

State Office

Attorney in Charge
Financial Fraud Section
100 Dept. of Justice
Justice Building
Salem, OR 97310
(503) 378-4320

Pennsylvania

State Offices

Director, Bureau of Consumer Protection
Office of Attorney General
Strawberry Square, 14th Fl.
Harrisburg, PA 17120
(717) 787-9707
(800) 441-2555 (toll-free in PA)

Consumer Advocate
Office of Consumer Advocate-Utilities
Office of Attorney General
1425 Strawberry Square
Harrisburg, PA 17120
(717) 783-5048 (utilities only)

Deputy Attorney General
Bureau of Consumer Protection
Office of Attorney General
27 N. Seventh St.
Allentown, PA 18101
(215) 821-6690

Director, Bureau of Consumer Services
Pennsylvania Public Utility Commission
P.O. Box 3265
203 N. Office Building
Harrisburg, PA 17105-3265
(717) 787-4970 (out-of-state calls only)
(800) 782-1110 (toll-free in PA)

Deputy Attorney General
Bureau of Consumer Protection
Office of Attorney General
919 State St., Rm. 203
Erie, PA 16501
(814) 871-4371

Attorney in Charge
Bureau of Consumer Protection

Office of Attorney General
132 Kline Village
Harrisburg, PA 17104
(717) 787-7109
(800) 441-2555 (toll-free in PA)

Deputy Attorney General
Bureau of Consumer Protection
Office of the Attorney General
IGA Building, Route 219 N.
P.O. Box 716
Ebensburg, PA 15931
(814) 949-7900

Deputy Attorney General
Bureau of Consumer Protection
Office of Attorney General
21 S. 12th St., 2nd Fl.
Philadelphia, PA 19107
(215) 560-2414
(800) 441-2555 (toll-free in PA)

Deputy Attorney General
Bureau of Consumer Protection
Office of Attorney General
Manor Complex, 5th Fl.
564 Forbes Ave.
Pittsburgh, PA 15219
(412) 565-5394

Deputy Attorney General
Bureau of Consumer Protection
Office of Attorney General
State Office Building, Rm. 358
100 Lackawanna Ave.
Scranton, PA 18503
(717) 963-4913

County Offices

Director, Beaver County Alliance for Consumer Protection
699 Fifth St.
Beaver, PA 15009-1997
(412) 728-7267

Director/Chief Sealer, Bucks County Consumer Protection, Weights and Measures
50 N. Main
Doylestown, PA 18901
(215) 348-7442

Director, Chester County Bureau of Consumer Protection, Weights and Measures
Courthouse, 5th Fl., North Wing
High and Market Sts.
Westchester, PA 19380
(215) 344-6150

Consumer Mediator, Cumberland County Consumer Affairs
One Courthouse Square
Carlisle, PA 17013-3387
(717) 240-6180

Director, Delaware County Office of Consumer Affairs, Weights and Measures
Government Center Building
Second and Olive Sts.
Media, PA 19063
(215) 891-4865

Director, Montgomery County Consumer Affairs Dept.
County Courthouse
Norristown, PA 19404
(215) 278-3565

City Office

Chief, Economic Crime Unit
Philadelphia District Attorney's Office
1421 Arch St.
Philadelphia, PA 19102
(215) 686-8750

Puerto Rico

Secretary, Dept. of Consumer Affairs (DACO)
Minillas Station, P.O. Box 41059
Santurce, PR 00940
(809) 721-0940

Secretary, Dept. of Justice
P.O. Box 192
San Juan, PR 00902
(809) 721-2900

Rhode Island

State Offices

Director, Consumer Protection Division
Dept. of Attorney General
72 Pine St.
Providence, RI 02903
(401) 277-2104
(401) 274-4400, EXT. 354 (Voice/TDD)
(800) 852-7776 (toll-free in RI)

Executive Director
Rhode Island Consumers' Council
365 Broadway
Providence, RI 02909
(401) 277-2764

S. Carolina

State Offices

Assistant Attorney General
Consumer Fraud and Antitrust Section
Office of Attorney General
P.O. Box 11549
Columbia, SC 29211
(803) 734-3970

Administrator, Dept. of Consumer Affairs
P.O. Box 5757
Columbia, SC 29250-5757
(803) 734-9452
(803) 734-9455 (TDD)
(800) 922-1594 (toll-free in SC)

State Ombudsman
Office of Executive Policy and Program
1205 Pendleton St., Rm. 308
Columbia, SC 29201
(803) 734-0457
(803) 734-1147 (TDD)

S. Dakota

State Office

Assistant Attorney General
Division of Consumer Affairs
Office of Attorney General
500 E. Capitol
State Capitol Building
Pierre, SD 57501-5070
(605) 773-4400

Tennessee

State Offices

Deputy Attorney General
Antitrust and Consumer Protection Division
Office of Attorney General
450 James Robertson Prkwy.
Nashville, TN 37243-0485
(615) 741-2672

Director, Division of Consumer Affairs
Dept. of Commerce and Insurance
500 James Robertson Prkwy.
5th Fl.

Nashville, TN 37243-0600
(615) 741-4737
(800) 342-8385 (toll-free in TN)
(800) 422-CLUB (toll-free health club hotline in TN)

Texas

State Offices

Assistant Attorney General and Chief, Consumer Protection Division
Office of Attorney General
Supreme Court Building
P.O. Box 12548
Austin, TX 78711
(512) 463-2070

Assistant Attorney General
Consumer Protection Division
Office of Attorney General
714 Jackson St., Ste. 700
Dallas, TX 75202-4506
(214) 742-8944

Assistant Attorney General
Consumer Protection Division
Office of Attorney General
6090 Surety Dr., Rm. 260
El Paso, TX 79905
(915) 772-9476

Assistant Attorney General
Consumer Protection Division
Office of Attorney General
1019 Congress St., Ste. 1550
Houston, TX 77002-1702
(713) 223-5886

Assistant Attorney General
Consumer Protection Division
Office of Attorney General
1208 14th St., Ste. 900
Lubbock, TX 79401-3997
(806) 747-5238

Assistant Attorney General
Consumer Protection Division
Office of Attorney General
3600 N. 23rd St., Ste. 305
McAllen, TX 78501-1685
(512) 682-4547

Assistant Attorney General
Consumer Protection Division
Office of Attorney General
115 E. Travis St., Ste. 925
San Antonio, TX 78205-1607
(512) 225-4191

Office of Consumer Protection
State Board of Insurance
816 Congress Ave., Ste. 1400
Austin, TX 78701-2430
(512) 322-4143

County Office

Assistant District Attorney and Chief of Dallas County District Attorney's Office
Specialized Crime Division
133 N. Industrial Blvd., LB 19
Dallas, TX 75207-4313
(214) 653-3820

Assistant District Attorney and Chief
Harris County Consumer Fraud Division
Office of District Attorney
201 Fannin, Ste. 200
Houston, TX 77002-1901
(713) 221-5836

City Office

Director, Dallas Consumer Protection Division
Health and Human Services Dept.
320 E. Jefferson Blvd., Ste. 312
Dallas, TX 75203
(214) 948-4400

Utah

State Offices

Director, Division of Consumer Protection
Dept. of Commerce
160 E. 3rd S.
P.O. Box 45802
Salt Lake City, UT 84145-0802
(801) 530-6601

Assistant Attorney General for Consumer Affairs
Office of Attorney General
115 State Capitol
Salt Lake City, UT 84114
(801) 538-1331

Vermont

State Offices

Assistant Attorney General and Chief, Public Protection Division
Office of Attorney General
109 State St.
Montpelier, VT 05609-1001
(802) 828-3171

Supervisor, Consumer Assurance Section
Dept. of Agriculture, Food and Market
120 State St.
Montpelier, VT 05620-2901
(802) 828-2436

Virgin Islands

Commissioner, Dept. of Licensing and Consumer Affairs
Consumer Affairs
Property and Procurement Building
Subbase #1, Rm. 205
St. Thomas, VI 00802
(809) 774-3130

Virginia

State Offices

Chief, Antitrust and Consumer Litigation Section
Office of Attorney General
Supreme Court Building
101 N. Eighth St.
Richmond, VA 23219
(804) 786-2116
(800) 451-1525 (toll-free in VA)

Director, Division of Consumer Affairs
Dept. of Agriculture and Consumer Services
Rm. 101, Washington Building
1100 Bank St.
P.O. Box 1163
Richmond, VA 23219
(804) 786-2042

Investigator, Northern Virginia Branch
Office of Consumer Affairs
Dept. of Agriculture and Consumer Services
100 N. Washington St., Ste. 412
Falls Church, VA 22046
(703) 532-1613

County Offices

Section Chief, Office of Citizen and Consumer Affairs
#1 Court House Plaza, Ste. 314
2100 Clarendon Blvd.
Arlington, VA 22201
(703) 358-3260

Director, Fairfax County Dept. of Consumer Affairs
3959 Pender Dr., Ste. 200
Fairfax, VA 22030-6093
(703) 246-5949
(703) 591-3260 (TDD)

Administrator, Prince William County Office of Consumer Affairs
4370 Ridgewood Center Dr.
Prince William, VA 22192-9201
(703) 792-7370

City Offices

Director, Alexandria Office of Citizens' Assistance
City Hall
P.O. Box 178
Alexandria, VA 22313
(703) 838-4350
(703) 838-5056 (TDD)

Coordinator, Division of Consumer Affairs
City Hall
Norfolk, VA 23501
(804) 441-2821
(804) 441-2000 (TDD)

Assistant to the City Manager
Roanoke Consumer Protection Division
364 Municipal Building
215 Church Ave., S.W.
Roanoke, VA 24011
(703) 981-2583

Director, Consumer Affairs Division
Office of the Commonwealth's Attorney
3500 Virginia Beach Blvd., Ste. 304
Virginia Beach, VA 23452
(804) 431-4610

Washington

State Offices

Investigator, Consumer and Business Fair Practices Division
Office of the Attorney General
111 Olympia Ave., NE
Olympia, WA 98501
(206) 753-6210

Director of Consumer Services
Consumer and Business Fair Practices Division
Office of the Attorney General
900 Fourth Ave., Ste. 2000
Seattle, WA 98164
(206) 464-6431
(800) 551-4636 (toll-free in WA)

Chief, Consumer and Business Fair Practices Division
Office of the Attorney General
W. 1116 Riverside Ave.
Spokane, WA 99201
(509) 456-3123

Contact Person, Consumer and Business Fair Practices Division
Office of the Attorney General
1019 Pacific Ave., 3rd Fl.
Tacoma, WA 98402-4411
(206) 593-2904

City Offices

Director, Dept. of Weights and Measures
3200 Cedar St.
Everett, WA 98201
(206) 259-8810

Chief Deputy Prosecuting Attorney
Fraud Division
1002 Bank of California
900 4th Ave.
Seattle, WA 98164
(206) 296-9010

Director, Seattle Dept. of Licenses and Consumer Affairs
102 Municipal Building
600 4th Ave.
Seattle, WA 98104-1893
(206) 684-8484

W. Virginia

State Offices

Director, Consumer Protection Division
Office of Attorney General
812 Quarrier St., 6th Fl.
Charleston, WV 25301
(304) 348-8986
(800) 368-8808 (toll-free in WV)

Director, Division of Weights and Measures
Dept. of Labor
1800 Washington St., East Building. #3, Rm. 319
Charleston, WV 25305
(304) 348-7890

City Office

Director, Dept. of Consumer Protection
P.O. Box 2749
Charleston, WV 25330
(304) 348-8172

Wisconsin

State Offices

Administrator, Division of Trade and Consumer Protection
Dept. of Agriculture, Trade and Consumer Protection
801 W. Badger Rd.
P.O. Box 8911
Madison, WI 53708
(608) 266-9836
1 (800) 422-7128 (toll-free in WI)

Regional Supervisor, Division of Trade and Consumer Protection
Dept. of Agriculture, Trade and Consumer Protection
927 Loring St.
Altoona, WI 54720
(715) 839-3848
(800) 422-7218 (toll-free in WI)

Regional Supervisor, Division of Trade and Consumer Protection
Dept. of Agriculture, Trade and Consumer Protection
200 N. Jefferson St., Ste. 146A
Green Bay, WI 54301
(414) 448-5111
(800) 422-7128 (toll-free in WI)

Regional Supervisor, Consumer Protection Regional Office
Dept. of Agriculture, Trade and Consumer Protection
3333 N. Mayfair RD., Ste. 114
Milwaukee, WI 53222-3288
(414) 257-8956

Assistant Attorney General
Office of Consumer Protection and Citizen Advocacy
Dept. of Justice
P.O. Box 7856
Madison, WI 53707-7856
(608) 266-1852
(800) 362-8189 (toll-free)

Assistant Attorney General
Office of Consumer Protection
Dept. of Justice
Milwaukee State Office Building
819 N. 6th St., Rm. 520
Milwaukee, WI 53203-1678
(414) 227-4948
(800) 362-8189 (toll-free)

County Offices

District Attorney
Marathon County District Attorney's Office
Marathon County Courthouse
Wausau, WI 54401
(715) 847-5555

Assistant District Attorney
Milwaukee County District Attorney's Office
Consumer Fraud Unit
821 W. State St., Rm. 412
Milwaukee, WI 53233-1485
(414) 278-4792

Consumer Fraud Investigator
Racine County Sheriff's Dept.
717 Wisconsin Ave.
Racine, WI 53403
(414) 636-3125

Wyoming

State Office

Assistant Attorney General
Office of Attorney General
123 State Capitol Building
Cheyenne, WY 82002
(307) 777-7874

Information in this section was taken from the *Consumers' Resource Handbook,* 1992 edition, U.S. Office of Consumer Affairs.

index

D

E